HELLO DARLIN'

HELLO DARLIN'

Tall (and Absolutely True)
Tales About My Life

Larry Hagman
with Todd Gold

SIMON & SCHUSTER
A VIACOM COMPANY

First published in Great Britain by
Simon & Schuster UK Ltd, 2001
A Viacom Company

1   3   5   7   9   10   8   6   4   2

Simon & Schuster UK Ltd
Africa House
64–78 Kingsway
London WC2B 6AH

www.simonsays.co.uk

Simon & Schuster Australia
Sydney

A CIP catalogue record for this book is available
from the British Library

ISBN 0-7432-0735-1

Typeset by Palimpsest Book Production Limited
Polmont, Stirlingshire
Printed and bound in Great Britain by
Clays Ltd, St Ives plc

I want to thank first of all Maj Irene Axelsson Hagman, my beautiful wife of forty-seven years. Without her co-operation, cajoling and her memory I would never have got this book out. With all my love and affection, thanks.

To Todd Gold, who has written many articles about me and was my collaborator on this endeavour and is a great friend and ally.

And Teri Prather, my assistant, who had to put up with all kinds of nonsense from me during the writing of this book.

And of course, to my liver donor, without whose *really*, *really*, *really* important contribution I would not be here to write this book.

INTRODUCTION

Everyone has a moment when life pulls a U-turn. Mine occurred in Weatherford, Texas.

It was the summer after my senior year of high school. I was seventeen years old. Two years earlier, I'd left a comfortable liberal school for rich kids in bucolic Vermont to be with my dad, a prominent lawyer in the small Texas town. I'd said I wanted to work as a cowboy. That time had finally come. I had my hat, my jeans, my boots . . . everything but a job.

My dad got me work in the machine shop at the Antelope Tool Company, a stultifyingly hot Quonset hut where I made a tool used in oil drilling that a machine behind me spit out at a rate a hundred times faster than I could make them by hand. Then I switched to unloading 100-pound cement bags from railroad boxcars under the fiery August sun, until the company's owner transferred me to his house—theoretically a promotion—where I was put to work digging ditches for sewer lines and a hole for his swimming pool.

But that was the toughest of all the jobs, and probably as close to hell as I've ever been. Shovels and picks were useless against the hard ground. Every few feet, we had to blast it with dynamite. One sweltering afternoon, as I leaned unsteadily against my shovel at the bottom of a 10-foot hole where guys much older and tougher than me were passing out from the heat and the dynamite fumes, I had an epiphany. The only horses I'd seen all summer were in the local rodeo. The hell with trying to be a cowboy.

"I think I want to be an actor," I told my dad.

Soon I was standing on my mother's doorstep in New York. My mother was Broadway star Mary Martin. It's hard to imagine anyone not knowing who my mother was, but nowadays, eight years after her death, I'll meet young people up to 25 or 30 who have no idea of the Mary Martin of *South Pacific* or *The Sound of Music*. But mention *Peter Pan* and their eyes light up. They can tell me how old they were and where they were when they watched it. When I tell them that Peter Pan was my mother, they light up but then look incredulous. One 18-year-old girl said, "That's impossible. Peter was a boy. And anyhow, he never grew up."

Such is the power of TV, and unfortunately they show *Peter Pan* very seldom now. So perhaps there will be many more children who will miss her extraordinary performance. Four of my granddaughters were watching the cartoon version of *Peter Pan* and halfway through, one of them asked, "When does the real Peter Pan come on?"

The real Peter Pan worked some of her magic to get me started. She also gave me some advice:

"Always know your lines. Hang up your own clothes. And try to be reasonably sober."

*   *   *

In this book, I'm going to describe how I did my best. A lot already has been said about me. I've been described as the Mad Monk of Malibu, the kooky actor in the caftan who led flag parades up and down the beach, didn't speak on Sundays, and occasionally roared up to the grocery store on a Harley while dressed in a yellow chicken suit. It's also no secret that I'm a recovering alcoholic whose life has been prolonged by a liver transplant.

It's all true, but there's more to say, lots more. Some of it's funny, some of it's serious, and some contains the wisdom that comes from discovering that having it all doesn't mean you *actually* have it all. In writing this book, I decided to throw all that mumbo in the gumbo, to stir in the stories, the little-known details, and the lessons I've learned, and I wanted to do it before I couldn't remember it anymore or we destroy the planet, whichever comes first.

I'm often asked how my liver transplant operation changed my life. Aside from saving it, nothing changed. It confirmed what I've always tried to do—live my life as fully as possible before the clock runs out. My happiness comes from being a husband, father, and grandfather of five, not from stardom, which is a fluke. I starred in two very successful television series. When people ask for my secret, I tell them it's been 20 percent hard work, 80 percent luck. I think a lot of life comes down to that. If you push too hard for something, it seems to retreat. If you hold on to something too tightly, it manages to slip away.

So little is in our control. I was once asked what were the three luckiest things that happened in my life, and I said, "Being born white, in the U.S.A., and in the 20th century." Even with all the luck in the world, you can't ignore fate. Sometimes it requires you to need a liver transplant. Other times all you need is a sense of humour. The other day I was in a restaurant and two young girls, 15 or 16, came up to my table and asked if I was the guy who played Major Nelson in *I Dream of Jeannie*.

When I said yes, one of them said, "You used to be really hot."

Real life is a roller-coaster, full of spills and thrills. As I see it, I've spent much of my life in the business of crowd control. Each night, millions of people are at home staring at a box, and I'm inside it. If they weren't watching TV, they'd be outside rioting in the streets, breaking windows and overturning police cars. I help keep them sedated, and at the same time I help sell cars, aspirin, deodorant, and feminine hygiene products. So far I've been pretty good at it. Hell, I even take a little credit for helping bring down the Eastern bloc.

Memories are like money—you can't take them with you, so you might as well share them. Between the ages of 10 and 18, I had a steamer trunk in which I kept all my most valuable possessions. When I struck out on my own to make it as an actor, I left it with a costume designer who had a large apartment in New York City. Ruth Morley was her name. She kept that trunk for me until she died, and then I lost all trace of it. All the stuff I'd collected was gone.

You don't have to be a shrink to see that I've spent the rest of my life replacing what was in that trunk with lots more shit. I'm a pack rat. Don't raise the subject with my wife. A few years ago we had six homes spread across L.A., Santa Fe, and New York, and she explained it was for all the stuff I'd accumulated. She was only half joking. I can't throw anything out. I collect hats because I have to. Same with flags and costumes. I have drawers and closets full of memorabilia. I can't even remember what memories are attached to most of this stuff, but it inspired a lot of stories for this book.

1

For Bob and Melinda Wynn, it was a big night. Maybe the biggest. Bob was a Texas wildcatter who'd made and lost fortunes and at the moment was flush enough to finagle his wife into being the chairperson of the Cattle Barons Ball, a cancer fund-raiser that was the hottest ticket among the social elite in Dallas. Bob's wife, Melinda, was exquisitely beautiful. He wanted the best for her, from diamonds to clothes (like the Bob Mackie gown she'd had made for the evening) to social status, which hosting the ball ensured.

Like so many of Bob's endeavors, it appeared to be working. Everyone who was anyone in Dallas was on the grounds outside of Southfork, the epicenter of so much sex, sleaze, and scandal on television's highest-rated series. It was exciting, like being on a Hollywood set. Even better, a fleet of helicopters swooped in, circling overhead, and then it began to rain money—one-hundred-dollar bills.

Within moments they knew that each helicopter carried

one of the stars from *Dallas* and that I was in the lead chopper, the guy in the white Stetson who was tossing out handfuls of the one-hundred-dollar bills with my picture on them and the saying "In Hagman We Trust." As all of us stepped onto the lawn, people cheered and waved. Some shouted, "We love you, J.R.," and I could feel the atmosphere turn electric. Out of the corner of my eye I caught Bob Wynn grinning.

But his good mood didn't last long. As I knew from having lost money in one of his oil deals, Bob's ventures often had another side, and this grand evening did too—rain. Not long after I arrived, the nighttime sky unleashed a storm of biblical force. It just poured. I was supposed to introduce the night's entertainment, country music legend Johnny Cash. By the time I arrived backstage, I had mud up to the crotch of my white Western-style tux, the power had gone off, and Johnny was telling Bob why he couldn't play.

"There's a damn good chance me and my band could get electrocuted out there."

Bob stepped forward until there wasn't any space between him and Mr. Cash.

"Look, you son of a bitch," he growled, "if you don't go out there and play, I'm going to blow your head off."

I have no doubt he would've done it too. Neither did Cash, who followed my introduction onto the stage, which, in the absence of electrical power, was illuminated by headlights from a bunch of Cadillacs and Rolls-Royces that were hastily moved into a semicircle. The introduction over, I hurried out to the audience, where my chair sunk into the mud. The woman next to me chuckled; hers was even deeper. We spoke briefly. She was from out of state, Cleveland or somewhere.

When the power was restored, and after a couple of

songs, the man seated behind the woman asked the guy in front of her to remove his 10-gallon cowboy hat. It was blocking his view. It was blocking everybody's view. When his request was ignored, he waited about 15 seconds, reached over the lady, and knocked the guy's hat off. She and I exchanged nervous glances as the man slowly turned around, asked for his hat, and put it back on. A few moments later the scene was repeated. But this time, before the hat hit the ground, the guy wheeled around and threw a vicious punch. It missed its target, who ducked, and instead hit the woman square on her forehead.

She tumbled backward in the mud. I saw a huge goose egg form just above her nose. I thought she was dead.

Meanwhile, the two men went at each other, fists flying and all that. As security intervened, I noticed Bob Wynn had taken over the microphone. He was asking everyone if they were having a good time. Despite the rain, it seemed like they were—except for the woman lying at my feet. An emergency medical team had rushed over and were working on her. A few minutes passed before she opened her eyes. She looked right at me without any recognition and asked where the hell she was.

"Texas," I said. "Welcome to Dallas, honey."

My arrival in Texas, though much less violent, would over time lead to moments of real drama.

I was born in Fort Worth, Texas, on September 21, 1931. My mother was 17. She had married and become pregnant almost the moment her marriage was consummated. She had no idea about sex. Nor did she have much of a clue about motherhood. It just happened as if it was supposed to, like so many events in life seem when you look back on them.

But Mom did things her way, and her way was rarely traditional.

Her father, Preston Martin, was a prominent lawyer in town. Her mother, Juanita Presley, had taught violin at the community college. Mother was born in the family's modest home. According to her, my grandfather signaled her birth to the neighbors by raising the bedroom curtain, and she liked to say, "Curtains have been going up for me ever since."

My mother was a good-looking child. She sang the words to every song the town band played on Saturday nights outside the courthouse. At 12, she took voice lessons. She would describe herself as the best customer at the Palace, the town's only movie theater. She began to dream about becoming a performer after seeing Al Jolson sing "Mammy", and soon she was able to mimic Ruby Keeler, ZaSu Pitts, and other stars of the day.

"Give me four people and I'm on," she said. "Give me four hundred and I'm a hundred times more on."

My father, Ben Hagman, had his own flair. He was a criminal attorney who, at six feet and 240 pounds, commanded a courtroom the way Mother did a stage. He once defended a man who'd gone into a sleazy bar on Jacksboro Highway and taken a shot at the bartender. While he missed the bartender, the bullet went through the bar's thin metal siding and killed a lady seated in a pickup parked outside.

Dad got a hurry-up call from the shooter, who'd been arrested on murder charges. Before the cops launched an investigation, my dad went into the bar and pulled two slugs out of the wood in the back bar. Then in court he argued that two or more shots would've been murder, but one shot was an accident—at least in Texas it was. As he didn't inform the court about the two extra slugs, Dad got his client a lesser sentence.

His family, originally from Sweden, owned lumber mills in Wisconsin before moving to Texas, shortly after the turn of the century. Dad's mother, Hannah, a Christian Scientist, died of cancer. His father passed away soon after. He had two brothers. One, my uncle Carl, was a retired army officer. The other, my uncle Bill, married a woman named Ruth, and both were so fat they needed special heavy-duty springs in their car.

My father was 19 when he met my mother, then 14. They didn't start dating until she was a high school senior. After a hot summer romance, my mother's parents attempted to lower the flame by sending her to Ward-Belmont, a finishing school in Nashville, Tennessee. Miserable there, she convinced her mother to come get her. For some reason, my grandmother brought Ben along, and then the three of them went to Hopkinsville, Kentucky, where my mother, 16, and Ben, 21, got married.

"How hillbilly can you get?" my mother would say later.

She had a baby at 17, but after a couple of months of playing mother, she was miserable. Maybe not miserable, but frustrated.

Not a big surprise. She was a kid herself—too young to be a wife, too young to be a mother, and too full of ambition to settle down.

My father joined my grandfather's law firm, and soon after, my mother opened Mary Hagman's School of Dance in an old grain loft, and I was handed over to my grandma. I called her Nanny. All of us lived under the same roof, in my grandparents' new home, a large, rambling, two-storey house. My grandmother took care of all of us.

* * *

Weatherford still had the flavor of an old Western town. Horses outnumbered cars, electric lights were new (not all the homes outside of town had them), and the big thing was watermelon. In front of the courthouse, there was a tin watermelon about 14 feet long, and outside of town there was another sign that said, "Welcome to Weatherford, Watermelon Capital of the World." That sign was regularly used for target practice. Every year they had to replace it, and one year they simply changed it to say, "Welcome to Weatherford, Home of Watermelons and Mary Martin."

Mother was very proud of that, but she'd joke, "Even in my hometown I can't get top billing!"

But that wasn't true. Everyone in town knew my mother as the talented, energetic dance instructor. I was two when she took the train to California, where she studied at Fanchon and Marco School of the Theater, a school for dancing teachers, in Hollywood. More trips followed. After she brought back new dance moves and the mystique of having seen the movie capital with her own eyes, her classes became more popular than ever.

Soon she opened a second school and began staging shows that made her name even bigger locally.

She was able to work so hard because my grandma assumed all the responsibility of raising me. It was as if I were her own child. My mother once took me for a walk and I was attacked by a swarm of bees. Another time I fell off a Shetland pony and broke my collarbone, and when my grandmother found out—three days later—she balled out her daughter, asking, "What'd you do to *my* Larry?"

I was always described as a good boy with a sweet disposition. I probably was. I'm still pretty easygoing. I can remember only one serious impropriety as kid. While playing in the sandbox, I stuck my tongue out at my grandma. She told my grandpa—who I called Papu—and he locked me in the cellar, a dank room that reeked of homemade wine and provided shelter to rats the size of Pekingese. "Larry, you stuck your tongue out at Grandma. That's no good."

First I heard the lock click. Then the lights went off. Then I started to think about the rats down there. I'd seen my grandpa trap some that were bigger than me—at least they seemed it. I naturally assumed the first sound I heard in the dark was a rat, and it scared the crap out of me. I ran to the door, terrified.

"I'm sorry. I'll never do it again," I cried.

The door flung open and I fell into my grandma's arms. She'd clearly had words with my grandpa.

As tough as my grandpa was, he never spanked me. Never once raised his hand. His punishment was much worse. He bored me to death with lectures. I used to say to myself, Why can't he just spank me and get it over with? His lectures were summations meant for a jury, not a five-year-old child. They also had an effect. I never did anything stupid a second time.

I was also raised by Billy Jones, a wonderful, very round, extremely loving black woman who'd worked for us so long she became part of the family. She'd raised my mother and her older sister, Geraldine, and then she got me too. She took me to the black church, which I liked better than ours. She also took me to the movie theater, where I remember the manager would let me and other white kids go upstairs with our nannies but the nannies couldn't go downstairs with us.

It didn't seem right.

"That's just the way it is," she said.

Still, I didn't understand why it had to be.

Even as a little kid I could talk all night, but Billy didn't always want to listen. At bedtime, she had a secret method of putting me to sleep. She'd blow out the pilot light in the gas heater and let the gas fill the room. Just enough to make me drowsy. That practice ended when my grandparents returned from a church barbecue and found us both passed out and the gas still flowing. Billy resorted to another trick. She filled a little cloth sack with sugar, dipped it in bourbon, and let me suck on it.

Was this the start of my alcoholism? Who knows?

As my mother grew up, she and my father grew apart. He wanted to have his own home and law practice, which he did. My mother quickly discovered she wanted her own career too. She zipped off to Hollywood every time she wanted to learn a new dance routine, but after a while it was pretty apparent she had aspirations other than becoming the best dance instructor in Weatherford and Fort Worth.

Finally she decided to give stardom a shot. She moved to L.A. with her devoted friend Mildred Woods. Between 1935 and 1937, she auditioned so frequently at Paramount, MGM, and the other studios that she earned the nickname "Audition Mary." Her first big job was singing at the Cinegrill, a bar at the Hollywood Roosevelt Hotel. Word quickly got back to Weatherford. Broadway was one thing. The movies were another. But working in a bar?

Concerned, my grandma packed me in the car and sped to L.A. She wanted to see what was going on for herself.

What she saw was my mother pursuing the life she'd

dreamed about. She was doing it without my father, whom she divorced amicably, the distance and diverging careers being too much of a strain on their relationship. My grandma and I moved in with Mother and Mildred. They had an apartment in the Highland Towers near the Hollywood Bowl. Mother was doing fairly well, making $400 a week singing at Gordon's nightclub, where she met the composers Oscar Hammerstein II and Jerome Kern. She'd also grown friendly enough with gossip columnist Hedda Hopper to have her baby-sit for me in a pinch.

One night I was awakened by a noise in my bedroom. Without stirring, I quietly opened my eyes and saw my mother and Mildred looking around my room. Mother picked up my piggy bank and handed it to Mildred, who broke it open and handed the meager amount to my mother. That night we dashed off to Palm Springs. As I recall, mother was fleeing from Val D'Auvray, a European businessman who was pressuring her to marry him.

Val was an interesting character, a strong, masculine, erudite man who made and lost fortunes and had influential friends all over the world. He loved mother and, I think, saw himself as her Svengali. She didn't give him the opportunity. However, for a time he did fill the space in my life that was denied to my father, taking me to the doctor, to amusement parks, and one time to Errol Flynn's yacht, which he said he'd once owned. And years later he would play an important role in my life.

Speaking of roles, the only one that ever gave my mother trouble was the one that concerned me, motherhood. But she tried her best. That Easter in Hollywood she and Mildred woke me up and said they had a surprise for me. Mother was holding the end of a yellow ribbon.

"Take the ribbon, Lukey," she said, using her pet name

for me. "Get up and follow it and you'll find a special treat."

I followed instructions and excitedly traced the ribbon through the house—from the bathroom into the living room, around the dining room table, and out through the kitchen. Mother and Mildred kept saying, "You're getting warmer. You're getting warmer." Finally, I opened the screen door in the kitchen and found the end of the ribbon tied to a little white bunny—splattered in bright red blood!

A neighborhood cat had chewed its head off.

I was traumatized.

I've been "allergic" to cats ever since.

2

In 1937, my mother was in the midst of a sold-out engagement at the Trocadero nightclub when she was discovered by the influential producer Lawrence Schwab. He offered to pay her way to New York to star in his next big Broadway musical comedy, *Ring Out the News*. Mom had Nanny take me to Weatherford and then she and Mildred went to New York, where they found out the play had been canceled. They stayed anyway and did well.

Mother opened in *Leave It to Me*, a Cole Porter musical starring Sophie Tucker, Victor Moore, and William Gaxton, and it turned out to be her big break. She stole the show in the second act with a risqué striptease while singing "My Heart Belongs to Daddy". Her scene, set in an Eskimo village, also featured a trio of chorus boys, including Gene Kelly in his first Broadway show and Dan Dailey.

That summer Nanny and I visited her, and when I saw

the show I was kind of embarrassed. By today's standards, her strip was not even a tease. She took off only her short fur coat and her gloves, leaving her in a teddy. Still, in those days, strippers were thought of as hookers, and she was my mother. But later, when she asked what I thought, I told her the truth. "You've got great legs."

Others thought so too. She was such a sensation that she made the cover of *Life* magazine.

By then I was back in Texas. That fall I remember my grandparents listening to the Mercury Theater radio drama *The War of the Worlds*. They believed every word of that legendary broadcast was true. That night my grandpa brought me into their bed and I fell asleep with Nanny on one side and Papu on the other. He laid his shotgun across his knees and if any aliens showed up, he was going to give them a Texas-style welcome.

A year later, Grandpa suffered a stroke. Mother was still in the show in New York. She flew to Weatherford on a Sunday but was back in Manhattan for Tuesday night's performance. Grandpa hung on only a short while longer. I heard about his death from the woman who boarded at their house. Her name was Shipp; she was a high school teacher who'd rented a room from my grandparents for years. I didn't have any idea what to do or say after she told me, so I made a joke.

"Why did Papu wear boots when he died?" I asked.

"What? What are you talking about, Larry?"

"Why did Papu wear boots when he died?"

"I don't know. Why?"

"So he wouldn't hurt his foot when he kicked the bucket."

She burst into tears.

I didn't think it was a great joke but I didn't think it would have such a dramatic effect on her.

Before Grandpa died, an owl took up residence in one of the two large cedar trees that stood outside the front door. According to Texas folklore, the owl was a sign of death. There was no need for any more bad luck. My dad went outside holding Papu's shotgun and blasted that old bird out of the tree. I remember the echo of that shot in the quiet of the night.

Dad came back in the house and said, "No more bad luck from that critter."

Soon my mother accepted a contract from Paramount Pictures to star in movies, and Grandma and I joined her in L.A. Nanny bought a home at 1287 Holmby Avenue, in Holmby Hills, a pretty neighborhood between Beverly Hills and Westwood. I still remember the address because mother made me memorize it so I'd know where the heck I lived if I ever got lost.

Mom made 11 films in just three years, including *The Great Victor Herbert*. I was enrolled in Black Fox Military Institute. Those regimented military schools were quite popular among parents, especially showbiz parents, back in the 1930s and 1940s. Among those in my class were the sons of Bing Crosby, Edward G. Robinson, Charlie Chaplin, and Harry Blackstone, the magician. I took to all the rules and the strict sense of order. A year later, I won the award for the small arms drill. Unfortunately, with America by then at war, medals were not being struck, to conserve metal, and I received a certificate instead. Since the school went under in the 1960s, I never did get my medal, which I still wish I had, and maybe that's one of the reasons I horde things.

Given my mother's rising-star status, she had many suitors, until she met Paramount story editor Richard

Halliday. They eloped to Las Vegas in 1940—just the two of them, without Grandma this time. On November 4, 1941, she gave birth to a daughter, Heller, so named because she kicked so much when she was inside Mother. ("Heller" is a Texas term for a hellion.)

When mother got her first real starring role on Broadway, in *One Touch of Venus*, the 1943 musical comedy with lyrics by Ogden Nash, music by Kurt Weill, and book by S. J. Perelman, the three of them moved to New York.

Since I was in school in L.A. and accustomed to living with my grandma, my mother was able to go off to her new life without feeling any guilt about leaving the two of us behind. She was 27, about the age when she should've started a family. I don't think she dismissed us as part of her old life, but Richard most likely did. He wasn't too fond of me. Nor was I a fan of his. He had to be in control of everything—an asset to Mother's career, but it made him a pain in the ass to be around if you weren't part of that little world.

And I wasn't, which was painfully evident when Grandma took ill and I moved into their Fifth Avenue apartment in New York City. The change happened suddenly and without any preplanning. Nanny went into the hospital for a gallbladder operation, and I was shipped east, shielded from the gravity of her illness. Mother and everyone else expected her to die during surgery, or soon after if she made it through, and they were right. Nanny died. I cried for days. She'd raised me through my first 12 years and her death broke me up. Without her, I was truly on my own in Richard's house.

A whole new life began for me. I was enrolled in Trinity, an old-fashioned prep school that I rather liked. All the students wore a jacket and tie and flannels. They called teachers "sir." It reminded me of military school. Homework was as mandatory as cleaning your locker or polishing your shoes had been in military school, and this kind of routine was familiar to me.

The same couldn't be said for my new Fifth Avenue home. The last time I'd lived with my mother, Nanny was still running the show. At that point, Mother had been a rising nightclub singer trying to make it in the movies. Now her world was completely different. She was a star. Her name was above the marquee on a new Broadway play, *Lute Song*. She was photographed in *Vogue* and *Harper's Bazaar*. She and Richard regularly socialized with Oscar Hammerstein, Richard Rodgers, Jerome Kern, and Leland Hayward—the biggest names in the New York entertainment world. It was everything she'd dreamed of, but none of what a kid like me found comforting, warm, or nourishing.

We didn't spend much time together. On school days, I got up at seven and knew to be quiet because she was still asleep. When I came home around four or five, she was getting ready to go to the theater. Usually she'd have a light dinner with us, and then she went to work as Richard called, "We've got to leave or we'll be late." I was asleep when she got home. On Saturday, a matinee day, she slept till 11, got up and vocalized, had a light lunch, and then went to the theater. She had the "21" Club send over dinner between shows. With no shows on Sunday, she slept till noon, her explanation being "Mommy needs her rest," and then we got to see her around two if she hadn't scheduled press or fittings.

The one time all of us did get together, for Sunday night dinner, was hell, as far as Heller and I were concerned, thanks to Richard. By five o'clock he was shit-faced. By six-thirty, he was shit-faced *and mean*. At the table, he would lecture us about proper manners. No elbows on the table, he'd snap. Eat with your mouth closed. Your fork goes in your left hand, the knife in your right. No talking at the table. Actually, we could talk—but only to answer one of his asinine questions. *When do children speak? When they're spoken to.*

He tormented us with ridiculous head games. He would ask questions just to try to catch us contradicting ourselves so he could berate us. He remembered everything we ever said. It was like he wrote down every utterance in his mind. He often could not remember what he had for breakfast, but he could recall what grade I got on a spelling test two months earlier. He verbally beat us over the head with this crap. He was never violent, just picky. Always picking, picking, picking—as if we were loose threads on a sweater.

My poor, sweet sister, Heller, only four, might've had it worse than me. Richard always got on her case for not eating her peas. He would watch with the demeanor of a pit bull until she ate every single pea on her plate, and Heller hated peas!

But she got the last laugh. She'd somehow hold the peas in her mouth and, after being excused from the table, spit them in the potted plant in the foyer. Finally, the man who tended the plants said, "Mr. Halliday, there's something strange growing down there. I don't know what it is. Look at all these moldly little green pellets."

I was given the task of building fires in the fireplace during the winter, a job I took to seriously and responsibly. In fact, my mother's friend Judith Anderson once showed me how to make perfect kindling by rolling up newspaper tightly and tying it in knots, a trick she'd learned in London when the war made wood scarce, and it was a trick that I copied.

One night, however, when Richard had told me to make a fire, we went in to dinner and left the fire blazing untended in the living room. Richard got a telephone call saying the apartment above ours was filling up with smoke. We hurried into the living room and found the switch on the electric fan controlling the flue had not been flipped to the proper setting.

"Larry, how could you be so stupid?" he scolded.

But I'd turned it on. I knew I had. That was my job and I did it properly.

It must have been Heller who'd flipped the switch to the wrong position. It had to have been. I'd seen her playing around the fireplace.

But Richard didn't care. He was convinced it was my fault and he wouldn't hear any arguments to the contrary.

"You are a dirty boy to pass blame like that," he said.

By then I'd had enough of him and decided to find a more pleasant life on my own. I would run away. I'd just read the novels about Huck Finn and Tom Sawyer and I decided to head to the Mississippi and raft down the river. I packed a bag with sandwiches, milk, and cookies, bundled myself up because it was cold, and took my Schwinn bicycle outside. The Metropolitan Museum of Art was across the street and I rode circles around the front. Round and round. I was trying to work up the nerve to ask someone where I could find the bridge to New Jersey.

After a few hours, the sun went down. I got very cold, went back home, and locked up my bike.

Now's not the time of year to run away, I said to myself. Maybe in the spring.

*   *   *

I had a lot of ideas about how to make my life more pleasant, but none as good or as final as the one I got that spring.

My dad had given me a .22 rifle for my birthday the previous year when I was in military school in California. The gun was my pride and joy. It had a telescopic site, perfect balance, and a great feel. Even after moving to New York, I still kept it polished as if ready for a military inspection.

One night, as Richard was taking Mother to the theater, I watched from my second-floor bedroom window as they went outside to their car. I happened to be cleaning my .22 and a thought came to me—one shot, that's all I need. I sat down on the windowsill and drew a bead on the back of Richard's head. While picturing the bullet going right between his ears, I told myself, I could shoot the son of a bitch and nobody would think a 12-year-old boy would do something like that.

But as I practised my alibi, I talked myself out of actually pulling the trigger. My story had too many holes, which in the final analysis meant one less hole in Richard's head. I went from thinking, What the heck are they going to do to a 12-year-old, to acknowledging, they just might throw my ass in jail forever. As a result, though, I do understand why kids snap and kill someone. They're tortured, abused, and see no other recourse. They're just like adults who go berserk.

Fortunately I wasn't that bad off. I just thought I was.

In the end I chickened out.

Somehow, despite my frustration, I came to see Richard was simply a goddamned necessary evil. Mother most likely wouldn't have had such a brilliant career without Richard in her life. He and I would never get along, and it prevented Mother and me from having a real relationship until he died. But knowing I had the choice to take him out if I desired was enough to get me through that day.

3

One summer my mother and Richard rented a house in New Canaan, Connecticut. It was a Roman-style villa owned by Stanton Griffith, a wealthy ambassador without portfolio. The marvelous home had lush, spacious grounds and an Olympic-size swimming pool. Whenever mother's best friend, Jean Arthur, visited, she swam laps at night and I was given the job of holding a flashlight over the water and keep an eye out for frogs and snakes. I always looked forward to her visits, since she swam in the nude.

But the summer was not as placid as the scenery. I'd followed the war news from Europe, as did my mother and Richard. Aside from theater gossip, it dominated conversation. People have forgotten how the war consumed virtually every aspect of life in America. Whether it was over cocktails or at the dinner table, the talk always got around to the latest news about the war. I absorbed everything I heard. The Nazis had to be defeated, and following the attack on Pearl Harbor, the Japanese were godless, inhuman ogres.

When America dropped the atomic bomb on Hiroshima, my mother burst into tears, crying over what I can still hear her calling "the slaughter of those poor people." Days later a second bomb was dropped, on Nagasaki. She continued to cry. I couldn't comprehend what had happened or what it meant until I was much older and knew that being remorseful and compassionate had been the correct way to react.

It wasn't the popular view. At the time, most Americans were brainwashed into having contempt for the yellow race, seeing them as inhuman, even subhuman, and I'm convinced that sort of conditioning directly contributed to our involvement in the Korean and Vietnamese Wars. Until many of us woke up during the sixties, we were led to believe we were correct in exterminating those people.

In the fall, my mother sent me to Woodstock Country School, a boarding school in Woodstock, Vermont. Though I'd been away 12 of my 13 years, mom was concerned about how I'd react to being sent away, but I was delighted to escape Richard. She drove me there in the Cadillac, the backseat filled with my trunk. I was assigned a roommate, Roger Phillips. Mother and I met him and his family as we unpacked. We had a good afternoon, laughing as we kept bumping into each other. The Phillipses seemed like a great family.

But just when I was nearly settled my mother took me outside in the hall.

"Larry," she said in a hushed voice, "I want to tell you something."

Since I'd never been to boarding school, I expected some sort of lecture.

"Yes, Mother?"

"You know that Roger and his family are Jewish?"

I had no idea what a Jew was. I'd never thought about such things. Mother didn't know me. How could she? We'd never spent any time together. With great bravado and fake worldliness, I said, "I know he's a Jew."

"I wanted to make sure."

"Don't worry. It's okay."

Not once in my life had I ever judged a person by race or religion, and I didn't start then. Nor have I since.

From the moment Roger and I moved in together, we've been best friends. We had something in common right away. He brought a beautiful white gelding named Stormy. He got me interested in riding, taught me how to ride bareback and vault a horse. I loved it so much I ended up working every weekend for two years at Fergie's stables, near school. I mucked out stalls for 50 cents a day, plus a great meal at quitting time and the owners' trust to exercise their horses.

At school, I also made another lifelong friend, Severn Darden. He grew up to be a well-known character actor, and we worked together many times. But Sev was already a character in school. I remember him visiting me in Connecticut over spring break. Though 15, he drove from New Orleans to Connecticut by himself. Not only that, he showed up in a 1937 Rolls convertible *and* he brought a bottle of Courvoisier for my mother.

Mother was somewhat taken aback. But she learned to love him, as we all did, for being an original till the day he died.

Compared to those two worldly guys, I had so much to learn. Woodstock was the first coed school I'd ever attended. It was a progressive institution, a bastion of liberal educational theory and thought where students created the rules. Yet, as they explained on the first day's indoctrination, there was no smoking, no drinking, and no sex. The three biggies, they called them.

I broke them all.

I didn't actually have to try. The school year was only a few months old when Klaus Heinmann, one of the boys in the dorm, taught us how to make applejack. We bought a barrel of cider for $16, added sugar and yeast, then let it set for a while in the cellar next to the coal furnace. After it fermented, we took it outside and let it freeze. The part that didn't freeze was pure alcohol. We got drunker than shit a few times. Then Klaus went blind for about three days after one batch, and that ended that experiment.

The other two rules toppled when I started going with "an older woman." She was a junior, and gorgeous. At 16, she was already a woman, light-years ahead of me in worldliness, relationships, everything. I wasn't even aware of it myself until I saw her smoke. That said a lot. She must've thought I had potential, because one day she offered me a cigarette. I said no. I wasn't going to smoke cigarettes.

"If you take a puff," she said, "I'll let you put your hand on my breast."

Well, I smoked for 20 years after that. I didn't stop until I was 34 years old.

The next year she took up with another guy, leaving me with a broken heart and a nasty smoking habit that nearly led to me burning down the boys' dorm. It was late one cold winter night, and Roger and I were smoking, flicking butts onto the roof of the porch outside our window. We didn't know there was an oil mop out there. One of the butts landed on it and within minutes the mop began to smolder. We didn't even notice.

A movie was just letting out directly across the street. A bunch of sailors were among the crowd bundling up as they hit the cold air. One of the sailors noticed the smoke and yelled, "Fire!" Soon the group was running toward the dorm as if they had been called to battle stations.

Hearing the commotion, I stuck my head out the window and saw the sailors staring at me. Then I noticed the smoking mop.

The dorm was a little wooden house, a 150-year-old tinderbox, and our room was on the second floor. Thinking I'd save the situation, I reached out the window, managed to grab the mob, brought it inside, and tried to shake the fire out. Sparks flew in all directions. In an instant, the curtains caught on fire, followed by the bedding, and soon we were engulfed in flame. I was so stupid.

Roger responded much better. He ran downstairs, grabbed the fire extinguisher, put the fire out just as the headmaster stepped through the smoke, and received the hero's congratulations he was due. I was suspensed for two weeks. I accepted the punishment but not the blame. I've always known the real culprit was my girlfriend, who let me touch her breast if I tried her cigarette.

Later that year my mother came to see me. She hired a horse and carriage to take us around the lovely Vermont town. I sensed she had something important to tell me because of the way she was acting. She told the driver to stop, collected her thoughts, and looked deep into my eyes. She told me that during the summer she was going on the road in *Annie Get Your Gun* and wanted me to come with her.

"There're a couple of small parts," she said. "Heller's going to have one. I'd love to have you in it too."

I went numb. I had no aspiration to be onstage. Worse, the thought of being with Richard for a year on the road made me dumbstruck.

Mother anxiously awaited an answer.

My mind was blank.

I remember staring straight at the horse's ass in front of me, and suddenly I got an idea.

"Mom, I really want to be a cowboy."

The thought had never entered my mind before. I was inspired by the horse's ass.

"I want to go live with Dad in Texas and be a cowboy."

My mother was disappointed but took it well. She said she understood.

"I know you want to be with your father. That's okay."

So that summer, after school ended, I took the train to Texas from New York all by myself. The trip was uneventful until I stepped onto the platform in Weatherford. Then it was like entering a new world. I didn't look anything like a 15-year-old from Texas. I wore a Brooks Brothers suit and tie, had thick glasses, and my hair was done up as was stylish in New York, in a big wavy pompadour.

"First thing we'll do is take a trip to the barbershop," said my dad, who kept his hair in the same buzz he'd been given upon joining the National Guard.

A buzz cut was unimaginable. I begged Dad to let me keep my hair a little longer. Eventually he said okay, but he made me agree to a deal.

"You have to play football," he said.

"Why do I have to play football?"

"Because in Texas, men play football."

I made the team as a second-string defensive end, but my gridiron glory was short-lived. In the first game I tripped over my own foot and broke my ankle. For the next few months I hobbled around on crutches, but that turned out to be a boon to my social life, attracting lots of sympathy from the girls on campus.

Then I met Joey Byers, who became my first love. She was beautiful and kind and a year older and much smarter than me. We were hot and heavy when my ankle healed and my dad told me that I had to go back to the football team. I didn't want to. I'd endured enough pain and suffering and asked if there wasn't something else I could do.

"The Golden Gloves," he said.

"What?"

"Boxing. You can box in the Golden Gloves tournament."

I saw what was going on, but there was no way I could be as tough as my dad. Ben Hagman was a two-fisted, drinking, good old Texas boy. He'd spent seven or eight days behind the German lines during the battle of the Bulge. He'd seen one of his closest buddies get shot in the head and blown out of their jeep. He'd come back a changed man.

From the day he returned home, he slept with a .45 under his pillow. One night the neighbor's cat climbed up on the screen of his bedroom window. Hearing the noise, my dad grabbed his gun and blew the cat to pieces. A couple shells went through the bathroom wall of the neighbor's house too. No one was hurt, but it scared the hell out of everyone.

Given the choice between football and boxing, I decided it was better to fight one guy than eleven. I chose the gloves. My coach was Jim Wright, the future U.S. Speaker of the House. I've always said I'm sure glad he was my boxing coach and not my acting coach. But he was a good boxing coach, big on strategy, always advising me to jab, jab, jab, "and when you see an opening, go for it!" I won a few fights as a light welterweight, which boosted my ego. Even better, I thought Joey, who liked me for my long hair, liked me even better for being tough in the ring. Later she told me it was barbarous. Go figure women.

So I kept at it. In the big boxing tournament, my first-round opponent was the toughest kid in the draw, the bootlegger's son. He was the toughest kid at school too. That kid liked to fight in and out of the ring.

I knew I was going to lose. A victory for me would be survival. But I did more than make it through the fight alive. At the end of three rounds, I was still on my feet, throwing punches, bouncing off the ropes, bruised but breathing. As expected, the bootlegger's son won the bout, taking the fight on points, but I'd broken his ribs with a flurry of punches and he had to forfeit his next fight. My so-called moral victory was the talk of school. After that fight, nobody made fun of my hair anymore.

When Dad ran for state senator, I helped "manage" his campaign, which was the epitome of a grassroots effort. My dad let me drive the two of us across the state while we sipped bourbon from the bottle and he told stories. Before we'd pull into a little town, he'd gargle some Listerine, and then he'd give his speech in the town square, his voice blasting out of the loudspeaker we stuck on top of his maroon Oldsmobile. After, I'd find a shady spot outside of town, pull over, and we'd take a nap.

I love to remember how much I learned from him. One

afternoon we stopped in the countryside to stretch our legs and I spotted a buzzard. Impulsively, I grabbed the .22 we kept in the back of the car and said, "Dad, watch this." I snapped a shot off. I didn't look or anything. But I killed the large bird midflight. It was a brain shot, right through his head. Probably the luckiest shot of my life. My dad, not happy, said, "Goddamn, boy, now we have to eat that son of a bitch."

"Huh?"

"Son, in Texas, we eat what we shoot."

He wasn't kidding. That night I ate buzzard for dinner. I learned my lesson. I never again shot anything I didn't want to eat.

My first big hunting trip was November 16, a day that many men regarded as sacred as Christmas, maybe more. It marked the start of deer season. I went with my dad and seven of his friends. Dad and his buddies leased twenty thousand acres that became theirs to hunt for 10 days. Their annual ritual began with a drive to Fredericksburg. We started out with three cases of hard liquor, 30 cases of beer, and something like 40 packs of cigarettes. These were the most important ingredients of a good hunt.

We had our own camp cook, a black man named Tom Simmons. The man was a genius with a Dutch oven, which we affectionately called Simmons' Pot. The first night in camp someone always went out and got a doe for camp meat. Once I shot six squirrels from a tree in 10 seconds, and they went into the pot. So did an armadillo I shot. And a rattlesnake. Simmons threw everything we brought him in the pot, let it simmer, seasoned with jalapeño peppers, onion, sage, garlic, and whatever else was handy, and he'd serve it over corn bread for breakfast, lunch, and dinner.

You couldn't breathe in that delicious aroma without getting hungry.

"Just lettin' the juices stew," he'd say and smile.

We slept in an old tin-sided fishing camp that had seven bunks. I didn't get one of those, thank you. Instead my dad handed me a sleeping bag and I made myself comfortable on the floor. It was fine for the first few nights, but then a norther blew in and the temperature dropped from 70 degrees to below freezing. Even with the tin sides tied shut and the stove cranked up, it was still so cold our big old hunting dog, Nora, curled up next to me, whimpering and shivering. I opened up my sleeping bag and let her get in. As soon as she got comfy, she pissed all over me.

I got up to get some dry clothes and when I returned, the bag was frozen solid. I woke my dad and asked if I could get in with him.

"Lukey, there's barely room in here for me," he said. "You can get some canvas out of the back of the truck and curl up with the dog."

I'd already tried that. From then on, Nora slept alone.

Such discomforts were forgotten as soon as I set out in pursuit of deer. I can still recall every detail of my first one. It's an event you never forget. I was seated in an outcropping of rocks when I heard a *thump-thump-thump*. Looking around, I saw about 30 deer on my right, running toward me. In those days, there were hundreds of deer. I once counted more than 800 in a single field at night with a spotlight. These particular deer had been spooked by something. I could tell from the way they ran. Then they stopped right in front of me and the biggest buck I'd ever seen was looking straight at me. I dropped him on my first shot.

Deer hunting is a rite of passage in Texas. I felt like I was now a man.

That trip also saw me go through another rite of passage. By the sixth day, we were out of booze and beer. My dad and his friends were unable to imagine continuing their trip without more firewater. They organized a liquor run to Piedras Negras, a little town across the border in Mexico. Dad turned to me and said something about the fact that I had a girlfriend who I'd been seeing for a long time. He was speaking about Joey. I said, "No sir, we don't get that far." And I wasn't lying.

"Well, son," he said, "we're going to get you laid."

I was thunderstruck. We drove straight into the red light district, which actually had red lights in front of the different bars, and we entered a dance hall. Nobody was dancing, but there were about 30 girls sitting around the bar. After drinking about four or five Carta Blancas, my dad told me to pick one out. I still couldn't believe this was about to happen.

"What?"

"We're going to get you bred down here."

It was a real situation. To save face, I wasn't able to say no. I glanced around at the girls and picked out one that looked nice—kind and pretty. Dad motioned to her, worked out a price (five bucks), and watched as she took me into a little cabin that was barely large enough for her bed, which I sat on with great trepidation. The cabin was lit by a string of Christmas lights and the walls were papered with magazine photos of saints and priests and nuns. The religious motif of her crib snuffed whatever ardor I had brought in, which wasn't much.

She took off her dress, letting it fall so that the

multicolored lights reflected off her white corset, which was all she wore. Without making eye contact, she unsnapped the crotch and lay down on the bed. Until that moment I'd never laid eyes on what I was looking at. While I was amazed, I wasn't excited, and the perfunctory way this girl presented herself to me put even more of a damper on my nonexistent ardor.

She nevertheless tried a few things, embarrassing me until I finally let her know that I wasn't interested. Instead, in my broken Spanish, we struck a deal. For an extra five bucks, she went back into the dance hall and told my dad and his friends what a powerful, virile young man I was. She was pleased. I was pleased. More important, Dad was pleased. Everyone congratulated me. My dad praised me on a job well done. Needless to say, I felt pretty good about the whole thing.

I'd passed the ultimate Texas test—I'd gotten my deer and got laid . . . kind of.

4

The combination of having a girlfriend and getting my first car, a 1943 Jeep, made me grow up quickly. I don't think any two things have a more profound effect on a young man. I was in love and mobile. When Joey went off to college, I was devastated but I still had my freedom. As a senior, I also branched out socially, writing for the school newspaper and acting in the school play, a production of a comedy *This Girl Business*.

On opening night, I got my first laugh. By the final performance, I had eight or 10 laughs. I'd learned that once the audience decides you're funny, they'll laugh at almost anything, a look, a gesture . . . it almost doesn't matter as long as they buy into what you're doing.

After graduation, I began working at the Antelope Tool Company. An opening had been created for me as a favor to my father, who in his law practice represented the company as well as its very wealthy owner, Jess Hall Sr. A former pro wrestler, Big Jess, as he was known, made

SENIORS 1949

LARRY HAGMAN
Los Hidalgos, Grass Burr Staff

GRETCHEN KEBELMAN
D. A. R. Representative, F. H. A.,
Melon Vine Staff

his fortune by inventing scratchers and centralizers, essential components in oil drilling. Scratchers kept paraffin from building up on the sides of the concrete pipes that brought oil up from the depths of the earth, and centralizers kept the miles-long steel drilling pipes from binding onto the walls of the hole.

Big Jess had four sons. For Christmas one year, he gave each one a Beechcraft Bonanza, a fast little airplane. Awhile later, one of the sons crashed his plane in Canada and was killed. Because the old man was ailing at the time, a battle ensued over who would assume control of the family's business. Jess Hall Jr.—known as Little Jess—a tough as nails good old boy who laughed and had a good time, emerged victorious in a drama that would sound familiar to me many years later.

But enough history. I began by making scratchers, alongside my friend Larry Hall, one of Big Jess's grandsons. The two of us worked inside an old metal Quonset hut, where afternoon temperatures inside surged well above the 110 degree mark. We turned out three or four springs for the scratcher a minute. If we had worked any faster, we would've keeled over from heatstroke. I spent nearly every cent I made in the Coke machine—and the Cokes were only a nickel apiece.

Shows you how much money I made.

Scratcher

The hut was filled with machines—which Big Jess had also invented—that spit scratchers out at three hundred a minute. They did a hundred times the work we did without breaking a sweat. Demoralized, after a few weeks I begged for another job.

"Sure thing," said Little Jess, who put me to work unloading one-hundred-pound sacks of cement from railroad boxcars that stopped outside Antelope Tool Company. Every bag had to be lifted by hand. Every fiftieth bag was broken, spilling its contents, making the conditions horrendous. I worked in cement dust up to my ankles, breathed the dirty air, and wiped it from my glasses. Whatever dust didn't make it into my lungs or eyes stuck to my sweaty skin and hardened. I'd never worked as hard or gone home as achy and sick.

After my first day, I worked up the nerve to get Mr. Hall to transfer me again. It was either that or die. He stuck me on the crew of laborers digging sewer lines and the swimming pool for his new home. The ground was cleechie, a hard sediment rock resembling cement. It was impossible to dig this stuff. You had to blast it. I would make a few holes by pounding a stake into the ground, then another guy would load it with dynamite and blow it up.

Gradually the hole got bigger. Once we got below ground, the lack of air, the heat, and the lingering dynamite fumes made working in it almost lethal. I got terrible headaches. Big strong men passed out every few hours. As the bodies piled up, I feared my turn was coming. Too soon for my taste. I didn't want to go having dug my own grave.

My dad understood when I quit, but he wouldn't let me hang around the rest of the summer, and so he found me a job bucking hay. That was basically more hard manual labor. I cut alfalfa, tied it in bales, loaded it on trucks, and then unloaded it in barns. The thick dust in the air and the heat made this job miserable too. But one guy told me not to worry about the heat. As he explained, Texas got the first harvest, then everyone migrated north to states with cooler climates. He was actually excited at the prospect.

"Larry," he said, "think about all the money we can make following the harvest all the way up to Montana."

I'd never seen a man as enthusiastic. He couldn't have been getting any more money than I was, and I got only 50 cents an hour.

And for what? Hay for some damn cow to eat.

I had another serious talk with my dad.

"I'm just not cut out for this kind of cowboying," I said. "I haven't seen a horse for two summers, except in a rodeo."

My dad was sympathetic. Taking pity on me, he suggested a hiatus until the fall, when I'd start college. But that itself was a subject we hadn't discussed. College. My dad laid out his vision. He wanted me to attend college, then law school, and then join his firm, eventually taking it over.

I wasn't a bad student but I wasn't what you'd call a disciplined student either.

"I don't think I have that studious quality that's required to be a good lawyer," I said.

"What are you talking about, Larry?" my dad said. "You do great in history. You remembered your lines in the school play. You'll be a great lawyer."

I don't remember the extent of our discussion. Nor do I remember exactly at what point I arrived at this next insight. But I realized I didn't have the facility most people had to plan for the future. I was more into living the moment. My dad worried that what I really meant was I didn't want to work hard. I don't think so. I was willing to break my neck for something I liked, something that I was passionate about doing, something I thought was fun . . .

"I think I want to act," I said.

He was silent, but his response was in his eyes. "Act?"

"I really like it. I want to give it a try."

Thank God my dad was an understanding man . . . or pretended to be.

5

D ad took me to the Greyhound station. With what was left of my summer salary, I bought a one-way ticket to New York City.

When I arrived, Mom offered me a choice between a new car or a trip to Sweden. Knowing I could always get a car, I opted for a trip with a group called Experiment in International Living.

Carrying a backpack and a small suitcase, I took an old steamship to Rotterdam and a train to Stockholm, where I was placed with a Swedish family. The Roones had never met an American until I walked through the door. I burst into their sedate family like ice cream over pickles. It was pure culture clash. We looked at each other with total bewilderment.

For my welcoming meal, they served me a bowl of curdled milk, a traditional dish called *filmjölk*. It smelled like old socks. When I spooned it to my mouth, a long, elasticlike string of icky goop remained in the bowl. My stomach turned. It pleaded with me not to eat it. The whole family watched as I put my spoon back down in the bowl. As reluctant and uncomfortable as I was in rejecting their culture and hospitality, I couldn't bring myself to eat this dish. I feared what might happen if I did.

Soon they feared me. That afternoon the Roones' son Nels tried teaching me to fence. He took it in school and was quite proficient. He taught me the old thrust-and-parry routine. After proving myself less than spectacular, I showed him my throw-the-sword routine, which I'd learned from the Zorro movies. We spent the rest of the day in the emergency room, getting his eyebrow stitched. Later that night, as penance, I dutifully ate my *filmjölk*. That the Roones put up with me the whole summer attested to their good Lutheran compassion.

And their patience. I didn't get out of bed in the morning till around 10, hours after the Roones were up and busy. The pot of coffee their eldest daughter left outside my door would always be cold by the time I rose. After a few weeks, I almost looked forward to my bowl of *filmjölk*, which was tolerable if I added enough lingonberries. Each morning they commented on how late I slept and wondered why I was so tired.

I had a good explanation. I'd met an American sailor who'd jumped ship after the war and had made Sweden his home. He loved Swedish women and aquavit, a liquor known as "the elixir of life." He took me to a party, where I met my own Swedish beauty and got to know her better over several glasses of aquavit. She was the daughter of a taxi driver. Her hair was the color of golden straw and her skin tanned to a honeyed brown.

Her family had a canoe and we took it for outings on

Lake Mälaren. In the summer, days lasted for 23 hours there. We had a great summer together.

Toward the end of my stay, my group took a 10-day trip into the mountains of Lapland, in northern Sweden. The scenery was spectacular. We drank from clear, icy streams that originated in glaciers high above the Arctic Circle and breathed fresh, crisp air. At night, I entertained by playing Burl Ives songs on my guitar. I had only one complaint—the giant mosquitoes that feasted on my American flesh.

The saddest day of my life was when the trip ended and I had to say good-bye to my girlfriend. She accompanied me to the train station. At 17, I didn't know if I'd ever feel as deeply about another woman in my life. Even though we promised to write, we never did, and all the fears I had that I'd never see her again were well founded.

As it turned out, I eventually fell in love with another Swedish beauty. She lived three blocks from the Roones. We took the same tram into the city, though our paths never crossed until I met her in London four years later. This time I wouldn't let her go.

In the fall, I entered Bard, a small college in Annandale-on-Hudson, New York, and it turned out I knew people there. Both Roger Phillips and Severn Darden, my roommates from Woodstock, were also freshmen. In fact, Roger had recommended Bard to my mother and Richard. I liked Bard from the start. Founded in 1860 as an Episcopalian school, it was a progressive liberal arts college that (I quickly realized) would allow me to continue my studies in drinking, smoking, and pursuing the opposite sex.

While everyone scrambled to pick their majors, hoping they were making the right choice, I chose drama and dance. The pretty girls were there and the few guys who signed up didn't seem interested in them. I sensed there'd be much greater opportunity in that major for me than in math, science, or English, and I was absolutely right. After a few months I'd had the best sex in my life, with young women who were kind, instructive, and eager to pass along their knowledge. Actually, they were eager to pass *me* along, which they did.

I was in several plays, often alongside Ted Flicker, who became a fast friend. My first real production was Shakespeare's *Twelfth Night*, in which I played Valentine. These plays were a big leap for me, and I remember feeling outclassed by the other student actors, sometimes like I had absolutely no business being onstage. Every night backstage, I noticed the girl on the book always seemed to be laughing, looking up, or talking to someone whenever I was around. Maybe I was paranoid, but I always thought she was about to expose me as a fraud.

However, I discovered that I enjoyed being onstage. The best thing I did, at least in my opinion, was a dance project created by one of the senior girls as her thesis. It was a modern ballet. I never had the kind of talent that would make anyone suggest I try out for George Balanchine, but my exuberance added a spark to the program. At least it did according to my very first review, which appeared in the *New York Times* and said something to the effect that Larry Hagman is outstanding.

That crumb of encouragement was enough for me.

We had January and February off from class in order to get real-world experience, and with my mother's help I got an apprenticeship with Margot Jones's prestigious theater group in Dallas. A lot of people criticize nepotism, but hell, it worked for me. Besides, after the door is opened, it doesn't matter. You're on your own.

Margot, known for giving playwright Tennessee Williams his start, had created a theater in the round, which at the time was a brand-new, almost radical idea and had attracted a diverse group of actors, including TV soap star Peggy McKay and actor Jack Warden, who was just starting out. We put on *Romeo and Juliet* (I carried a spear) and Sean O'Casey's latest work, *Cock-a-Doodle Dandy*. Despite long, hard hours, I realized I had an affinity and an appetite for the stage.

I also acquired experience outside of the theater. I lived at the YMCA, a pretty rough place in those days. I'd been warned that only gays lived at the Y and they attacked innocents like me. But I had no choice; I couldn't afford to stay anyplace else, and what the hell, I figured nothing would happen. Just to be safe, though, before going to bed I bolted my door, braced it shut with a chair, and then worried all night. I didn't sleep much.

After four weeks, I was exhausted, and though untouched, I was still uneasy. I moved to a boardinghouse recommended by one of the guys at the theater. It seemed nice and safe. Your basic boardinghouse. In other words, it was teeming with weirdos. On my first night, someone told to watch out for "the bear."

"The bear? What's the bear?

"Just watch out," he said.

For what? My room, the Ritz of boardinghouse rooms, was on the top floor. I jokingly referred to it as a second-floor penthouse. On my second night, I returned from a grueling day of rehearsals. Exhausted, I flopped onto the bed and went to sleep. Around one, I felt a thud against my bed. Then this something climbed into bed with me. It scared the crap out of me. I wasn't able to move, that's how frightened I was. Then this thing took my hand and placed it on its enormous breast—actually, a mound of hair.

That's when I remembered: the bear!

"How do you like that, honey?"

I recognized the voice. It was my landlandy. She wanted me to massage her hairy chest. Maybe she wanted me to do more than that, but I didn't want to go that far even in my imagination. After I got her out of there, I got out myself and bunked with a friend from the theater. One night he took me out for White Castle hamburgers, and we were hanging out at the stand when a song came on the jukebox. He told me to listen.

"Who's that?" I asked.

"Just listen," he said.

I looked around. The girls were going wild.

"What is it?" I asked.

"Rock and roll," he said.

It was "Blue Suede Shoes." I didn't get it. I was into Stan Kenton and Glen Miller. I obviously had a lot to learn.

I finished out the year at Bard, doing more of the same: building sets, learning about lights, sewing costumes, and a lot of acting. In June, when my mother asked how I'd enjoyed college, I told her that there'd been some good moments onstage but I'd imagined doing something else. When I'd left Texas, it had been for Broadway and the excitement of New York City, not small-town college life along the Hudson. My instinct told me to move on and I worked up the nerve to tell my mother I wasn't going back.

"It's just not what I want to do," I said.

"You don't want to be an actor?" she asked.

"No, I still want to. I'm just not cut out for school."

She looked at me and must've seen that bit of herself at 17 and 18 years old, that girl who, despite a husband and a child, knew her future was in Hollywood.

She smiled. No matter her age, her smile remained mischievous and youthful. She never really grew up.

"Let me see what I can do," she said.

6

I spent the summer with Margret Webster's acclaimed Shakespeare workshop in Woodstock, New York, where I worked in about six or seven plays with many excellent teachers, like Lucia Victor, and actors like Nancy Marchand, who went on to memorable roles on TV in *Lou Grant* and *The Sopranos*. I remember being in an Irish play, in which I was playing a dead man, and I forced the guys who were carrying me to take me onstage. I kept saying, "Goddamn it, get me out there." I was so anxious to get out there. Except I was four pages too early.

I was always jumping my cue. That was my biggest problem. I couldn't wait to get on.

But I also remember receiving some decent reviews for a small part in *The Taming of the Shrew*. Though my notices were more about being the son of Mary Martin, who was getting raves in *Annie Get Your Gun*, I finally started having the kind of acting experience I'd wanted.

It was a great eight weeks, except for one nagging

concern. The Korean War started that summer and I felt the threat of being drafted for a real war. The threat was real and it consumed everybody over 18. It filled young men in the 1950s with a paranoia that was hard to shake.

Then I moved back in with Mother and Richard in Connecticut. That lasted a very short time, and for good reason. I was drinking pretty heavily at the time. It was a skill I had picked up at Bard and honed in Dallas. One night I got a tape recorder and read all of James Thurber while consuming a bottle of gin. At that time I drank salty dogs—grapefruit juice, gin, and salt around the rim.

For the next few days, I was extremely sick. It was not a pretty sight.

Mother thought I had a walking pneumonia and called the doctor.

"Mrs. Halliday," he said, "I have to tell you that your son does not have walking pneumonia. He is going through alcohol poisoning."

Mother faced me down.

"If you drink like that, you can drink on your own," she said none too happily.

I did not know what to say. I had been drinking on my own—and doing a hell of a good job.

"Larry, I'm going to give you 50 dollars a week, and you can go find a place of your own," she said. "Visit me backstage when you can."

Getting kicked out of the house was the best thing that ever happened. I had just finished reading *The Catcher in the Rye*. I felt I was a misunderstood teenager, which of course I was, so I packed my one suitcase and I left without any hard feelings. However, I suspected Mother was a litle disappointed in me, to say the least. Dragging my suitcase, an old leather satchel that weighed 50 pounds empty and about triple that full of clothes, I took the train into New York City.

As soon as I got off the train, it started to rain. I walked into one hotel after another, looking for a place with a room for $50 a week. Eventually I arrived at the Knickerbocker Hotel, which was so old it still had DC current in the rooms, a fact I discovered when I plugged in my tape recorder and fried it. The room was afford-able, just $34 a week, leaving me $16 to eat and drink.

I was allowed to observe classes at the Actors Studio and watched people destroy one another's performances with stinging critiques. Knowing that was not for me, I flopped around a few other acting classes, but nothing stuck. When Mother saw I was at least making an effort, she put me in touch with Lawrence Schwab, the producer who gave her her start on Broadway, and he put me in touch with his partner George Eckles, who went by the name St. John Terrell.

His name was pronounced *Sinjin*. He was a wonderful teacher and mentor. I sat in his office while he looked me over, like a man looking at hieroglyphs for the first time, and he seemed absolutely perplexed.

"What are we going to do with you, kid?" he muttered.

"I'm a helluva dancer," I said.

"Dancers are a dime a dozen, kid."

But Sinjin knew much more than he let on. He produced a slew of musicals that changed weekly, and he signed up a revolving cast of stars for the lead parts. They would do a week, then leave; the show would change, and a new star would perform. It was a tidy little formula, but Sinjin profited, and occasionally he shared bits of wisdom.

"I'm going to tell you something, Larry, and remember

this," he said. "You don't have to pay actors and dancers that much."

"You don't?"

"No, because no matter how much you pay them, when the rag goes up"—the rag was the curtain—"they're going to do the best they can. They can't help it."

Sinjin didn't have anything for me at that moment, but before Christmas he came up with my first job. He was producing musicals for the annual winter musical circus in Saint Petersburg, Florida. He wanted me to drive the show's choreographer, Ken MacKenzie, his wife, the lead dancer, their three Pekingese, two chorus girls, a newly hired secretary—let's call her Frances—and her Great Dane down there in a 1941 Navy surplus Woody station wagon that looked ready for the scrap heap.

I told him fine.

Fine was probably not the right word, but on the day after Christmas we loaded up the wagon and took off. With all of us crammed into the car, plus our luggage and assorted dog food bowls, which were half in the car and half tied to the roof, it was crowded, to say the least.

A short ways into the trip—and mind you, it was snowing and sleeting the whole way; it was just a damn shit storm is what it was—I realized those tiny Pekingese could not stand the Great Dane and he could not stand them. There were problems right away.

The trip was supposed to take three days. Sinjin had given me $150 to ensure we slept comfortably at night. I started down the New Jersey Turnpike, wishing either the Great Dane would eat the two Pekingese or they would annoy him into jumping out the window and hitchhiking to Florida on his own. I had never heard noise like that in a car. And that was the pleasant part of the trip!

About 300 miles later, somewhere in Delaware, I got my first blowout.

Boom!

"What was that?"

Yap-yap-yap-yap!

Grrrrrrrr!

"Is everything okay?"

No, it wasn't. It was about two in the morning. It was colder than hell, it was snowing, and I did not have a spare tire. I walked about three miles in the dark to a filling station and bought a new tire and a used spare. Changing tires in that weather was a real learning experience.

Ready to go, I drove a couple hundred more miles down the highway before finally stopping at a motel for the night. When he gave me money, Sinjin had not figured the cost of a flat that would require me buying two tires. Nor had he figured the cost of motel rooms for so many people. And never mind the dogs. None of the motels we stopped at would take them.

"But Larry, they can't sleep in the car," Millie MacKenzie, the choreographer's wife, said. "They'll freeze to death."

So, after everyone settled into their rooms, I had the two chorus girls come on to the motel manager while I smuggled the dogs into the rooms.

The next day, following a short night's sleep, I told everyone that I wanted to make up for the time we lost the previous day. I drove as fast as possible in the terrible weather. Spirits in the tightly packed car were not quite as high as they were the day before, when they had been extremely low. People did not get along as well. Neither did the dogs. Somehow, though, all of us managed to tolerate one another until we crossed the line into Georgia.

That's when we suffered another blowout. Unlike the last time, no one asked what that noise was. The dogs did not growl. We knew. There was a collective groan.

Oh no.

Again, it was nighttime, cold, and miserable. I saw a light from a filling station far ahead, and as I tried rolling toward it another tire slowly lost air.

Oh shit.

Luckily a guy came along in a pickup. He stopped to see what was up with us. He saw the chorus girls, who were bundled up but had beautiful faces. I saw they triggered his interest. I stepped up and introduced Willard to the girls, who by this time knew the procedure. They whimpered helplessly, and I said they needed help.

"Yup, I'll give you a ride down there to the fillin' station," he said.

I walked in and the man running the place, one of those Southern mountain men who had no teeth and wore overalls that barely covered him, was sublimely drunk.

"Whatchay need, boy?" he asked.

"Tires."

"Well, we got tires here," he said. "What kind you want?"

"The kind that won't blow out," I said.

"Well, what kind of car you got, boy?"

"One with pretty women in it," said the guy who picked me up, smiling hopefully.

About an hour later we had been driven back to the station, the car had been towed, and I was back in the office talking to Jethro.

"Where y'all stayin'?" he asked.

"We need to find a motel. Know of any nearby?"

"We've got a motel right here," he said, eyeballing the chorus girls. "In fact, we got two rooms open."

Just two, I thought. But what were my options?

"Okay," I said. "How much?"

Whatever amount he told me was more than I had when I added in the tires and the money I would need for food. Ignoring the surge of panic I felt, which might have convinced me that I really was an actor, I struck a deal with the guy, promising to be out of the rooms by noon the next day. Then he gave everyone a taste of the local moonshine he said he made and we settled into the rooms.

They were adjoining rooms with a dank smell. I put the MacKenzies, their Pekingese, and the chorus girls in the larger room, which had two beds, and then the secretary, Frances, and I took the other, smaller one, which had only one bed. Frances promptly claimed it, and her Great Dane hopped on just to make sure I knew my place was on the floor—the cold floor again.

A few hours later I heard a noise that sounded like moaning. My first thought was terror. I thought maybe Jethro or Willard or both had sneaked into the room and were molesting Frances. I turned on my little flashlight and raised my head just slightly enough to see that Frances and her Great Dane were in the midst of a—uh—well, they were having a moment together. In truth, it was more than a moment. Frances had her eyes shut tight, was having a wonderful time, and it made my jaw drop lower than that Great Dane's.

I put my head down, covered my ears, and thought, Oh God, what am I going to tell Mother when she asks how work is going?

"How was your night?" Jethro asked the next morning. We were in the bar for breakfast. He had clearly been up all night. I could see our car in the garage. It looked almost refitted with tires. After scrambling up some eggs and frying bacon, he went back outside, leaving us to eat in relative peace and quiet. Everyone looked tired, except the Great Dane, who, I swore, had a smile and looked like he might want a cigarette.

But apparently his mood wasn't that good. When one of the Pekingese went after a piece of bacon that dropped on the floor, the Great Dane thought it belonged to him and started chomping on the little dog. The other Peke attacked the Great Dane. And all hell broke loose. Chairs and dishes toppled and broke.

Jethro heard the ruckus and came in.

"You aren't getting ready to leave, are you?" he asked.

At some point he had fallen in love with Frances. Now he sidled up to her, real close, and gave her a goofy look that showed he was truly dangerous.

"How's it going with the car?" I asked, knowing we had to get out of there.

"Coming along," he replied.

"We just needed two tires." I was being bold. "It should be ready by now."

Somehow I convinced him to tighten up the final lugs on the tires and we took off faster than Napoleon fleeing Moscow. I ended up borrowing gas money from the MacKenzies and cash for food from the chorus girls. But we finally arrived in Saint Petersburg. I phoned Sinjin to say we'd made it and to ask for more money to pay everyone back. But he beat me to the punch by asking how much cash I had left over.

"Left over?" I replied. "I had to borrow like a hundred bucks from these people to feed them."

Sinjin was incredulous.

"I didn't tell you to feed them," he said. "They're on a per diem. They feed themselves."

Whatever. I was pleased with myself. This was my first professional job in the theater, and I'd been successful. Though it would take me six weeks to pay back the money I'd borrowed, Sinjin was a great teacher. I got everyone where they were supposed to go in one piece—except for one of the Peeks, who was missing a small chunk of his right ear.

7

In Saint Petersburg, I had one of the best theatrical experiences of my life. Sinjin staged good solid musicals like *Desert Song*, *No No Nanette*, *Die Fledermaus*, *Showboat*, *Up in Central Park*, and *Carousel* under a tent large enough to hold fifteen hundred people. Based on my successful jaunt cross-country, he made me the assistant prop man—at no increase in salary, I might add. I still made only 28 bucks a week. He also put me in the chorus, letting me sing, dance, and play bit parts. Sinjin knew how to get his money's worth.

Sinjin also thought I should know how to put up the tent and maintain it, so in addition to everything else, he assigned me to work under the tutelage of the tent master, Joe Pelican. He'd learned all there was to know about big tents from years with the Ringling Brothers Circus. I learned how to drive nine-foot stakes into the ground while swinging a 14-pound sledgehammer from the top of a ladder. That was another learning experience. You miss the stake, you go flying off the ladder. After a couple of misses, I had perfect aim. I'm not kidding.

Between setup, daytime rehearsals, and nighttime performances, plus two matinees a week, tent maintenance, and numerous other assignments, I crammed 35 hours of work into 24—and somehow I still managed to get in some playtime with one of the chorus girls I had driven down with.

She was a bona fide nymphomaniac. I remember telling Sinjin I liked her a lot! Smiling, he said that he did too. So did the general manager, the carpenter, the head parking attendant, and several of his assistants.

"I like working the winter down here," I told her.

"I like the work you do down there too," she replied. "Now hush up, cutie, till I tell you it's time to take a break."

This was not an easy gig, though. The show was closed when a hurricane hit and ripped the tent apart. The enormous tent poles, weighing over a thousand pounds, were blown down and one of them landed on the wardrobe mistress. That tragedy, combined with dreadful box office sales, convinced Sinjin to move the show to Miami, where he had another tent on the Seventy-Ninth Street Causeway.

After what little remained of the lighting equipment was packed up and shipped off, I found myself with a two-week break before I would be needed again. I also found myself without a salary, as the always frugal Sinjin stopped paying me those weeks.

So on the way to Miami a few of us stopped in Sarasota, the winter home and headquarters of the Ringling Brothers Circus, which I'd always loved. With a few days to kill, and broke, I found one of the managers and asked if I could work for a couple of weeks.

"We need a ticket taker for one of the sideshows," he replied.

"Done."

On my second day of work, the circus staged their annual winter parade through town, advertising the start of the winter season. It was about a hundred degrees, one of those Chamber of Commerce days when Floridians put on their Bermuda shorts while the rest of the country is snowed in. A guy told me they needed some help with the animals.

"Animals? I'm pretty good with animals," I lied.

"Good, try this on." He gave me a lion's suit.

At 10 A.M., I got into my suit, practised a few growls. The parade started. It was hot and humid. By ten-thirty, I swear, the temperature had passed 140 degrees inside my lion's suit. I do not recall how long I managed to keep growling and marching. I remember sweat poured off me. I was wetter than when I had showered that morning. Next I remember about halfway through the parade being on my back and looking up into a clown's face. They had taken my head off and thrown a bucket of water on me.

"What's going on?" I mumbled.

"You got heatstroke," the clown said.

A lot of people had crowded around, apparently thinking it was exciting to see one of the lions passed out on the asphalt. As I staggered up, pausing on all fours, some kid sprinted out from the crowd and ripped off my tail. It was no easy task. The tail was so long that it had a wire that ran from my neck to my ass to keep it in the air. But he snatched it right off, almost strangling me, and I was too groggy to give chase.

"Where's your tail, lad?" the costume guy asked later on when I returned my suit.

"Some kid ran off with it," I said.

"Well, that'll cost you thirty-five dollars."

"I'm not even making $35 a week. Not even close."

"I know," he said with a smirk. "I'll give you a break. You'll have to work here another week for nothing."

I was quickly learning that theater and circus management have something in common—they're all heart.

Once I got to Miami, the intensity of everything, from the work to my life, ratcheted up. You could not live in that city for my salary, $28 a week, so I bunked in the men's latrine. I threw up a cot between the urinals and put up a tent of mosquito netting. The latrine was a major breeding ground of Miami's mosquito population. I dated a member of the corps de ballet whose father was a U.S. Customs officer, and every two weeks he confiscated a stalk of bananas for me. She kept me alive. All I did in my time off (ho-ho) was drink rum, eat bananas, an occasional hamburger, and that pretty little dancer.

My day started at 6 A.M. when I checked the tent to see if the wind had come up at night and caused any damage. Then I sat in on rehearsals in my various capacities as chorus member, actor, assistant prop man. It was a lot to do, and yet I felt lucky to have the job. These musicals often boasted a talented cast headed by Elaine Stritch and solid characters like Iggy Wolfington and George Britton. My night didn't finish until very late, and I somehow had the energy to party all night, drinking and dancing and so on.

I'd never been as poor, tired, or happy. I had a lot of stamina. After all—I was 19.

*   *   *

Toward the end of summer, the area suffered a freak cold wave. There was even a sleet storm. Not surprisingly, between sleeping in the latrine and the crazy hours I kept, I came down with pneumonia. I felt like I was going to die. Iggy and George took me into the little house they rented and got me to a doctor, who gave me a shot of penicillin, which was still a relatively new drug. That got me through it.

By the time I recovered, though, the season was over.

I headed north, where Sinjin had me work in his productions in Lambertville, New Jersey. It was "the original musical circus in the round," where he had started out. By now I'd won my spurs and he made me the assistant stage manager, a position whose salary was regulated by the Actors' Equity Association. I don't remember the amount, but it was a helluva lot more than $28 a week. Best of all, it allowed me to get my Equity card, a big step for me in those days.

I was also playing very slightly bigger parts and feeling more confident about myself onstage when Mom called to ask me about an actor named Wilbur Evans. She was about to reprise her starring role in *South Pacific*, and Wilbur was set to be her leading man. I'd worked with him in Florida. She said she was concerned that he wasn't as tall as Ezio Pinza, her costar on Broadway. I assured her that he was a fine actor who would do well in the part. But it turned out she actually had something else on her mind. My mother could be crafty like that. She said there was a small speaking part open in *South Pacific* and I could also be in the chorus if I was interested.

I didn't have to think about it. I jumped at the offer.

The hard part was telling Sinjin, but he magnanimously let me go, saying mine would be hard shoes to fill. Indeed, he was going to have to pay at least three additional people to do the work I did. But knowing Sinjin, I felt confident he'd find another sucker.

8

Mother, Richard, Heller, and I sailed to Southampton from New York on the *Media*, a small passenger liner belonging to the White Star Lines. During the voyage, I met an air force Catholic chaplain, Captain O'Rourke, who was on his way to his post at the U.S. base at Bushy Park, England. We drank and joked all the way across the ocean and that connection would prove to be a great help to me a short time later.

The sailing was not as smooth during the brief family vacation we took before starting rehearsals. At one point we were at Castle Combe, a fine countryside hotel, and once again Richard was on my case. He saw me vault on a horse in the stable area and ride bareback. This sort of riding was apparently too wild for the proper form around the stable and caused quite a stir. At dinner, Richard informed my mother that I'd been misbehaving as usual, and it became an issue between us.

"The woman at the stables says you are harming the horses," he said.

"I didn't know that," I said. "I learned to do that back in Vermont and I've seen it in every Western movie ever made."

"I don't care how many Western movies you've seen. You're here now and there are very different customs."

Things got very heated and I went to my room. It must've been embarrassing to them in front of the other diners, but I was beyond caring. About three o'clock in the morning, I started down the back stairs, trying to sneak out quietly, except I kept knocking the walls with my heavy leather suitcase. I was like a bull in a china shop. Mother was waiting for me when I got to the bottom and asked what I was doing. I told her that I was getting away from *him*.

Mother convinced me to stay. She wouldn't admit Richard was a son of a bitch to me, but she emphasized that having me in the play was very important to her. Though she didn't say it outright, it was a way for us to have a relationship. I know she wanted me to see her in London, the scene of many triumphs, and I have to admit it felt like a homecoming when we checked into the Savoy Hotel a few days later.

Once rehearsals began, Mother was quickly drawn into her own world. She was so focused, so consumed with breaking in a completely new cast, doing interviews, and she was just plain remarkable when it came to handling the pressure of getting things together in less than a month. It was the first time I'd ever watched her this closely and I saw how much she loved it.

Richard was also busy, planning her schedule, dealing with producer and the press, and generally getting on everybody's nerves.

For some reason, he brought up the Castle Combe horse-vaulting episode again and this time I couldn't take it and left. I was on the street again, looking for a place to stay, when I got an offer from Archie Savage, the show's lead dancer. He was the only other American in the company besides Mother, Wilbur, and me. Archie had a great place on Belgrave Square and said I could stay there. I knew Archie from New York, where I'd once rented his Third Avenue apartment. He was a gay black man with impeccable taste. I remember him saying that he'd been turned away by several hotels in London, so he'd found a beautiful 20-room mansion to rent, and he opened it up to an array of boys, some of whom were in the show, others who were off the street.

The night I arrived Archie called everyone together for a meeting. He introduced me to the group. They were a colorful crowd, to say the least.

"Here's the deal," Archie said. "Larry has this room up there on the second floor and if anyone touches him, or even tries, I will beat the shit out of him."

"It's nice to meet all of you," I added.

And it was. They were great. That mansion was hopping 24 hours a day. I was there for two weeks, then hooked up with Ted Flicker, my friend from college. He had a nice little flat in Saint John's Wood and was looking for someone to share the expenses. It was the perfect arrangement. He went to the Royal Academy of Dramatic Art during the day, and I was in *South Pacific* at night. We seldom got in each other's way.

Director Josh Logan, the original director on Broadway, came in for the last week of rehearsals and gave the show its finishing touches. I had a nice little part. In a scene when the captain talked to his aide-de-camp, I was to come in through the door and tell the captain that Ensign Nellie Forbush—Mom—was there to see him. I handled that with ease—until opening night.

Everything was wonderful. Mother stood behind me in the middle of the stage, concealed behind the cabin that was the captain's office. She was bursting with pride as I waited to go on. I was so goddamn excited. The audience was filled with royalty, famous actors, and important British dignitaries. I was riding the rush of such a thrilling evening. Then I heard my cue, opened the door, and walked in front of the audience, and behind me, at the moment I started to speak, I heard Mother whispering, "No, not yet."

She was right. Overanxious, I had once again jumped my cue. The actor playing the captain stared at me like I had lost my mind. He ad-libbed. "Tell her to wait." I did an about-face and walked off chagrined. Mother didn't say anything. Her laugh was sufficient. A moment later, I opened the door *again* and introduced her at the proper time.

Afterward, the audience applauded thunderously. There were at least two dozen curtain calls. It was tremendous. They also threw coins on stage as was the custom at Drury Lane and showered Mother with loving shouts of "Mary! Mary!" It was exhilarating to stand out there.

Then all of us went to the Savoy for the party, where I had one of the thrills of my life. As Laurence Olivier led Mother across the dance floor, I danced with Vivien Leigh. My God, talk about a beautiful woman. I was so enamored of her I worried my knees might give out. Even though I had grown up around celebrities, I was starstruck, and Mother chuckled about it later.

"How was it, Larry?" she asked.

"Oh my God, Mom, I was dancing with Scarlett O'Hara."

After each night's performance, I got on my bicycle and rode ten minutes to the Irving Theatre, off Leicester Square, a late-night theater where I earned an extra three pounds a week by singing and dancing in a musical revue. Around 1 A.M., the tube closed, so I caught a cab back to my flat, using up the money I'd earned that night. I was always tired and broke. But happy.

"This beats the hell out of getting your ass shot in Korea," I said to Ted.

Oh my God, was it ever. The Korean War was going full tilt. I'd registered for the draft in Texas and constantly thought about my chances of being called up for service. They were higher than I wanted to know. From what I'd heard, the military liked the boys from Texas. They had a reputation for being good soldiers. While that was a reason to be proud, there was also a downside to being a great soldier. Occasionally you got killed. I wasn't interested in either fighting hard or getting killed. But when the letter arrived calling me into service, I couldn't disregard it.

I went to a U.S. military base in Germany for a physical. The doctor asked about *South Pacific* while reading through my papers.

"So you're in the theater?" he asked.

"Yes sir."

"Are you homosexual?"

"No, I am not," I replied.

"Why don't you say you are?" he asked. "Then I can get you out."

Okay, I admit it, the idea sounded good for about a quarter of a second. But back then people had different attitudes about gays, especially in the military. As bad as it is today, it was worse then. I worried that if I answered yes, it would be on my record forever. So I exclaimed, with the proper sense of outrage, "I can't do that!"

"Aw, come on," the doc said. "Who's going to know?"

I came up with another idea.

"I'm nearsighted," I said. "Without my glasses, I can't see a damn thing."

"Okay, I'll give you an eye test tomorrow."

That night I stayed in the barracks. Almost a year had passed since the opening night of *South Pacific*, and as I lay on my cot I marveled at how quickly time had gone by. One night I was in the Savoy, dancing with Vivien Leigh, and now I was going to sleep in a nearly empty Luftwaffe military barrack in Germany. Only one other guy was bunking in the barrack that night, and the next morning we hit the shower at the same time.

"You got any soap?" he asked.

"Sure," I said and tossed a bar his way.

Then I heard it drop. I saw him glance around for it.

"Hey, listen, can you find my glasses?" he asked. "They're on the shelf over there."

I handed him his specs. I noticed the lenses were thick as Coke bottle bottoms. I thought, My eyes are perfect compared to his.

"What do you do?" I asked.

"I'm in the army. A machine gunner's assistant."

"But you can't see."

"That don't mean nothing," he replied. "I carry the ammo and feed the belt in the machine gun. You don't have to see real good to do that."

There goes my chance of getting out of the service.

"What are you in?" he asked.

I thought about it for a moment and said, "I'm in deep shit."

9

When I got back to London I looked up Captain O'Rourke, who was stationed at Bushy Park, and asked if he knew of any way that I could get based in London. He did. Bribery.

"If you can get tickets to *South Pacific* for all the brass—the generals and the colonels—you'll probably be able to get any posting you want," he said. "Knowing who your mother is, I suspect those tickets ought to be relatively easy."

"I'll do my humble best, sir," I said.

Since Bushy Park was the enlistment center for the U.K., Captain O'Rourke walked me through the whole procedure like the good drinking buddy he was. While I was in basic training in Wales, he spoke to the general, and eight weeks later I was back in London, posted to the Third Air Force Headquarters, in South Ruislip, Middlesex, a convenient forty-five-minute subway ride from the apartment I shared with Ted Flicker. Then Ted was drafted and had to go back to the States for his basic training in the army. Before he left, Teddy found me a new roommate, his friend Henri Kleiman, a young, smart, stylish Englishman who wore pinstriped suits and a bowler hat. We became lifelong friends.

I belonged to the Remington Raiders, named such after the typewriters we used in the office. I was assigned to Special Services. Nowadays, that means a crack commando unit. In those days, it was different. I was in the entertainment division. I reported to a civilian who ran a ticket bureau for the military. If a VIP came to London and wanted tickets to a show, they called her and she tried to take care of them. But on my first day, I realized she couldn't get anything done when she turned to me in a panic.

"I got a general and his wife who are huge Mary Martin fans," she says. "Do you have any way of getting tickets to *South Pacific?*"

Obviously the scuttlebutt hadn't reached her. She had no idea of my relationship to the show or its star. That's how out of the loop she was.

"It's a popular show," I said.

"The hottest ticket in town."

"I'm not promising anything, but I'll do my damnedest."

I understood how crucial it was to make myself vital to the war effort right from the start.

She looked relieved when I said, "Why don't you let me deal with the general directly on this one?"

I met the general, who told me that he wanted six tickets. I informed him that the show was sold out every night, which he already knew, but I said I'd do my best to get him seats. A few days later, I delivered the prized tickets. Needless to say, that put me in very good standing with the general of the Third Air Force.

Soon I took over the ticket business. My boss was upset, but she was a civilian and didn't have to worry about the gunfire and mortar shells on the thirty-eighth parallel, so I didn't really care if her nose was out of joint. I just wanted to do a good job getting tickets for VIPs and keep my own ass from getting shot off.

By the end of the year I was put in charge of all the entertainment in the United Kingdom, which involved providing entertainment for sixty thousand men and their dependants. I produced *Stairway to the Stars*, a talent contest that drew from aspiring entertainers in the army and the air force. Dozens of acts were brought to Bushy Park, including comics, jugglers, barbershop quartets, tap dancers, magicians, jazz combos, and vaudeville routines. I put the winners of each category from *Stairway to the Stars* in another show, called *The Spotlight Review*, and toured it successfully across the 27 U.S. Air Force bases in the U.K.

I traveled with the show as producer, director, and coordinator—training I'd learned from Sinjin in Florida. Through these trips, I met the people who ran the service clubs, and they spread the word that the show was great, and soon I was bringing the show to military bases in France, Germany, Italy, and Austria. It was a great scam.

I also came to handle all the NCO and officers' clubs, too. I might have been only an airman second class, or the equivalent of a PFC in the army, but I could take advantage of a staff that included a major, a lieutenant, a captain, several sergeants, and three civilian secretaries. I also dressed in civilian clothes most of the time and lived in my own apartment. For the military, it was the good life. No one had a clue what I actually did—nor, most of the time, did I.

For the most part no one bothered me, because I was successful, but there were a few hard-asses who tried to put me in my place. One lieutenant, an escort officer with a USO group, which I also handled, came on the base for a week and made my life miserable by demanding one thing after another as if my sole purpose were to take care of him, not the other way around. As soon as he left I had my buddies in Personnel Services, the department in charge of the records, get even for me. They lost his pay records, threw out his medical records, and arranged a transfer to Thule, Greenland, which was the armpit of the Air Force.

As for my social life, I specialized in nighttime maneuvers. During my first year in the service, I dated actress Joan Collins, who was then 17 years old and so breathtakingly beautiful I thought she made Elizabeth Taylor look like a boy. I met her through Ted Flicker when he was going to the Royal Academy of Dramatic Art. Almost 20, I was a lark for her, since she normally dated older men, in their twenties and thirties. But we had some fun. I also went out with her sister Jackie, who was just as stunning. I never got anywhere with them, but boy, they were lots of fun.

Two years later I met Maj (pronounced *My*) Axelsson, a 25-year-old Swedish girl who was a successful clothing designer for a major wholesaler. She was my roommate's friend, part of Henri's cultured little group that liked to meet at pubs and coffeehouses, discuss important social issues, and attend the symphony. Henri told me she was a beautiful blonde, sharp, funny, and sensible. I liked what I saw from the moment I looked into her blue eyes.

And Maj? She thought I was cute. She gave me that much. From what she later told me, she liked a lot of things about me, including my sense of humor. Mostly she liked that I was very different from anybody she'd ever met and that I seemed to make my own rules.

"Almost everything is right," she confided to Henri.

"What's wrong?" he asked.

"Larry's an American. He couldn't be more American."

She'd lived in England for three years. During that time, she'd assumed the snobbery of her clique, and all of them looked down on the American servicemen they saw in Picadilly. She quoted the popular saying at the time. "There are three things wrong with them," she'd say. "They're overpaid, oversexed, and over here."

But she thought I was different. She'd flipped when I played her a George Shearing album, and she liked that my record collection also included Vivaldi and Gregorian chants. She also liked that I was able to sell her black market cigars for her boss, which incidentally helped pay for my rent. In any event, I seemed to have taste and connections, so when I finally asked her out, she said yes.

For our first date, I took her to the Colony Club, a very posh nightclub on Berkeley Square. It was freebie for me, since I was looking for acts for the NCO clubs. Everything was comped, from champagne to dinner. Maj seemed to be very impressed. Eventually we went out three or four nights a week to clubs around London, always free. I was constantly searching for new acts, and I wanted to see Maj as much as possible. It worked out well.

My travels to the continent with *The Spotlight Review* often kept us out of touch for long periods of time. I let her know I was thinking about her by sending her notes on the back of menus. She claims there were only three. When I was around, we were almost inseparable and had a ball. We ran all over London on my Vespa scooter. We hung out in coffeehouses and pubs, always running into people we knew, as if London were a small town. I was pretty serious about her, but I was constantly going away on trips and she worked hard.

About six months into our relationship, I went away on another long trip, this one lasting three months, and during that time Maj rented my apartment from me. She cleaned it up, repainted it, and slipcovered all the furniture. Clearly she improved my life. When I returned we planned to celebrate my twenty-third birthday by going to the theater. It was raining that night, a hellish downpour, and I waited for Maj in the NCO club at Burdrop Park, about sixty miles outside of London.

She was late. Several hours went by. I figured she was having trouble in the weather. The whole base knew she was late. When Maj arrived at the front gate, the guard told her that I was waiting for her in the bar at the NCO club. Indeed, I was—having my third or fourth martini. Finally, Maj pulled up in front in a little Morgan sports car. The top and the windshield were down. She was drenched, but explained she could see better with the top down.

With great difficulty, we put the top up, bailed the car out, and I got into the sopping wet driver's seat. I was intent on making the second act.

"I'll drive," I said, not thinking that as I put the sports car into reverse my blood was higher proof than a Molotov cocktail.

Once outside the base, I made a wrong turn and drove onto a field that had been used for practice by the British army's Tank Corps. The ground had been churned into a muddy quicksand. The little Morgan immediately sank up to its hubcaps in this muck. We could not budge. I stared

out the window, into the darkness, and then turned to
Maj, shaking my head in disgust.

"This is great. Just great," I said.

Maj nudged my shoulder lightly.

"At least we don't have to rush anymore," she said with
a laugh.

Suddenly our situation brightened. Nothing changed
except my outlook. For the past few months, I had mulled
over the idea of asking her to marry me. I had gone from
debating whether or not I should ask to contemplating the
perfect time and place to pop the question. I had only one
concern. What if she said no?

That was a possibility. I had no idea Maj had serious
reservations about getting involved with a guy from a show
business family. She worried she was in too deep and was
thinking about ending it before she got in any deeper. In
other words, she was in love with me. But thank God I
did not know, otherwise I never would have found the
nerve to say what I felt in my heart.

"Why don't we get married?"

She didn't say anything. She says she was too shocked
to respond.

"I think it would be very hard to live without you," I
continued.

She was still silent.

"You know, if we got married, I'd get an off-base living
allowance. And with your salary, we could have a great
life."

Finally, she took a deep breath and said yes. It was the
total reversal of what she'd planned on saying to me. We
kissed and steamed up the windows celebrating. When the
rain finally let up, I slogged across the field in mud up to
my knees and stood by the road until I flagged down a

farmer driving along on a big tractor. I explained that I'd just proposed and my girl had said yes, and he was only too happy to help launch us into the next stage of our life as a couple. But some help it turned out to be. He pulled the car out of the quagmire, yet in the process he ripped the Morgan's bumper off, causing Maj to gasp.

"Oh shit, now we're in a jam," Maj said, as if we weren't before.

"Why?" I asked.

"The car's borrowed."

Since Maj was a Swede living in England and I was now an airman first class in the U.S. Air Force, we had to wade through miles of red tape before we could get married. After the official papers were finally sent to USAFE headquarters in Wiesbaden, Germany, they were returned, refused. I was told enlisted men were prohibited from marrying officers. They thought "Maj" was an abbreviation for "major". It took another month to straighten out that mess before we set our wedding date on December 8, 1955.

A week before the wedding, I got in trouble with the WAF captain. In my four years of service, I did only two stints of guard duty. Ordinarily when you pulled guard duty at night, they let you sleep in till noon the next day. I thought that was standard operating procedure. So when I failed to report for duty until noon the next day, she nailed me. I was sent before the squadron commander, who was brand-new and did not know how to play the game, or at least my game. She restricted me to the base for a week—the only seven consecutive days I'd spent on the base in two years.

It took me out of the wedding loop, forcing Maj to plan the whole thing by herself. Actually, we had two ceremonies. The first was a civil ceremony witnessed by my best man, Staff Sergeant Bill Bolmier, and his wife, Shirley, who have become our lifelong friends. The second was a religious service at London's Swedish church in Marylebone. Henri Kleiman was my best man, and Maj's younger sister, Berit (Bebe), and her father, Axel, attended. Mother sent me an Austin-Healey as a wedding present.

Our honeymoon began the next day. We took a boat to Gothenburg, Sweden, unloaded the Healey, and drove to Eskilstuna, Maj's hometown. It was time for me to meet the rest of her family, and there were a lot of them, including her sisters Lillemor and Eva. I visited with her grandfather, who was ailing, but I think he liked me, because after we talked, he told Maj, "You got yourself a sturdy one."

After Christmas, we said good-bye to her relatives and drove to Wiesbaden, Germany, where I celebrated New Year's by nearly killing myself when I climbed down three balconies at our hotel—drunk, of course. We went skiing in Garmisch, in the Bavarian Alps, and then traveled to Salzburg, where I knew of a gorgeous resort. It turned out to be closed for the winter, but the owner, a former German U-boat captain, let us stay, provided we fed ourselves (I had several cans of baked beans in the car) and didn't mind the lack of heat, and then he spent the night regaling us with stories about how he'd blown Allied ships out of the water during the war.

Finally we ended up in Belgium, and with our last $10 we had what I think might be the greatest meal of my life, a steak with perfect french fries. We returned to our flat in London, at 82 Clifton Hill, with nothing but coins, having had the time of our lives.

We settled into married life as if it were a nonstop party.

Our door was always open. We bought a player piano for five bucks. As I'd promised, my air force salary combined with the 25 pounds Maj earned each week by designing dresses made us feel rich by British standards. At that time, a top private secretary got five pounds a week, or $14. Lunch in those days would cost us a shilling and a half. We'd also go to parties at NCO clubs, and as the party began to wind down, Maj would position herself outside a window with a large bag and I'd shovel into the bag the hams and turkeys and other food that was going to be tossed. Friends who couldn't get that kind of food waited for us to get home so they could feast.

About six months after we were married, Mother was starring in a Theater Guild production of Thornton Wilder's *The Skin of Our Teeth*. It also starred Helen Hayes, George Abbott, Lee Remick, and other luminaries. Mother said there were two walk-on parts available, and it would be an ideal opportunity to meet Maj. I took a two-week leave from the war effort, loaded our Austin-Healey on the ferry to France, and booked into what the American Express travel agent assured me was the cheapest hotel in central Paris. The Star Hotel, right off the Etoile, lived up to its billing. It cost a thousand francs, or about $2.80, a day—or an hour. But we had clean towels and hot water all the time.

We'd timed our arrival to meet Mother, Richard, and Heller when they got off the plane from New York. Mother and Maj adored each other. Maj was slightly in awe, but she'd never seen Mother perform and didn't understand the magic until the next day, when all of us were invited to the ambassador's residence for lunch. When the musicians there spotted Mary, they began to play "Dites Moi" from *South Pacific* and she walked up and sang. The whole place went gaga. At lunch, she sang more songs.

As for the play, it was Maj's debut and farewell performance in the theater. Opening night her knees were knocking so hard I literally had to push her onstage—just to walk across in the background. I was secretly relieved that Maj didn't want to make the stage her career. Offstage, for the first time in my memory, both Richard and I were on good behavior. There were no contretemps between us.

Those lovely two weeks included daily breakfasts at cafés on the Champs-Elysées with Peter Stone and Art Buchwald, who'd write his newspaper articles at the table while we talked. In fact, Art wrote one about Peter doing what he described as "the three-minute Louvre." You'd leave a cab running, sprint into the Louvre, visit the *Mona Lisa*, *Winged Victory*, and *Venus de Milo*, and return to the cab. When Art asked Peter for his secret, Peter replied, "Sneakers."

I think his record still stands.

We spent our first anniversary dancing at the Savoy. Earlier that day, as Maj was getting herself prettied at the Dorchester, I barged into her treatment room in the beauty parlor, opened the curtain, and dropped a matching pair of .38 revolvers. As I said, "Happy anniversary, honey," I thought the little girl tending to Maj was going to faint. Not even the London bobbies carried guns. "It's all right, darlin'," I said. "I'm from Texas."

In the summer of 1956, as my hitch came to an end, the WAF captain quite rightly still had it in for me for getting away with murder for four years and she refused my promotion to staff sergeant. She felt if I wasn't going to stay in the air force, which I wasn't, there was no sense in promoting me, and she was quite right. However, that meant Maj and I would have to take a troop ship home rather than fly, which seemed like she would get the last revenge.

Once we boarded the ship in Southampton, we were separated. Maj was put in a room upstairs with two women and a baby; she was miserable. I was down belowdecks, with six hundred enlisted servicemen, and just as miserable. We were permitted to see each other once a day; military rules. There wasn't any alcohol allowed on board either; also military rules. But on the second day out at sea, there was an announcement on the ship's PA asking if Mrs. Hagman could take tea with the ship's captain. Everyone was curious.

Maj was escorted to the captain's private cabin, and it turned out he was Swedish and wanted some Swedish company. He poured her aquavit, not tea. Soon he had me up too, and appointed me the ship's official entertainment director. I staged a show the night before we docked. Getting that ready was a welcome diversion, as was the fact that every day at teatime the three of us got shit-faced, which made the eight-day voyage almost tolerable.

We arrived in New York with mixed emotions. The U.S. dockworkers were on strike, delaying everything from being taken off the ship a full day. Then we discovered the battery of our Austin-Healey had run down. When I came back from looking for a new battery, I found Maj sitting in the driver's seat of the disabled car, crying that she wanted to go back to England. I reached in my jacket pocket, pulled out a pint of gin the captain had slipped me, and I handed it to Maj, saying, "Here honey, drink this. You'll feel better."

We drove from Brooklyn to Times Square. By the time

we were in the center of the lights, Maj was feeling no pain. In fact, she was pretty enthusiastic about the city, the taxis, the people, the excitement of the night, and she said, "Now this is more like it. One day I want to live here. Right here. In the middle of the hustle and bustle of New York."

That would happen, but first I took Maj to Mom's in Connecticut. Mom and Richard weren't there. We were greeted by Richard's sister, Didi, who was the opposite of him, warm and loving. She was a friend to us until the day she died. She helped us settle into the guest house, a darling place that Mother referred to as the Peter Pan House because it had been constructed as a present from producers after she spent a year in the role on Broadway and then starred in the classic 1955 TV special. According to Mother, Peter Pan is the most important thing she ever did in the theater. Never mind it was a hit or audiences smiled through the whole thing. For her it was a role that allowed her to play herself. Mother was someone who had dared to follow her dreams from Weatherford to stardom; she followed her heart; she refused to see any limitations. I figured that's as close to flying as humans get. In spirit, she really was Peter Pan.

Maj was also curious about my father. The opposite was also true. From the time he heard I came back to the States, he wanted to know when he was going to meet "the foreign bride." His tone implied that he was not ready to accept her into the family the way he would have been a gal from Texas. No, first he had to check her out.

Finally we arranged a visit. We flew down on one of those four-engine prop planes that took forever. It was 2 A.M. when we finally arrived at Amon Carter Field. My stepmother, Juanita, greeted us, explaining that my dad was in Jacksboro defending her cousin on a murder charge. About two hours later, my dad came through the front door talking about how he had driven all night to meet the foreign bride.

"Where the hell is she?" he bellowed.

First Juanita asked about the trial. Dad was happy to tell her, since he had saved her cousin's skin from a death sentence.

"I convinced the jury it was an accidental shooting," he said. "They gave him seven years."

"Seven years!"

"For godsakes, he shot a woman to death!"

. Dad was already at the liquor cabinet, reaching for a bottle of bourbon.

"Where's Larry's foreign bride? I'd like to have a drink with her."

It was 4 A.M.—a perfect time to drink in Texas. Maj was all smiles as Dad poured shots with the look of a Roman emperor who had just ordered the games to begin. After half the bottle was gone, and before breakfast, Dad took her outside to throw bayonets into a wall. She had to make them stick; she did. Then they graduated to hatchets. And then my dad got out his shotgun, handed Maj a .22, and announced they were going out to shoot doves.

"Dad," I said.

Maj gave me a dirty look.

"Larry," she said grinning. "I'm going dove hunting!"

We were in the middle of town when my dad spotted a dove. He pointed it out to Maj; then ordered her to "shoot that son of a bitch."

Maj turned out to be a crack shot, impressing my dad

and surprising the hell out of me because I knew she'd never shot a gun before. She made it a bad morning for several doves. We had them for breakfast, finished the bourbon, and went to bed. After a nap, Dad wanted to show Maj what a real oil well was like. There was one outside of town ready to come in. Dad was on a retainer to the company that was drilling and had a small piece of the action. It was one of the few oil wells he ever invested in.

We had to drive about 20 miles to get to it. The temperature was well above one hundred, almost unbearable. Only my dad's description of the excitement of watching a gusher come in and seeing people go bonkers over their newfound fortune distracted us from the discomfort of the heat. I listened with anticipation; Dad's description was exciting. I remember him telling Maj that there was nothing like that taste of oil fresh out of the ground.

Soon we were on the oil field. My dad watched as Maj put her tongue to a handful of dirt.

"You taste the oil?" he asked.

"No, it tastes like salt water," she said.

Dad was not happy with this news.

We waited out there nearly all afternoon as the investors saw their hope of a gusher dry up faster than a speck of water on that hot plain. We could have spent six months there waiting for oil and never seen it. Like so many oil wells, the only thing in there was all the money that people poured in it. The hole was dry.

There was a wonderful lake next to the well and we all jumped in. After a nice warm bath, we drove home and barbecued dinner. Dad toasted Maj's official welcome to the family with a bottle of Jack Daniel's. He said he did not know what they put in the water back in Sweden but she had strength and spirit. She could also hold her liquor. He liked her. Hell, he loved her.

We had terrible hangovers the next morning, but they were mild in comparison to what might have been if we had swum any longer the day before in the lake where we had decided to cool off. According to a story in the morning paper, just a few hours after we left the lake, a man who went swimming was bitten by more than 150 poisonous cottonmouth water moccasin snakes. His was an agonizing death.

"Jesus Christ, it was exactly the same place we were," I gasped.

"That's a sign, Larry," Maj said. "I think it's time to get out of Texas."

We headed for Brazil, where Mother and Richard owned a ranch. A few years earlier, their dear friends Janet Gaynor and her husband, Adrian, had invited them to visit the Moorish-style home they had built on ranchlands in Anápolis, and they had been immediately hooked. After being swindled in their first attempt to purchase property, they finally bought about a thousand hectares with a pretty but rustic adobe house, and turned it into a first-rate ranch, where they could unwind, ride horses, and enjoy the solitude of rolling green valleys and hills in every direction.

On a clear day, Mother would look out from the highest point on the property, a view that stretched for a hundred miles, and swear she could see where the earth began to curve.

You had to be hearty to enjoy it there, as luxuries weren't scarce, they were nonexistent. Life in Anápolis was the equivalent of America in the latter part of the nineteenth century—with dirt roads that were sometimes impassable in the rainy season, no telephone, with no electricity other than the power, about two hours' worth, from a crude little hydroelectric dam. We picked our coffee beans and roasted them in the morning. There was one little refrigerator, which ran on kerosene. Our food was cooked on a wood fire in the kitchen.

Yet it was exactly what I'd been looking for. They had horses and ran some cattle on the land. They also had ten thousand chickens and were the biggest supplier for Brasília, the soon-to-be new capital of Brazil. I had a feel for the ranch; the unbelievable beauty really touched me. The dirt was red the way it was in Weatherford, Texas. Mother noticed the effect it had on me and said that if I liked it that much, I could take it over and run the place.

The offer sounded good until my first blowout with Richard. Early on he and I got into one of our fights, and suddenly I was the guy in the old Hollywood Western who snarls, "This town ain't big enough for both of us." Only I did not have to say it. As much as the ranch touched my soul, I knew it was no use. There was no changing Richard. No talking to him. He was just a pain in the ass—and that was when he was at his best. He was worse once the booze and the speed kicked in.

After eleven o'clock in the morning, he was impossible. Later I found out one of the reasons Richard liked Brazil so much was that he could buy almost any medication over the counter, including amphetamines. After he died, Mother would find bags of speed stashed amongst his belongings; she never knew how bad his habit was; it explained a lot.

Maj and I took off for Rio, where we spent a month living

a carefree bohemian life, drawing money occasionally from a few thousand dollars Nanny had left me. and that Richard's accountant had invested wisely. In those days, you could survive nicely on very little money. For $12, you got a first-rate hotel room on the Copacabana in Rio. For four bucks, you ate steak and lobster and drank wine. Behind the Copacabana, in a backstreet alley, we found a bookstore that had novels in English, and we got hooked on Gore Vidal. We read everything he had written. Later, he became a good friend.

For a while, we considered staying in Brazil. The country was wide open and things were happening down there that made life look exciting. But I was eventually scared off by the wild fluctuations of the currency. One day you had $10, and the next day it was worth 10 cents, without any apparent reason for the change. There was another factor that made me decide to leave: Maj got pregnant. I didn't see us as pioneer types raising a family on the frontier. Unfortunately she miscarried on our way back to the States.

Still, the few weeks she carried the baby had an effect on me. If it was time to start a family, it was also time to get serious about my career.

10

Back in New York, we rented a basement apartment in Greenwich Village. We fell in love with the place. The building, owned by Irving Marantz, an artist who had a wife and two great kids, overflowed with character. Supposedly it had been constructed by Aaron Burr, the former vice-president of the United States and famous duelist who shot Alexander Hamilton. We had two rooms. One was the bedroom/living room/dining room, and the other was turned into Maj's sewing room. She brought in good money designing costumes for entertainers.

We also took over a neglected patch of dirt and weeds in the back. Maj turned it into a palette of bright flowers.

The rest was up to me. I knew to make it as an actor I needed a combination of talent, thick skin, luck, and connections. I believed I possessed talent and thick skin. Luckily, it turned out, I also had a connection. Ted Flicker. Teddy, my roommate from London, was directing William Saroyan's play *Once Around the Block* at the Cherry Lane

Theatre, and he gave me a job playing a cop. Every night I would run around the block two times before making my entrance in the first act so I'd really seem out of breath from having chased a burglar, as my character was supposed to have done.

The first part that allowed me to show what I was capable of was in an off-Broadway production of *Career*, James Lee's play about an actor determined to succeed on Broadway. It was at the Seventh Avenue Playhouse. I had a small part as a serviceman returning home from the European theater. At the top of the third act, I had a four-minute scene that stopped the show. The audience howled. That part enabled me to get a great agent, Jane Dacy, who also represented George C. Scott and James Dean, both of whom were also starting out.

Career ran for about a year, and during that time Maj became pregant again. We were ecstatic. We were also broke. At one point, we were paying for groceries with money that Maj's sister Bebe—who was living with us while she got her New York nursing license—got for selling her blood to the Red Cross. I could've asked my mother for money, but pride wouldn't let me. We were also estranged since my fight with Richard in Brazil. At the time, she was rehearsing for a new show, and some days the two of us were blocks from each other, yet we didn't communicate.

One day Maj finally picked up the phone and called her. My mother was a little tentative at first, wondering why Maj was calling.

"Mary," she said, "I come from a family where, if you have a difference, you work it out."

My mother was silent.

"It's a shame that you and Larry are gonna be this way,"

Maj continued. "We're going to have a baby. You're going to be a grandma."

More silence.

"You should talk to him," Maj said.

"It's up to him," my mother finally said.

That was the opening Maj needed. The two of them talked for about 45 more minutes. I think my mother was impressed that Maj had the guts to phone her and mediate a problem that the two of us were too stubborn to confront.

"Look, if I can make Larry go over to where you're rehearsing, will you talk to him?

"Yes."

That was the beginning of a better relationship. The next day I saw her backstage. The hard part had been taken care of by Maj. All my mom and I had to do was talk about the future . . . how Maj was feeling, the baby, the excitement, and work. We built from there.

Maj built too, but her due date arrived without any hint the baby might be ready to come out. She hadn't felt a single labor pain. We went from wondering where her water was going to break to what it would take to break it. We were invited to a party at a friend's apartment across the city. Given her condition, I didn't think it was a good idea to go, but Maj insisted. She was tired of being cooped up, fat, and uncomfortable.

We had two vehicles, our Austin-Healey and a Vespa motor scooter. Maj made me get out the Vespa so, as she said, she could feel the wind against her face.

It was against my better judgment. Nonetheless, I loaded her onto the back.

"Larry, it's like when we were in London," she beamed. "Let's go."

She held on tight and we scooted into the night. Less than a mile later, I drove over a pothole and Maj's water broke. It was probably the first time a pothole proved useful. Instead of the party, we ended up at Lenox Hill Hospital, where doctors told us the ride had induced Maj into labor.

Unfortunately it wasn't an easy one. After several false alarms, the doctors sent me home and promised to call when the action started. I went outside and saw the ground was covered with snow, two feet of it. There was no traffic in the streets. New York was at a standstill. Rather than go all the way downtown to the Village, I stayed at Val D'Auvray's apartment, which was just three blocks away from the hospital. A lot of years had passed since Mom had cracked open my piggy bank to flee from him. He'd contacted me when we moved to New York City and he and his wife, Jane, had become fast friends.

When the doctor finally called, about 3 A.M., it wasn't with good news. He said Maj was having trouble. The baby was stuck in her pelvic area and he needed permission to take the baby out with a C-section. That was major surgery. I worried about Maj and the baby and felt helpless and scared.

"Jesus, do you have to?" I asked.

"Do you want your kid to be able to count to ten?" he said.

"Take the child."

I saw Heidi Kristina Mary in the nursery while Maj was still under anesthesia. She was adorable. As Maj woke up, I was able to tell her our baby was perfect. After spending a week in the hospital, Maj and the baby were ready to come home. My mother, not wanting to think of me cramming Maj and the baby on the back of the Vespa, made sure her granddaughter traveled in style. She sent her Rolls-Royce and chauffeur to the hospital to take all of us home.

A week later, I received the bill for Maj's surgery and hospital stay. It was about $1,000. We didn't have a cent. We couldn't pay the bill. No way.

I met with the hospital's head accountant, a nice woman who glanced through my paperwork while I told her that I felt terribly embarrassed about being unable to meet my obligation.

"Larry Hagman?" she asked.

"Yes."

"Do you remember a guy named John Salmon?"

John Salmon. I hadn't thought of him for years. But sure, I remembered him.

"He was one of my best friends at Trinity."

She smiled warmly. "Well, I'm his mother."

The news immediately put me at ease. She worked out a payment plan, and I went home just as broke as before but feeling relieved. A few weeks later, I sold the Austin-Healey for $1,200, used the bulk of that to pay off the bill, and still had $200 left over. Suddenly we were rich.

Things got even better. My agent, Jane, came through with a job, getting me a role in the Ziv production of *The West Point Story*, an important show at the time. I got my part, learned my lines, and was supposed to report at 8 A.M. Monday morning at West Point, where the series was filmed. Embarrassingly, I miscalculated how long it would take to get there and arrived two hours late for my first TV job. I was appalled, but not to the point where I gave up.

Off in the distance, on the drill field, I saw what looked like a film crew, not that I'd ever seen one, and to make up for lost time I drove right up to it. As I jumped the curb, I pulled off the car's muffler and roared across the drill field. I was greeted by the first assistant director, who threw his hat down and said, "Who the hell are you? Don't you understand we're shooting out here and can't have that noise! We've got six hundred cadets out here marching behind our actors, and you ruined the shot!"

I told him who I was and he said, "Go to costume and makeup and get back here as soon as you can." I started the car up again and drove across the vast expanse of the field again, noticing everyone behind me covering their ears and shaking their heads. I somehow got through the two days I was shooting and was never asked to reappear on *The West Point Story* again.

However, Ziv had another series shooting in Florida, with Lloyd Bridges. It was called *Sea Hunt*, and a couple weeks later I went down there to do one show. Either they liked me or there weren't many actors who could scuba dive, because they kept me there for two more shows. Lloyd was a wonderful man who had the patience to help a neophyte like me learn the ins and outs of working in front of a camera. I also remember his two little boys were down there, Jeff and Beau, and both would become terrific actors just like their dad.

I returned home to Connecticut, to the Peter Pan house, where Maj, Heidi, and Bebe were staying while I was away. Mom was on the road at the time too. Anyway, I came back with a fistful of per diem, which Maj was happy to see since she was so broke she'd had to borrow five bucks from my mother's butler in order to buy groceries. I looked into the doll's carriage outside on the porch and there was my daughter, Heidi, pink and rosy, covered with a light dusting of snow. I was furious.

"She's going to freeze," I said.

"No, it's healthy," Maj said. "She's getting fresh air. It's good for her."

When Richard found out that Maj had borrowed five bucks from the butler he blew up at Maj. Big mistake. It was one thing to get angry at me, but an altogether different thing when he targeted Maj. She handed him his head, and we moved back to the Village apartment, which was suddenly way too small for the four of us. We had to move. Maj opened up the newspaper and searched the ads.

Though we hated to leave our beloved two-room, Aaron-Burr-slept-here place in the Village, our new apartment, located at 159 West Forty-ninth Street, between Sixth and Seventh Avenues, was smack in the middle of the Times Square district. It was exactly what Maj and I had wished for the day we arrived in New York. It was also one of the greatest bargains ever. For $269.60 a month, we got four bedrooms, three bathrooms, two living rooms, a kitchen, a rooftop terrace, and the aroma of being right above the Sun Luck Chinese Restaurant.

We never ate there because they kept shutting off our heat and hot water. We had a running feud with them.

However, we did eat right next door, at the Canton Village, which was run by Pearl, a very sophisticated Chinese lady who'd come to the States with a Chinese dance act. She danced on huge wooden balls three or four feet in diameter and played some of the best vaudeville theaters in America. When the act moved on, Pearl stayed in New York City. She was a kind and wonderful person who let us run up huge bills. Years later, when I got *I Dream of Jeannie*, I was in New York on a press junket and paid her $2,500, plus a 15 percent tip for her staff, for all that I owed, and we stayed friends forever.

Our new apartment also came with a history. Prior to us, it had been a bookie joint, and before that it had been a whorehouse run by the famous madam Polly Adler. We took advantage of having so much space by constantly offering friends a place to stay. But there were so many other people knocking on the door from its previous incarnations that we had to be extremely vigiliant about locking the door.

Not that it always worked. One night I was awakened by a noise. It was around three or four in the morning. We didn't have any guests at the time, so I got out of bed and cautiously searched the apartment. I went room by room until I found an old drunken sailor pissing in the back bathroom. He was irritated. He didn't even wait for me to ask what he was doing in my house.

"Where's Polly?" he asked.

"Huh?" I said.

"Polly Adler."

"She's gone."

"Well, goddamnit, she had the best whorehouse in Manhattan."

"I can't help you. Sorry."

The apartment couldn't have been more convenient when I was cast in the play *Comes a Day*, a new drama by Speed Lamkin. It took one minute and 20 seconds to walk from my front door to the theater in which I made my Broadway debut. The production also starred Judith Anderson, George C. Scott—in his first Broadway play too—and Brandon De Wilde, the child actor from the movie *Shane*.

My proximity to the theater didn't matter much, as I learned that working with George created many unexpected detours. He was brilliant in the play. He was nominated for, and should've won, the Tony Award. But his life offstage was far more dramatic than anything he did on it. I'd worked with George before, on *The Alcoa Hour*, a television show. One day George came to rehearsal limping. He was clearly in pain. I asked if he had a problem. George lifted up his shirt and I saw the side of his body, from shoulder to waist, was black-and-blue.

George explained that he'd beaten up a cop. Actually, he'd started with one and then taken on three or four— he couldn't remember the exact count—who then beat the crap out of him with sand-filled socks, bruising his kidneys. As a result, he came to the studio pissing blood. But the point is, he came to studio and he turned in a great performance.

He was no more together when we previewed the play in Philadelphia. He asked me to do him a little favor by picking up his pregnant wife at the airport between shows. Then he wanted me to take her to a room on the 14th floor of his hotel. Not his room, mind you, but a room I was to say was his.

No problem.

I didn't have a problem because he'd already cornered the market on problems. George couldn't pick up his wife because he had to meet an old mistress in the coffee shop . . . and the child he had with her . . . and her new husband.

Later, after I'd settled his wife into her/his room, he tracked me down. He had another problem.

"Larry, can you go downstairs and ward off Colleen

Dewhurst? She just showed up. They called me. She's in the lobby."

"Anything else I should know?"

"She's pregnant too. So please go down there and spend some time with her until I can get out of the coffee shop. I'll meet you in the lobby."

That was just a warm-up for New York. On opening night, George roared into our dressing room ready to explode. He'd spent the day with Colleen, who was due to give birth at any moment. Moments earlier, at the stage door, he been served with divorce papers by his wife. As he finished delivering a brilliant soliloquy about his day, he whipped around and punched his fist through the window. The glass was reinforced with chicken wire. It opened up every vein in his arm. He bled like a stuck pig.

We had less than an hour before the curtain went up.

For some reason, everyone looked at me to do something. I sprinted downstairs to the Turf, a famous restaurant on the corner, and asked for a bucket of ice. The guy behind the counter wanted to know why before he handed me a bucket. I told him an actor in the theater down the block had cut himself pretty severely and the show was about to start. We had to stanch the bleeding.

"Who's going to pay for it?" he asked.

"I am," I said.

Then I realized I was in my costume. My money was upstairs.

"Just give me the bucket," I said. "I'll bring it back."

After arguing for a few minutes, the manager got me the bucket and I ran back to the theater. Someone had wrapped George's whole arm in bandages. He plunged it directly into the bucket of ice. Right before the curtain went up, we rebandaged his hand and then shoved him onstage. Though drunk, pissed off, and bleeding, he still gave one of the greatest performances I've ever seen on a stage.

He expected the same from us—and hadn't lost his sense of humor in the way he let us know that. Moments before my entrance, he came up behind me and as I heard my cue, he put his hand on my shoulder and said, "Larry . . . about your performance . . . oh shit, never mind, I'll tell you after the show."

I stepped on the stage of my first Broadway show slightly stunned but I somehow managed to get through the night.

I learned that George was a little unpredictible too. One night I went out to a bar and the guy on the other side of him struck up a conversation. They talked, laughed, and suddenly in midconversation George picked up a plate of canapés and smashed the guy on the side of head. The blow nearly severed his ear. There was blood all over the place. I couldn't figure out what had triggered George. Probably nothing. From then on, I made it a rule always to sit real close to him, so he couldn't wind up and punch me. Not that he ever would've . . . maybe.

You never knew with George. One day George and Brandon came to my apartment between shows to unwind. I was barbecuing on the roof. After some drinks, I went downstairs to get the salad, and when I returned a few minutes later, George was dangling Brandon by his heels over the parapet, a five-floor drop to the pavement. George was screaming at the top of his voice.

"You little son of a bitch! If you ever step on my line like that again, *one of my best lines*, I'll drop you on your fucking head!"

I stayed calm. Showing how cool I was, I turned the

steaks on the grill. Poor Brandon was crying buckets, justi-
fiably terrified, while promising never to do it again. I
didn't know what George was going to do. I don't think
George knew. But if he let go, Brandon was dead.

I pretended there was nothing wrong and announced
that dinner was ready.

George glanced over his shoulder and nodded, "Oh,
okay." He reeled in Brandon, sat down, and cut into his
steak, while Brandon disappeared.

"Helluva of a good idea, steak, Larry," said George as
if nothing had happened.

I just marveled at the man. You don't meet many people
like him. George had charisma and power onstage as well
as in film, a rare talent that he proved in everything he
did. I was always in awe of him.

11

I've always said there were no down periods in my life—just out-of-work periods. That attitude has carried me through thick and thin, the only difference being the availability of cash. Mostly we didn't have much, and most of the young people we knew were in the same boat.

Take Carroll O'Connor. We formed a lifelong friendship when Burgess Meredith cast me in the play *God and Kate Murphy*, a depressing Irish story about faith and love starring Fay Compton and Lois Nettleton. Carroll was the assistant stage manager. While we were doing the show in Boston, he would chase my little daughter, Heidi, up and down the hotel hallway, the two of them laughing when he scooped her up in his arms. Except for being thinner and having darker hair, he was the same then as he was after his work as Archie Bunker in the landmark series *All in the Family* made him the TV equivalant of the Beatles. He was bellicose and funny, 100 percent Irish.

There was only one difference over the years. At the time we met, Carroll was so broke he couldn't afford more than a cold-water flat on Forty-sixth Street. Once the play reached Broadway, he and his beautiful wife, Nancy, made it a habit to come to our apartment several times each week to take a hot bath, which is when I first said, "Friends who bathe together stay together."

While we stayed friends for 40 years, the play closed mercifully after two weeks. Aside from Carroll, I remember it largely because I won the Clarance Derwood Award as the most promising new actor of the year, one of the very few awards I've ever won.

Work was so much more important than money, which I remember as more of an annoying necessity than a goal. One day I came home with two bags packed with groceries and Maj, pregnant with our second child, asked if I'd knocked off a store. No, the truth was, I'd found a five-dollar bill in the gutter.

We lived off the kindness and trust of the owners of our neighborhood stores. The Italian grocers let us run a tab, otherwise we wouldn't have eaten. The owner of Maj's favorite fabric store—an opera lover named Louie—also let her pick out whatever she needed. "It's no problem," he always said. "Pay when you can." The guy at the hardware store was just as understanding when Maj went through a nesting compulsion during her eighth month of pregnancy with our second child.

It seemed like every day she was recarpeting, repainting . . . something. I came in one day and found her standing on top of a ladder, painting the ceiling. Later that week we bumped into several of her doctors at a party, and the following day our pediatrician, Dr. Andy, called both of us into his office. He looked at Maj and said, "I heard about the ladder. You're grounded." Then he turned to me. "Make sure she stays on the ground till she has that child."

A few weeks later Maj went into labor. She needed another cesarean. It was a little easier this time since we knew she was going to need the C-section. When the doctors came out and told me the baby was a boy, I was overjoyed. We named him Preston Benjamin Axel, after my grandfather, my father, and Maj's father. He weighed ten and a half pounds, so big that Maj couldn't get over the fact that something that large had been inside her. I was so thrilled about our new arrival that, according to Maj, I went into Texas mode: when we left the hospital I carried my son and she carried her two suitcases by herself.

Shortly after we brought Preston home, Maj had a dress delivery going to Tallulah Bankhead. The costumes she designed and sewed kept us afloat. Singer Jane Morgan and Tallulah were two of her best customers. Obviously unable to deliver the dress herself, I went in her place. Maj warned me that Tallulah was extremely particular about who she'd let touch her, and she preferred Maj. But as I found out, Tallulah wasn't as particular about who she let see her. Or maybe she was simply expecting Maj. In any event, she answered the door stark naked, holding a glass of gin. It wasn't a pretty sight, at least from my perspective. But I don't think she cared. With a naughty purr, she told me to step inside, and in a reverse strip, she slipped the dress on right in front of me. She looked a lot better with it on.

Then I got the play *The Warm Peninsula*. Julie Harris starred with Farley Granger and June Havoc, Gypsy Rose

Lee's little sister. I played opposite June, who was in the role of a beautiful actress on the slide. I was her young lover. The play made tons of money on an extended pre-Broadway tour, but probably lost it all during the three weeks it was on Broadway. The cast was wonderful. I learned a lot and made enough to keep my family afloat until my next venture, which came soon after.

It was a musical called *The Nervous Set*, based on a book by Jay Landesman. My buddy Ted Flicker was directing it. The lyrics were by Fran Landesman and the music by Tom Wolf. Ted had presented it very successfully in Saint Louis and then cast me in it when he brought the play to Broadway. It was another great stage experience for me, but the run lasted just two weeks, again. This time, though, I'd learned not to pay for my friends' tickets on opening night, which kept me from going in the red.

Then I got what was in those years the greatest chance ever invented for an actor. I was cast on the daytime soap opera *The Edge of Night*. For more than two years, I played Ed Gibson, a young cop studying at night for his law degree. Done in a studio on upper Broadway, the soap was extremely hard work. It was trial by fire. I started out working three days a week, then four, and eventually I was on the set five days a week. By the end of the first two months, they were handing me 26 pages of dialogue every day.

The shows were broadcast live. There were no second takes. You had to know your stuff, and as soon as you finished one show, they gave you a script for another. It required intense discipline, so I developed a routine. After the show, I'd go straight home, make a martini, then sit down with my tape recorder and read my script into the microphone. After memorizing as much as I could, I ate dinner, and then went to bed. At 3 A.M. the recorder automatically clicked on and replayed my lines on a loop tape, over and over again, till I woke up.

About a month or two into it, I started to hallucinate. A doctor told me it was due to a lack of sleep and advised me to quit playing the tape at night, which I did. I didn't have time to listen anyway. I started driving to the Bucks County Playhouse in Pennsylvania every night to act with Bert Lahr in S. J. Perelman's comedy *The Beauty Part*. I'd finish *The Edge of Night* at 4 P.M. and drive 80 miles to the theater. The play was a smash hit, and it was a great role for me. I was on the stage for all but four minutes of the entire production. But Bert, a wily veteran, made sure that he had the lion's share of attention. I started out with six really boffo laughs, but gradually, after a show, Burt would say, "You know, that line is not really your character, kid. It's really my character."

By the end, I had two laughs.

But between the play and the soap I was getting invaluable training. You can't underestimate the value of working every day. Nothing compares to it, especially the soap opera. That really kept me on my toes. Besides all the lines, there were 20 or 30 characters involved in complex relationshops, and you had to keep track of every one of them. The shows were live. If someone forgot their lines, you had to know what was going on in the story in order to ad-lib without blowing the whole premise. Every day I seemed to learn something new about cameras, blocking, how not to upstage people, or how not to be upstaged, and also diplomacy.

I had a terrible time with the leading man, John Larkin. He made fun of me at every opportunity. He was full of little put-downs and slights that were probably his way of keeping a younger guy like me in check. Finally I faced him down and we became good friends. When he left the show to try his luck in Hollywood, they offered me the leading role and said they'd increase my salary just $500 a week. John was making considerably more than that, so I thanked them and got it in my head that I should start making plans to leave for Hollywood too.

I resigned from *The Edge of Night* when I rejoined *The Beauty Part* for its Broadway production. There was no way I could've done both. On opening night, Alice Ghostley decided she'd been in the business a lot longer than me and she wanted a dressing room closer to the stage, namely mine, which was two flights up from the stage. The new room they gave me was on the sixth floor. That didn't leave me any time to get offstage, go back to my dressing room, change clothes, have a cup of tea, and whatever during the brief break. That meant I'd have to spend the whole time in my changing tent on stage right.

I was pissed. Alice had a nice part, but nothing like mine. I was onstage all but four minutes of the play. Charlotte Rae heard what happened and asked if I wanted to share her dressing room. She was just one flight down, in the basement. I said, "Wonderful."

For the whole run of the play, Charlotte and I shared a dressing room, and I was very happy with that. She was a wonderful lady. But the way Alice pulled rank showed me that the business could be callous and uncaring, and also that I should not expect any special treatment. Talent didn't mean anything. It was all about how much clout you got.

Bert had plenty. The star of the play, he was still as diffi-cult as ever, maybe more so, and this time working with him was downright painful. Bert had a lot of lines and at his age he was having a difficult time remembering all of them. He didn't go through a single performance without going up somewhere. Each time that happened, he'd grab the back of my arm in a panic and squeeze until my eyes teared.

"Kid, what's my line?" he'd mutter.

Worse, he somehow made it seem as if I'd gone up and he was saving me.

This happened every night.

Then one night while I was taking a bath Maj saw the green-and-purple bruises on my arm.

"What the hell, did you get rolled or something?" she asked. "Look at the marks on you."

I looked over my arms and gently rubbed them.

"That's Bert," I winced.

"What do you mean?"

"That's where he grabs me and pinches me and gets the lines out of me."

"How are you putting up with that?" Maj wondered.

A good question.

"I'm thinking of getting out of the business after this show," I said. "This is too hard."

Bert had no clue what he was doing to me. As with most people who are brilliant, funny, and demanding, he was in his own world, operating from his own agenda. In this case, he had a piece of the box office. Before the first act of each show he stood backstage, peering at the audience through a hole in the curtain. Unwrapping a hard candy, he would count the house—always coming within 10 people—while providing an equally accurate critique: "A bunch of losers tonight." Or, "Okay, we've got a bunch of jewels in the front row. A first-class audience. There's money out there."

I learned a lot from Bert. He was driven and had a toughness that was acquired from years of playing the Borscht Belt. In *The Beauty Part*, he had a great advantage—after all, he had been the Cowardly Lion in *The Wizard of Oz*. The audience adored him before he stepped onstage. He was also a great comic and it was hard not to break up onstage every night.

He'd work a laugh till the audience was crying. Some nights the curtain would ring down 20 minutes later than normal because Bert was on a run. Nobody left the theater wanting their money back. He might approach the curtain before it went up like a man walking the last mile without energy, worried and glum; however, when the curtain did go up he turned into a dynamo with the energy of a 19-year-old boy. When the performance was over, he was wired.

He taught me what it was to be a straight man, which is essentially what I was on *I Dream of Jeannie*. He also taught me to hang tough when I felt like my career was collapsing. If you wanted to succeed, you had to be strong. I owe a lot to Bert, and after a while, like in most of life, the bruises disappeared.

The show had bad luck, though. We got great reviews, but there was a newspaper strike so nobody could read them. Then we moved theaters. Because of the newspaper strike, nobody knew where we'd moved to. The show should've run a couple of years, but we closed after about 10 weeks, and as they say, that's showbiz.

Before it closed, though, director Sidney Lumet saw a performance. Afterward, he offered me a part in *Fail Safe*, a movie he was about to film that was adapted from the best-selling novel about a runaway U.S. bomber with orders to drop an A-bomb on Moscow. He had lined up, among others, Henry Fonda, Walter Matthau, and Fritz Weaver, and he said there was a part for me if I wanted it. I signed on then.

He asked if I had read the book. I said no, but got it, read it, and knew I'd lucked out.

For my first movie, I could not have wished for better experience. We rehearsed for a month, a length of time practically unheard of on movies. I played Buck, the Russian-speaking translator for the U.S. president, who was portrayed by Henry Fonda, and the two of us were locked in a bomb shelter. I was the go-between, listening to the Soviet prime minister on the phone and then interpreting for the president. I must have done all right since everyone thought I really did speak Russian, though I never spoke a word of it in the film.

Henry gave me a few pointers, the kind that only a veteran would pass on. I thought it would be smart if my character smoked, given the tense situation. But as soon as Sidney cut a scene, the prop man rushed over and snipped my cigarette so it would match when filming resumed. I ended up smoking six or seven packs a day. As Henry pointed out, even for a smoker, that was a lot of nicotine to inhale, enough to make me sick, and I never smoked again in a film. Henry also told me not to act with my hands, if at all possible. If you gestured with them, you had to match the move in all the shots, and that took a lot of remembering. Sure enough, when I watched Henry, he just sat there with his hands crossed. He was a master of simplicity.

Columbia Pictures purchased *Fail Safe* in order to protect

another film still in production, Stanley Kubrick's master-piece *Dr. Strangelove; or, How I Learned to Stop Worrying and Love the Bomb*, which they wanted to come out first. They stuck *Fail Safe* on a shelf and no one saw it for two years. I felt betrayed. I was just naive. It was sound busi-ness on the studio's part.

12

Despite the frustration, I liked making movies. If you are around the right people, moviemaking is just the most fun an actor can possibly have. I wanted to do more. I called up director Josh Logan, a longtime family friend, and asked if he had any parts for me. He was about to shoot *Ensign Pulver*, the sequel to the terrific film *Mister Roberts*, and said he'd find a part for me when it began shooting in Acapulco.

Before it began, Maj and I took the kids and our Irish nanny, Peggy Ryan, and turned our trip to Acapulco into a vacation. We started by driving across the country to California in a Jeep station wagon. Right at the start, as we crossed into New Jersey, we had trouble. I'd put an emegency can of tire inflator under the front passenger's seat. It was right above the muffler, which heated up, caused the can to explode, and blew out the bottom of the Jeep.

It was a setback, but not enough to delay us. We kept

driving across the United States with one-hundred-degree heat radiating up off the asphalt and into the car. The hottest stretch was between Las Vegas and Los Angeles. But before we got there, we stopped at Yellowstone National Park. I pitched our tent in a crowded campground and Maj started cooking dinner inside it while Peggy watched the kids. At some point Maj felt someone leaning against her from outside the tent. She thought it was me, said, "Cut that out, Larry," and threw an elbow.

Suddenly she heard an angry growl. It was a bear, not me. Curious, Maj went outside the tent and saw five guys white as a sheet. When she saw me, I was holding a flashlight, trembling, having seen the bear destroy our ice chest and saunter off into the woods with a bag of marshmallows. And Peggy, who'd emigrated from Ireland and never been south of New Jersey, had the kids, one under each arm, as she dashed into the car, locked the door, and said Hail Marys all night.

She wouldn't let us in.

"No, no, I got the babies," she said. "They're all right. You two can sleep in the *tent*."

When we got to Los Angeles, we stayed in Carroll and Nancy O'Connor's house in Studio City. They'd gone to Rome, where he was acting in the film *Cleopatra*. One day a friend of ours, actor John McGiver, invited us to lunch at a home he was renting on the beach in Malibu Colony. A few days earlier, Maj had said she didn't think she could ever live among all the brown in L.A., but after a few hours out at the beach, she turned to me and said, "Now if we have to stay in California, we're going to live in Malibu."

It turned out to be prophetic.

After a couple weeks, we flew to Acapulco to start *Ensign*

Pulver. The movie starred Burl Ives, whose songs I'd played my entire life, Walter Matthau, Robert Walker, and Tommy Sands. I was fortunate to be given a pretty fair role as one of the ship's officers. The role was about the same size as the one Josh gave Jack Nicholson, who had already written and directed several movies. Once shooting began, he emerged as an off-screen ringleader among the cast of up-and-comers that included me, James Farentino, James Coco, and Peter Marshall.

It was swelteringly hot in Acapulco, nothing that I would have called paradise. The ship's deck was like a skillet. If you spilled water, it disappeared instantly with a sizzle. Prior to the first day of shooting, Josh assembled the whole cast and crew on the main deck and then delivered an address that reminded me of James Cagney talking to the crew in *Mister Roberts.* If we ever saw him sitting alone, he said, we were not to disturb him. If he was by himself, he explained, he was thinking about the film, lining up shots, or as he put it, "creating," and he did not want to be bothered.

Josh failed to mention he was taking lithium, at the time an experimental drug, which had side effects like drowsiness and lethargy; if you took enough, it caused a coma-like stupor. On the first day of actual work, he lined up a shot, did the scene, and then sat down on the deck to ponder the next shot. Josh, who was tanned even during the coldest New York winter, positioned himself facing the sun, all the better to enrich the deep, dark color of his face. He sat there for quite a while without being disturbed. Nor did he move when lunch was called. Neither did he appear to have moved when we returned after the break.

Finally the first assistant director went over and asked if he was all right. Not only was Josh not all right, he was completely zonked, basically unconscious save for some unintelligible mumbles, and so severely overbaked that his eyes were swollen shut and his lips had puffed up to the size of pomegranates. He was loaded onto a boat like a sack of rice, taken back to the hotel, and given a couple of days to recuperate before he was ready to shoot again.

At least he recovered. I cannot say as much for the birds. We had a scene in which one of the sailors, played by Tommy Sands, is on his way back home, and as his C-47 transport plane circles the boat, we were supposed to release dozens of white doves. It was to be a loving gesture as well as a striking cinematic moment. After five days in cages in the sun, those birds might as well have been on lithium too. When the C-47 was overhead, their cages were opened but the birds would not fly. Some actually got up in the rigging, but most would not budge. They had sunstroke, dehydration, or both.

We tried again in the afternoon, but still none of them would fly. So when the plane made a second pass, Josh had some of the crew get rifles and start shooting in the air in the hope the noise would scare them into flight. It made sense. By this time, though, the poor birds were so sick and weak they flew all right, but fell into the ocean like planes running out of gas. They littered the ocean, scores of sick white birds, fluttering and sputtering. It was the saddest, most frustrating thing I'd ever witnessed.

No, wrong. The saddest thing was when the sharks came. They arrived in threes and fours and started eating the birds as if they were Kentucky Fried Chicken. There was nothing any of us could do to help. We could not dive in. We did not have nets to scoop them out of harm's way. Taking a boat out would not help. As we watched this pathetic scene, the water churning with bloodstained feathers, some of the guys sobbed while others screamed, "Save the fucking birds!"

A few days later we nearly lost Josh the same way. During lunch, he decided to go for a swim. A ladder was let down and he dove into the ocean. He began a leisurely freestyle alongside the boat. Then someone noticed a dark shadow tailing him. Soon a bunch of us were watching, our mouths agape. It was a shark, at least an eight-footer, trailing Josh like a tailgater on the freeway, taking his sweet time while riding his bumper. All of us started to yell: "Josh, get your ass in here."

"What? I can't hear you."

"Get your ass on the boat." We pointed behind him. "Shark!"

Then the shark surfaced. Josh saw it about 12 feet behind him and swam for the boat as if trying to break an Olympic record. Once he got close enough, some guys pulled him in, otherwise it could have easily been the last of Josh Logan.

For his birthday, Maj and I gave him a half dozen baby chickens, which he raised in his hotel penthouse till nearly the end of filming, when the hotel's manager pressured him to put them on a farm. Another afternoon, while in a lithium-induced daze, he stood on the roof and tossed plate after plate into the swimming area, 10 floors below. The day before, we had showed him how to play Frisbee, which he could not throw to save his life. But he was murderous with those plates. The hotel manager, having noted we were friends, asked me to go to the roof and calm him down before he caused some serious damage.

If anyone actually came close to dying, it was the first assistant director, when he tried to chintz us out of a decent dinner. About 80 of us were being ferried back from the ship after a long, hot day when this AD declared that by the rules of the Screen Actors Guild he could serve us left-over box lunches for dinner. The lunches consisted of inedible bean paste sandwiches. Maybe he saw the homicidal looks the crew gave him, or heard somebody mutter something about shark bait, but he reluctantly added that any of us who did not want to eat the box lunch could stay on the dock until they brought us a proper supper.

Well, along with Jack and Peter Marshall, I had been bringing my own lunch, so we weren't particularly hungry. The three of us glanced at one another. This was a no-brainer.

"We're staying on the dock," Jack said.

It was as close to a mutiny as you could get on a movie set. The other guys opted to go back to the hotel, leaving just the three of us on the dock. We ordered lobster from the food stands and got shit-faced on beer and tequila. Finally, about three hours later, the first assistant director returned in a car and found the three of us holding one another up at one of the food stands. Because of us, he was having to pay meal penalties to about a hundred actors, at a cost of several thousand dollars. He was pissed.

"I want you idiots to get in the car and go to the hotel," he said. "You've cost us a shitload of money."

Back at the hotel, he continued to rant, promising none of us would ever work for Warner Bros again.

"And if I can help it," he added, "you'll all be out of the business."

"Fat fucking chance," Jack said as we turned back to the bar and toasted the end of our careers.

I did not need much of an excuse to toast anything. On

that movie, I was seduced by the carefree, party-time atmosphere of being in the tropics. I had never been anywhere like Acapulco, where holding a piña colada, mai tai, daiquiri, or some other alcoholic fruity concoction with a spear of pineapple and a cute umbrella on top just felt natural. I had found paradise. Everyone down there had their pleasure. For me, it was booze. My pal Bobbie Walker did tai chi. I remember asking him about the weird movements he was doing on his balcony, something I'd never seen before, and soon I was hooked on that too. Josh had his own thing. Others had their vices. I didn't pay much attention to any of it until Jack made a comment to me.

"Hag, you drink too much," he said.

"I don't think it's a problem."

"Neither do I. I just think you ought to try something else."

"Like what?" I asked.

"A little grass. I'll go out and get some."

"Marijuana?" I said. "I can't do that."

Jack, who could tell I was ignorant and frightened of pot, accepted my answer and went his own way. A few days later, he came up to my room with a newspaper folded under his arm. When I told him Maj was down at the pool, he flashed a devilish grin and set the paper down on the coffee table. I asked what was in it. He said, "Acapulco Gold." Whoa, not in my room, I said, then suggested we go up to his room. A few other guys joined us, and then Jack got to work, sounding like a Vegas dealer as he said, "Well, let's roll it up."

At first I did not feel anything. About an hour later, after smoking more, I asked when the stuff started to take effect.

"Hag, you just asked me that," Jack said.

"Huh?"

"You just asked me that for about the twelfth time."

"I did?"

"Yeah."

"Well, when does it start taking effect?"

"Now."

"No shit."

"What do you think?"

"I think I'd rather have a martini."

Then the fun started. I went downstairs to see Maj, who was swimming laps in the hotel pool, which was extremely large and deep, something like 15 feet. I had absolutely no idea that I was extremely high as I jumped in the pool, grabbed Maj, and told her to swim with me to the bottom. Once down there, I started to take off her bikini top, something she resisted while at the same time trying to get me to understand she was running out of air and needed to surface quickly. But when you are as high as I was, time does not mean anything.

Finally Maj dragged me back to the surface, gasping for air and pissed off.

"What the hell have you been doing?" she asked.

"Well, Jack turned me on," I said.

"Larry, we had a deal," she said. "You always said you wouldn't do anything like that unless you did it with me."

"I'm sorry. But don't worry, there's more."

We went up to Jack's room, where everyone was still in their same seats, puffing away, except for one guy, who vanished without anyone having seen him leave. Instead of searching for him, we ordered food and beer from room service. After the guy delivered it, we became paranoid that he'd turn us in to security for smoking pot. Then there was a knock on the door, and it freaked us out. It turned out to be the missing guy, a stuntman, who had climbed down 10 floors to the ground on the outside of the hotel without being spotted. It's what he liked to do when he was high.

For me, the real fun came when Maj turned on. We went back to our room with some grass and had a great time. We ate, put on some music, and then started to make passionate love. We had such a good time I started to levitate. I rose up off the bed, high enough that I could look down and see the two of us on the king-size mattress. Then the wall next to my head opened up and I saw about three inches of blue sky.

"Jesus Christ, this stuff is fantastic," I said. "I've never had anything like it in my entire life!"

"Wow!" Maj exclaimed, laughing.

Eventually we wanted dinner and headed down to the restaurant. We had to take the stairs because the elevator was out. When we got to the lobby, it was jammed. Someone from the movie company hurried over to me and asked if we were okay. I got paranoid. Did they know I had smoked pot all day? Could they tell? It was best to act as if everything was normal. I said we were fine and asked why.

"Didn't you feel it? We just had a huge earthquake."

It was news to me. The quake had knocked out all the power and damaged the hotel, including the roof over our room, hence the crack of blue sky I'd seen. And I thought it had been the grass. It's probably lucky that episode came toward the end of shooting there, but then we went back to L.A. to finish up the film at the Warner Bros studio. One day the prop master mixed up a batch of jungle juice that we as the ship's crew were supposed to have made. But he added too much purple coloring and after a couple takes, everyone's tongue turned deep purple and they had to suspend shooting for a few days.

13

We'd sublet John McGiven's rented house in Malibu for a couple of weeks while I finished up work. Maj had really fallen in love with the beach, and the kids were old enough to enjoy it. We were next door to Jascha Heifetz, which might sound exciting, but hearing him practice one sequence over and over and over for hours was enough to drive you nuts. But I admired him as the first guy I ever met who owned an electric car.

As we celebrated my birthday on the beach, I received word that I had gotten another movie, *The Cavern*, a World War II movie that was going to shoot in London and Italy. Maj's sister Bebe was going to take the kids to Sweden, so we had to be back in New York within four days. Despite having paid for a few more weeks at the beach, we packed up the Jeep, the floor now repaired, and took off for New York.

After driving all night, we were near Midland, Texas, around 3 A.M., needing gas and food. I pulled into a truck stop, and while I filled the Jeep with gas, Maj went for hamburgers. She came back in a lather, complaining they wouldn't sell her hamburgers. I asked where she went. She said to the hamburger stand. I looked over and saw she had been at the blacks' window. I told her to go around the front and get them.

"I'll be damned if I will," she said.

She'd never run up against segregation, and she was infuriated that there would be separate windows for whites and blacks. She was going to stand at the blacks' window and demand to be served. I said, "Look, Maj, you're in segregated territory. It's not right, but you will be arrested and that means Dad will have to be woken up, drive five hours to bail us out of jail. It's going to be a lot of money, a lot of trouble, and we've got the kids. It's just not worth it."

Finally I quieted her down, went around to the white section for hamburgers, and we were on our way. Before leaving, though, Maj threw her burger out the window. A few hours later, we stopped in Weatherford to see Dad, slept a bit, and took off again.

We got to New York just in time to load Bebe and the kids on the plane to Sweden so she could show them off to their Swedish relatives. A few days later, Maj and I flew to Europe, stopping first in London to see Henri Kleiman and some other friends. One night I got bombed and jumped into the Serpentine for a moonlight swim, and the next day I had a cold that turned into a deep hack by the time we made it to Trieste for the start of *The Cavern*.

The film, directed by Edgar Ulmer, was about a group of soldiers—two U.S., one Italian, one British, one German—and a beautiful Italian woman who take refuge from bombing in a cavern the Nazis have stocked with booze, cigarettes, and enough food for a regiment. But eventually they go nuts and kill one another.

Edgar began shooting in the caverns at Posumia, Yugoslavia, and then moved to Trieste. We had a large, talented, multinational cast and crew, including John Saxon, Brian Aherne, Italian actress Rosanna Schiaffino, and Nino Castelnuovo, who had won an award for his work in *The Umbrellas of Cherbourg*. There were also actors from France, Germany, and Russia.

Edgar got very concerned about my health. My cough was a sickening hack. Every time I drew a breath I felt stabbing pains in my chest. Finally Edgar told me that he thought the cough was pretty serious. He said I better get an X ray. He was right, but his concern went beyond friendly. I had a momentary suspicion that the producer of the movie might be more interested in finding something that would stop production, like an accident or serious illness, which would allow him to collect insurance money rather than finish the picture. After *Fail Safe*, I knew movies were business endeavors, and all of us knew this wasn't going to be a blockbuster.

Edgar sent me to get an X ray. Maj and I went to a place in downtown Trieste, a beautiful old city but a backwater village when it came to medical facilities. The doctor's office was on an upstairs floor of an old, decrepit building. We stepped into the elevator, an old cage that did not inspire confidence as it very slowly creaked upward.

Once at our destination, we were met by a little woman about four feet tall who had a thicker mustache than mine. The doctor did not speak a word of English, but he motioned us into place. Maj had her chest done, since the company was paying, and then I had mine. I coughed my head off for an hour in the freezing cold office till the results came back.

The doctor had a very serious, grave look as he put the plates against up against the lights. Maj's X rays were clear, but mine was filled with arrows pointing to spots. There was also a two-page, single-spaced report written in Italian, which I could not decipher. But I figured it was my death sentence when the doctor handed it to me and went off on an intensely serious explanation in Italian. I kept asking what it meant, what he was saying, until finally he drew his finger across his throat and said, "Signor Hagman, *niente fumari . . . Morte! Morte!*"

I interpreted only the throat-slashing gesture, and fainted.

After coming to and getting my head bandaged, I was made to understand that I would have to stop my two-pack-a-day cigarette habit. In the meantime, the doctor gave me antibiotics for my infection. Maj said the doctor felt I would be better in a week. On the set, everyone expressed relief at my diagnosis, except for the producer, who tried to cover up his disappointment.

Then disaster did strike. While shooting the bombing sequence that forced us into the cavern, a scene that had all of us running through a path between explosions, Joachim Hansen, the actor playing the German officer, accidentally stepped inside one and it blew him sky high. The blast did not kill him, but it knocked him flat out. The producer looked like a kid watching Fourth of July fireworks, his face the picture of hope, like someone who thinks he might have the winning lottery ticket—at least until he heard the crew guy who had rushed over scream, "He's okay! He's alive!"

I always contended that since I did not have double

cancer of the lung, they had to figure out a way to stop production. And poor old Joachim literally walked into it.

They were not spending a whole lot of money on this movie. There was not much in the way of creature comforts. They packed three of us—me, John, and Peter Marshall—into one trailer. It was so small the three of us could not change in there at the same time. Two of us could, but not three.

So one day, after we had spent hours shooting by the side of a mountain, we were driven back to base camp. It was cold as hell outside. I was waiting for my turn in the trailer when Brian came by. The veteran actor had taken a liking to me and said he wanted to talk to me confidentially. I said fine.

"My darling wife has procured the trailer that Elizabeth Taylor used in *Cleopatra*," he continued, "and I was wondering if you would share it with me."

"What?"

"Yes, I feel rather bad about it because I really don't have room for all the other actors."

I was flattered. I knew there had to be a catch, and there was.

"If you share my trailer, you would take the job of my batman."

"What the hell is a batman?" I asked.

Brian seemed a bit surprised I had not heard the term.

"Well, all British army officers have an enlisted man who is their batman," he explained. "He draws their baths, pitches the tent, makes the cot up, strings up the mosquito netting. All the things that a batman does."

I spent a moment thinking about the position he described. He wanted me to be his goddamn butler. Brian went on:

"Dear boy, this profession we're in requires a great deal of facility. There are feast years and then there are famine years, and it's always good to have the knowledge of an additional job. If you are my batman, I can teach you how to be a proper man's man."

At that point, I saw John and Peter exit our trailer and wave it was my turn to change clothes. I imagined the cold wind whipping through our trailer.

"Say, Brian, does your trailer happen to have heat?" I asked.

"Yes, it does."

"Then I'll be your batman. It sounds right up my alley!"

For the next six weeks, I worked as Brian's batman. If I was not in front of the camera, I was doing chores in our trailer. I learned how to serve tea to a field officer, turn down his bed, and press pants without an iron, which is a nifty trick. You carefully set the pants between the mattress and box spring, go to sleep, and by morning they are perfectly pressed. I was never a batman again, but Brian was right, I learned a lot of practical skills and put them to good use 10 years later when I played a butler in the TV series *The Good Life*.

One night at the end of November, Maj and I had dinner at our favorite restaurant in Trieste. We'd had a wonderful time. We walked back to the hotel arm in arm, laughing and talking, not a care in the world. Some of the cast were in the lobby when we walked in. They gave us a look that asked how we could be enjoying ourselves so much at the moment. Then Edgar said, "You killed Kennedy! You killed Kennedy!"

"What?" I said.

"Yes, yes, you Texans. You've killed him."

At that moment we learned that President John F. Kennedy had been assassinated in Dallas. Maj and I were devastated. We spent the next few hours in our rooms listening to the BBC news on the radio. Our grief and sadness was profound. The next morning Maj and I went to the U.S. consulate in Trieste and paid our respects by signing a condolence book. When we finally got back to the States, the country was different, and though we didn't immediately recognize it, so were we.

Maj picked up the kids from Bebe in Sweden, and then we spent Christmas in Rome, where I finished *The Cavern* and we visited with our writer friend Gore Vidal, who lived around the corner from our apartment in Piazza Margana. It was a magical time. I remember our housekeeper, an old Italian woman, always barged through our bedroom door and asked, "Amore?" wondering if we were making love.

Though I worked hard, I liked that the Italians always found time to break for long, delicious lunches and indulged in equally long dinners. There always seemed to be a party with fascinating people who would talk till three in the morning. Maj made sure the kids saw every important museum and ruin. She also had accounts throughout Rome; shopkeepers sent bills addressed to *la bionda signora Americana con due bambini*, or the blond American lady with two children. She also rented a Fiat, and needed three or four new bumpers on that car by the time we left town two months later.

It didn't seem as if life could get any better, and I was right.

Back in New York, I met with Otto Preminger, who was about to direct the World War II epic *In Harm's Way*. He had the biggest desk I'd ever seen in my life and afterward I learned why. You'd need to have a trampoline to vault it and strangle him. That man knew enough to make his throat inaccessible. But over dinner and in a meeting, he was the epitome of charm. Once the camera started to roll, though, he turned into a dictatorial ogre.

He gave me several weeks of work on the movie, which shot in Hawaii. it seemed every male star in Hollywood was in it: Henry Fonda, Duke Wayne, and my friends Burgess Meredith, Patricia Neal, and Carroll O'Connor. Tom Tryon was the star. Every night a bunch of us met in one of our rooms for cocktails and we discussed ways we could murder Otto. We fantasized about putting massive amounts of Ex-Lax in his coffee, loosening the threads on the back of his director's chair so when he leaned back he'd topple overboard, and countless other schemes.

For me, he was at his worst while shooting a scene on the bow of a ship. There were at least a dozen of us in the shot, but it centered around Tom Tryon. Tom was a talented actor who had worked with Otto in *The Cardinal*. All Tom had to do in this scene was take a piece of paper from a sailor who'd run down from the radio shack and then read the message. The first take was fine, and Otto seemed pleased. But then he asked how it was for sound.

"We're getting a lot of paper noise, Mr. Preminger," the soundman replied.

"Wet down the paper," Otto said.

The prop man spritzed the paper with water and we tried take two.

"Are we still getting the rattle?" Otto asked after the second take.

"Yes, Mr. Preminger."

"Wet it down again."

By the sixth take, the paper disintegrated and we'd fallen two hours behind schedule. All of us still had a line or two. Plus we had reverses, over-the-shoulders, close-ups. We were going to be on the bow of that ship all day. When I asked Tom if I could do anything to help, he looked around nervously and asked if the microphone was on.

I checked.

"No, we're okay," I said.

"Otto makes me so fucking nervous that I tremble and it shakes the damn paper," he said.

"Didn't you just make *The Cardinal* with him?"

"Yeah."

"Is he always like this?"

"It gets worse."

Indeed, the longer it took, the more things went wrong. The light changed, planes flew overhead, clouds drifted in and out. With each delay, Otto grew angrier, louder, and more temperamental. Waiting for my close-up was like standing on a firing line. He made everyone so overwrought and anxious they screwed up, including me.

When my close-up finally came, I blew it.

"Mr. Hagman, I understand you are a Broadway actor," Otto said. "Is that correct?"

"Yes sir," I said.

"So how come you are so . . . ineffectual?"

"Oh shit, I'm sorry."

Otto stared at me with astonishment.

"Do you always swear at your directors?" he asked.

"Oh fuck, I'm sorry, Mr. Preminger."

"What?!" he exploded.

Actors didn't speak to directors like that, especially to him. But I was on a roll.

I really started to swear. "Shit, I can't get it. I'm an asshole. I'll try to do better."

"That won't be necessary," said Otto, dumbfounded.

He thought I was having a fit. He turned abruptly.

"Print it and let's move on."

He never bothered me again. He never gave me another close-up either. All of us swore we wouldn't work with him again.

I called Maj in New York to tell her how it had gone. She had just gone to the theater with Burgess, who'd finished his work on the movie about a week earlier, and she told me that she'd asked him how it had gone in Hawaii. She laughed while recalling how he'd said, "I'll never work for that son of a bitch again." Three months later, they were making another film together. What does that tell you about our profession?

14

There wasn't much work when I got back to New York, and we didn't have much money either. Not a good combination. Earlier, I'd signed with the big agency GAC, and I didn't think my New York agent was paying enough attention to me. One day I sat in his office while he took one call after another without talking to me. For about two hours, I listened to him talk on the phone. Finally, I went into the foyer and called him. He picked up.

"Hi, this is Larry Hagman," I said.

"Hi, Larry, what's going on?"

"What's going on is you're fired," I said.

"What for?"

"I was just sitting in your office for two hours, listening to you talk to other people instead of me, and I got tired of it. So good-bye."

He rushed out, got me to cool off, and said I had to learn how the business worked from his perspective. That was fine, but then I explained my perspective—I was down to my last 30 cents and I had a family to feed. Not too long after, he called and said there was a good part for me in one of Alfred Hitchcock's television dramas in Hollywood.

"Oh God, I was just in L.A.," I said.

"Timing's everything, kid."

Then I went through the routine. I asked to see the script. He asked, "Does it matter?" I said it didn't. Then I asked about the money. Again he said, "Does it matter?" When you haven't worked for nine months, what do you say to that except no, it doesn't matter?

The offer was $2,500 and a round-trip ticket. I went back to L.A. knowing full well that they'd never actually air the script, never mind finish filming it. It was about a young couple who move to L.A. from Illinois. The husband had suffered a war injury that left him unable to consummate the marriage. He hooked up with a cult of hoodlums looking to sacrifice a virgin. They drugged him and made him watch while they carved his wife's heart out and then burned down the house.

Good stuff, huh?

Well, I knew it wasn't going to go. Sure enough, we rehearsed the first act, broke for lunch, and when we came back they told us the network had read the script and canceled that show. At least I got to keep the money, which I promptly sent home.

That left me in L.A. without a job, or even a prospect, but I called Maj and told her that I thought I should stay out there and look around. George Peppard, who I knew from New York, was red hot then. I was also very good friends with his girlfriend at the time, Elisabeth Ashley. We hooked up and George made it a special project of his to introduce me all over town. Nothing came of it, but I met a lot of people and you never know what comes from things like that.

One of the people George introduced me to was actor Lee Marvin. We met on the set of *Ship of Fools*, which Liz Ashley was also in. While George was visiting with Liz, I started talking to Lee. We went out for drinks afterward and he invited me to visit his house. Soon Lee and his wife, Betty, and I became fast friends, and they helped me settle into town. They were among the dozen or so friends I invited to have Thanksgiving dinner with me at my house, which I borrowed from Ted Flicker, who was renting it from his old Bard roommate, *1776* author Peter Stone, in the Hollywood hills.

For Thanksgiving dinner Lee drove up to my house in a brand-new Lincoln convertible that Betty had given him as a birthday present, and he quickly got shit-faced. He was funny when he was loaded, but he was also a bit reckless and quite a bit unpredictable. That turned out to be bad news for my turkey. I'd never cooked a turkey before, but I took this one out of the oven and placed it on the table to a chorus of ohs and ahs. Lee took one look at my masterpiece, picked it up, and threw it in the pool.

"Let's see if the son of a bitch can swim!" he said.

I watched the bird sink like a bowling ball, trailing a film of greasy dressing across the water. After a moment of shock, I dove in with all my clothes on and rescued the bird from the bottom of the pool. On the way back to the kitchen I used the old joke, "Don't worry, I'll get the other one." I got it in the kitchen, patted it down, spooned in the remainder of the Stove Top stuffing, and reentered to a not-so-enthusiastic chorus of ohs and ahs.

Actually, it tasted pretty good, with a slight hint of cilantro . . . and chlorine.

The party broke up in the wee hours, and Lee topped his earlier performance by backing his car through the three-foot-high curb that protected the parking area from a 30-foot drop. His brand-new Lincoln teetered over the edge, looking like it was about to fall. I had a bunch of guys stand on the front bumper while I unloaded Lee out the back. Then we tied down the car and had a tow truck come haul that boat back to level ground.

Before driving off, Lee said, "Great party, kid. Happy Thanksgiving." Then he roared off into the night.

Soon after, my agent sent me scripts for five pilots. I chose to read for *I Dream of Jeannie*, a new sitcom created by Sidney Sheldon for Screen Gems, which already had a hit with *Bewitched*. I had a feeling this was the right project. It was 100 percent instinct, but I liked the premise of *Jeannie*. It was good, wholesome, escapist fun, with a healthy dose of sexual tension.

When I showed up, they'd signed Barbara Eden and had looked at many actors for the part of Captain Nelson, including Robert Conrad, Darren McGavin, and Gary Collins. I had two readings. I thought I nailed the first one, done for the casting director, and called Maj and told her that I had a good feeling. She made a suit for Jane Morgan in exchange for the airfare to L.A., and arrived the day of my second reading, which was in front of Sidney Sheldon. I thought that went equally well. Maj shared in the excitement when they called me to do a screen test.

I went in confident. When I stepped in front of the camera, Edward Wandrink Swackhamer, the director, saw

I knew my stuff and did me a huge favor by stepping back and letting me do my thing. Afterward, I felt great. I went home and told Maj that I had a feeling in my gut. "I've got this one."

"If you feel that way, then I'll go home," she said.

Between us, we had less than $35. But as Maj says, we had a lot of faith.

A few days later, my agent called with great news. I got the pilot.

Hot damn! I knew it was going to go. I couldn't see any reason why not. Before I even got in front of a camera, I made my deal for the series. I signed for $1,100 an episode, the standard fee unless you had a big name. I was thrilled.

I rented a tiny, two-bedroom cottage in Rustic Canyon. You had to cross a little wood bridge that spanned the flood control channel to get in the front door. I remember doing the Royal Canadian Air Force exercises there and running a mile every morning at 4 A.M.

I was in great shape when we shot the pilot.

Sidney Sheldon said he knew *I Dream of Jeannie* would be a hit when his nine-year-old daughter gave his original script a thumbs-up. I agreed. The premise was great and the cast's chemistry was there the day all of us met for the first time at the studio. Barbara was gorgeous, a marvelous professional, and a really nice person. Bill Daily had the timing of a great comic and a gift for improvisation. And Hayden Rorke was the droll anchor on- and offscreen. I knew if I did my job as the straight man with the proper sense of silly I'd get as many laughs as everyone else.

I respected Sidney, who'd won a best original screenplay Academy Award for Cary Grant's *The Bachelor and the Bobby Soxer*. Sidney had also created *The Patty Duke Show* for TV. He dreamt up *I Dream of Jeannie* after Screen Gems executives asked him to come up with a series like *Bewitched*. He was smart, tough, diplomatic, insightful, and he meticulously jotted down notes in a little book whenever anyone passed along a suggestion, idea, or complaint. If he wrote it down, it got done. I was personally responsible for filling several volumes.

In the pilot, which was delightfully simple, astronaut Tony Nelson's space capsule make an emergency landing on an island where he finds a bottle containing a two-thousand-year-old genie, who announces that he is her master for life. When he's rescued, she hides in his bags, and the both of them end up back at his Cocoa Beach, Florida, home, where he's forced to keep her a secret.

The show was timeless, clean, innocent, and to my way of thinking, it had all the elements of a hit.

There was one problem. During rehearsal, Bill and I were extemporizing, adding sight gags and physical business, and it irritated the hell out of the director, Gene Nelson. He wanted to call all the shots, and he was against deviating from the script. He also wanted to take all the credit; that's another story. I didn't care who got the credit, I simply wanted whatever got on film to be funny.

At another point during the pilot, I offered a suggestion to Gene, and he told me to shut up and let him get "the thing done." I replied, "This isn't a thing, it's a comedy," and I explained that as far as I was concerned, it was supposed to be fun. When all was said and done, I felt like it was fun. We did a great job on the pilot.

But with Gene's attitude, I didn't see how he could direct a comedy. He felt the same way about me. From the start, we were like oil and water. Luckily, we only had to shoot the one show and then see if it sold to the network.

I spent Christmas in New York with Maj and the kids and Bebe. We'd decided to take a chance that the pilot would sell, and move to L.A. Maj had made enough money to buy a white Plymouth station wagon for $2,500. Val had a connection with Chrysler and got it at a huge discount. We packed up the kids and Bebe and started the drive cross-country. We stopped to see my dad in Weatherford and had a full Texas experience for New Year's at the country club.

The country club was the only place you could drink in Parker County. Parker County was dry. You weren't allowed to buy liquor there. Nor were there any bars. But because of some obscure law, you were allowed to have a locker at the club where you could keep liquor. You'd buy your setups at exorbitant prices and could pour your own drinks among your friends.

Juanita, after a few, or perhaps more than a few, libations, took an interest in the band. Dad and Maj and I were hanging out at our table with some of his old cronies, who were inspecting my foreign bride, as they still called Maj, and the bandleader came over and spoke to my dad.

"Mr. Hagman, could you ask Mrs. Hagman to come back to the table? She spilled a drink on the drums and they're sounding all soggy."

Dad dutifully went over there and guided Juanie back to the table. Everything was fine until we noticed she was missing about half an hour later. Soon a dreadful smell permeated the room. The bandleader came back over, livid and literally shaking.

"Mr. Hagman, your wife has just puked in the electric piano. She shorted it out. That's the odor you smell."

Dad again dutifully retrieved Juanita and we all called it a night. But the night wasn't quite finished. While Dad loaded her in the car, he slammed the door and broke four of her fingers. We spent the rest of New Year's at the hospital. But that wasn't the worst of it. She did all of his legal typing, so she had to spend the next few weeks learning how to type his torts with one hand.

After we finally arrived at our little brown cottage, Bebe said good-bye and flew back to New York while we settled into our new home. Three months had to pass before I heard whether *Jeannie* was going to be on the fall television schedule. In the meantime, I had to earn a living.

About that time, *Fail Safe* was finally released into theaters and it was seen by Bob Walker, a casting director for Four Star Studios. After seeing the movie, Bob swore that I spoke Russian and he tracked me down for a voice-over part in an episode of *The Rogues*, a popular TV series starring David Niven, Charles Boyer, and Gig Young. The part called for someone who spoke Russian. I never told Bob that I didn't know one word, and he didn't ask.

But I pulled it off by finding a Russian actor who kindly tape recorded my dialogue, and I learned the proper pronunciation by mimicking his accent. It worked. They liked me. There were a couple shows left in their season, but Gig had a previous commitment that he couldn't get out of. Shooting on *The Rogues* had gone weeks over and the producers were in a bind. Bob Walker persuaded the producers to bring me onto the show as Gig's character's cousin. In essence, I took over for Gig.

My first episode in that role had the famous actor George Sanders as its guest star. On the first day of shooting, he wasn't prepared when the director asked if he knew his lines, and I was amazed that an actor of his stature arrived on the set like that. But George was unfazed; in fact he had what to him was a perfectly good explanation, saying, "You didn't expect me to learn my lines on *my* time, did you?"

I always knew my lines. They liked me, and maybe they would've used me more often on *The Rogues*, but the program was canceled.

We still hadn't heard about *Jeannie*, so I had to try hustling more work. It wasn't out there, at least for me, and one morning I turned to Maj and said, "Honey, I think you have to go back to work." She said no. She told me that she was taking *my* children to the beach for the day. Instead, she told me to continue looking for work. "Stay positive," she said.

I took her advice. I spent the day trying to find work, talking to my agent, networking with friends, and trying not to think about Maj and the kids on the beach. As it turned out, Maj wasn't on the beach. She'd come home in the afternoon, and soon after, the phone rang. It was Sidney Sheldon. He asked if we had a bottle of champagne. She said, "Sidney, we don't even have a bottle of Gallo."

Just then I walked in through the door.

"Sit down, Larry," Maj said. "I have something to tell you."

"What?"

"Sidney just called and said the pilot sold, the network ordered twenty-two, and it starts shooting right away."

We were so happy. I was so relieved.

"That's called having faith," Maj said. "Trust your instincts. They're always right."

15

The show didn't need to start off as a battle, but it did.

In the spring of 1965, NBC green-lighted *I Dream of Jeannie*, and it seemed as if forces were conspiring against us. First, Barbara announced she was pregnant, making it necessary to shoot the initial 10 episodes as quickly as possible. NBC signaled they didn't have much faith in the series by insisting on shooting the first season in black-and-white to keep costs to a minimum. Or at least that was how it was explained to me. The network was also worried the censors would go nuts every time Jeannie said she wanted to "please" her master. Finally, to my way of thinking, the director was all wrong.

In short, it was the TV business as usual, and that's exactly what I wanted to avoid—business as usual. My goal was to make the best sitcom ever. It was an obsession that I brought onto the set and into meetings by questioning everything and making suggestions, always with the same goal—to make it as good as possible. I never criticized anything without making a suggestion I thought was different or better. I was driven. Gene Nelson misinterpreted my behavior as that of an ego-driven actor chasing stardom. But the cast knew better. I made it very clear that my interest was only in the show. If *Jeannie* did well, all of us would benefit.

I think I had my points. After a while, the scripts contained the same jokes week after week. I got frustrated. Billy and I would create physical gags so we wouldn't be just talking heads. But our efforts at creating something off the page irritated Gene. As far as I was concerned, he didn't understand the kind of comedy we were trying to create. He also blew up one day when I insisted that we couldn't simply let Jeannie blink people away without showing where they went. Otherwise viewers might think she killed them. I suggested we always blink them someplace amusing and get a laugh. Ultimately Sidney decided, and he went with my idea.

After the first 10 shows, Gene wanted me fired. He must've given an ultimatum because Sidney asked me how I felt about Gene returning as director.

"You can bring him back if you want," I said. "But I won't be here."

Apparently Gene had gone to Sidney and suggested writing an episode in which Jeannie's bottle was lost and then found by someone else, who would become her new master. As far as he was concerned, that would solve the Larry Hagman problem. But Sidney told him that NBC didn't have a problem with Larry Hagman. In fact, the network loved me. As a result, one of my problems was solved. Gene didn't return after we finished those 10 episodes.

*   *   *

But there were other problems, which made me like a volcano set to erupt. One in particular vied for my attention with the show. My father was very sick in Weatherford. His condition was brought on partly by age, partly his own negligence. Toward the end of spring, he'd gone to the Weatherford Country Club, had some drink, and as he would often do, he stripped down to his Skivvies, and dove into the pool. Nobody had told him they'd drained it.

He survived, but a short time later, while fishing with his friend James Porter McFarland, he had a stroke and fell out of the boat. Somehow James got him out of the water and drove him to the hospital.

He recovered. But about three months later he suffered another stroke, this one massive, and it left him in a coma. His weight dropped from 265 pounds to 120. He was a helpless skeleton. We were told he had absolutely no hope of recovering. He just lay in bed and had no awareness of anything as far as anyone could tell. He wouldn't have wanted to be in that condition.

I visited him as much as *Jeannie*'s tight schedule allowed. Dad was in a room with four other guys. One of them, a man named Walter, had tried to blow his brains out 13 years earlier, but his attempt had been only partially successful. He'd given himself a perfect lobotomy. Consequently, he sat in a chair grinding his teeth, sweating, and talking some indecipherable language. Whenever I visited Dad, I'd always say, "Hello, Walter," wipe his mouth off, and try to figure out if the sounds he made had any meaning.

All of us hated seeing Dad in that condition. At the time I knew a guy who had access to pharmaceuticals, legal or otherwise. He could get anything. So before I went to visit Dad for what turned out to be the last time, I had him get me the kind of drug that U-2 pilot Gary Powers was supposed to have swallowed when the Soviets shot him down.

Dad was the same as always. But we had a nice visit. I gave him a shave, as I always did, and I told him what was going on in my life. I had no idea if he understood. Probably not. Then came the moment that I'd thought so hard about. I got up from my chair, opened up Dad's IV, and took out the pill I'd brought. I was scared to death. My hands shook and sweat poured off me the way it did Walter, who I noticed was staring right at me.

Suddenly I lost my nerve. I knew that if Dad expired, Walter was going to yell his first intelligible words in 13 years. He would point at me and yell at the top of his lungs, "He did it."

I closed the IV, kissed Dad, and left the hospital, never to see him again. Mercifully, he passed away on his own about a month later. He never saw the premiere of I Dream of Jeannie on September 18, 1965.

I was in New York promoting the series, walking up Fifth Avenue, when I bumped into director Sidney Lumet. We were delighted to see each other. He was carrying a script for his adaptation of Mary McCarthy's novel The Group. He described the story, about the lives of eight girls from Vassar in the 1930s, suggested there might be a role in the film for me, and told me to read it and pick one out.

I'd never been given that freedom before, and naturally I picked out a part that ran through the entire movie. Sidney was surprised at the role I selected. He said it wasn't what he'd had in mind. I didn't explain my reasoning—

the longer the role and the bigger the part, the more I got paid. It was Candice Bergen's first movie and she was gorgeous. But of course, all the girls in the film were drop-dead beautiful. I looked forward to going to work every single day.

After the movie, Maj and I got a camper and drove the children all through Canada on our way to Seattle, where Mother was performing. One day we were going through a desolate stretch of highway when I stopped for gas. The station attendent noticed our California license plates and asked if we were by any chance from Los Angeles. I said yes. He showed me a Canadian newspaper whose front page was plastered with pictures of L.A. on fire.

Great columns of black smoked filled the sky. Watts was burning, the result of devastating riots. I was really shaken. Maj was too. It was very emotional, thinking of how miserable and enraged black people had to be to burn their own homes, stores, neighborhoods. We cut our trip short, stopping briefly to see Mother in her show in Seattle, and then made a beeline to L.A.

In October, work started up again on *Jeannie*, without Gene Nelson. In his place, Sidney brought in Edward Swackhamer, my favorite director. He also hired Claudio Guzmán, a veteran producer who knew how to handle me. Ted Flicker even came in to direct. Everything I wanted was mine, and I was excited and happy to be a part of a successful show. In general, I was having fun. Still, it didn't stop me from pushing for better scripts.

I was naive. I didn't know that once you got a good thing, you didn't change it. But I always felt we could make the show even better, and I pushed for it. I didn't know how to settle. On two occasions I got so frustrated that I called Maj from the set and told her to start packing,

I was ready to quit. She took it in her stride, as did the others. After the second time, Hayden Rorke gently massaged my shoulder and offered some good advice.

"Anyone who quits a successful show is seen as insane," he said. "You'd be crazy to leave. It's so hard to get a successful show like this. Nobody will ever trust you again."

Fortunately, my cast mates were always supportive. Barbara, who was like a rock all the way through the series, also wanted better scripts but she never complained. It wasn't in her nature. Billy was right with me; we had so much fun creating our shtick. Whatever I wanted, he was for it.

Sidney was the guy responsible for the whole thing, and he patiently accepted the fact that I could be difficult. I think he put up with me because he understood I battled for all the right reasons. As he said, "Larry's problems stem from his being such a perfectionist. He wants to own the world and own it this afternoon."

In truth, I was in a hurry, but there was a reason. After the birth of our son, Preston, Maj had been prescribed a medication called Bontril to help her lose weight. She'd had no idea the pills were uppers. Neither did I when I started taking them around the same time to keep my own weight in check and for energy, which, boy howdy, they gave me.

Throughout *Jeannie*'s first season, I took them twice a day without knowing the psychological effects they were having on me. After we started the second season, Maj tried to refill the Bontril prescription. The pharmacist refused, explaining there was a new state law that prohibited selling that particular drug. Maj said he told her that it was because it could become habit-forming.

"That's a lot of bullshit," I said. "I've been taking them every day for years and . . ."

Suddenly I heard what I was saying and a lightbulb went off. We stopped Bontril and tobacco at the same time. The effects were devastating. Coming down off nicotine is hard enough. Add amphetamines and you have serious problems.

I certainly did.

They were so obvious that one day on the set Ted, thinking I was flipping out, strongly advised me to go see his therapist, Sidney Prince.

I pooh-poohed it until one day on the set I lost it all. I don't know what triggered it, but I had a breakdown. I was crying, vomiting, and shitting at the same time. Even the wax from my ears was coming out. I was exploding. I decided right there I'd better go see Sidney Prince. They put me in the back of a pickup because I was such a mess nobody wanted to put me in their car. They took me to Sidney's. He talked to me gently once I'd calmed down.

"I'm going to tell you something and you may not realize it now, in fact you probably won't realize it, but try to focus on it," he said.

I nodded, waiting for words that would solve my problem.

"Don't worry about it," he said.

"That's all?" I said. "I'm paying you a hundred dollars an hour and you're telling me don't worry about it?"

"Yeah. Don't worry about it." He paused. "Look at it this way. You're in a golden prison. You're getting paid a couple of thousand dollars a week to do something you love, and you only have to do it nine months out of the year. What could be better than that?"

*   *   *

The next time I saw Sidney, he gave me a copy of *The Joyous Cosmology*, Alan Watts's landmark 1962 book about alternative ways of perception, consciousness, and spirituality. It was an influential guide for those on the leading edge of the changes taking place in the culture, but hell, I couldn't make any sense out of it no matter how many times I read it.

Sidney also introduced me to Zen and other alternative ways of thinking I never even heard about. He told me about Esalen, the Big Sur outpost known for its workshops, encounter groups, and hot tubs. Maj and I went for the hot tubs, lectures (we heard Ray Bradbury there), and tai chi lessons. Another time, when I was on a camping trip with Preston, we walked into Esalen, ducked into a lecture hall, and there was Alan Watts himself, speaking in his lovely English accent. After listening for about 20 minutes, I still didn't understand what he was talking about, but he made me curious.

I finally met Watts at a friend's house in Malibu. When he came in, my friend asked what he wanted to drink and I expected this erudite, charming Englishman to ask for herb tea. Instead he requested a very dry double martini, and I was blown away.

Maj and I also took up flying. Now that I had some money I indulged in flying lessons for us. I'd always dreamed of learning to fly. Since we had only our student licenses, we always had to rent two planes if we wanted to go anywhere together. But we got a kick from flying side by side. One time we flew to Santa Barbara for lunch, and when we landed back at the Santa Monica airport, the guy who'd rented us the planes asked how was lunch.

"Great," I said. "We had hamburgers and shakes."

"How much was it?" he asked.

"About two hundred and eighty dollars," I said, adding in the cost of the planes.

One time I flew over the set of *Jeannie* on a day when I was upset about something. I opened the door and tried to piss all over Columbia Studios. But I didn't account for the wind, and the spray blew right back at me. It should've taught me something about vindictiveness. Another time, when we were on location in the Mojave Desert, Maj circled the site for about 15 minutes, causing us to shut down because of the noise. The director was standing on the ground shaking his fist and threatening to call the FAA until I recognized the numbers on the plane as the one we'd been using, and I knew it was my wife.

One day in therapy it hit me. I didn't have anything to complain about. Not anything real.

"How do you sit there and listen to the woes of people like me?" I asked.

"I've trained all my life for it," he said. "What else am I going to do? Besides, it's my living."

Then Sidney put away his notes. The hour was nearly done. It was the time in our session when he summed up what we'd talked about or cracked a joke that put things into perspective. This time he did neither. Instead he held up my file so both of us could see how thick it was and then asked if I felt better or worse for all of our talks. I had no answer.

"Exactly," he said. "You've been coming here for a couple years and we could be in therapy for as long as you want. But you're troubled by the same things you were when you came here three years ago. As I told you then, you're in a golden prison. But life is not so bad, is it?"

"No," I said.

"Right. You don't need therapy as much as a lot of other people. I know what you should do," he said.

"What?"

"Why don't you drop some acid?"

16

The idea of trying LSD lodged in my brain and wouldn't go away. Then Maj and I went to a party at Brandon De Wilde's home in Topanga Canyon. Peter Fonda was there. We'd met years earlier in New York and we were glad to see each other again. We led Peter to our van and told him that we'd recently seen him in *The Trip*, a movie Jack Nicholson directed about a man going through a bad divorce, who in an effort to understand himself better takes LSD. We told Peter we really liked the film and thought he was great in it.

I also explained that I'd been thinking about taking acid myself.

A few days later, Peter took me to see Crosby, Stills and Nash in concert. After the show we went backstage and visited with David Crosby. I expressed my desire to turn on, and before we left, David handed me a handful of tabs. This wasn't ordinary LSD. It was the purest acid available, made by Stanley Owlsley, the famed underground chemist from San Francisco.

I kept them for close to a month before the time seemed right to trip. My friend Larry Hall, the grandson of Big Jess Hall from Weatherford, was in L.A. He'd dropped acid a few times before, and for my initial journey I thought it would be wise to try it with someone who knew the ropes as my guide.

The two of us met on a Saturday morning at my house. Maj was out with the kids. I wanted the environment comfortable and secure, since I'd been told that acid stripped you of all emotional and psychological protection. I wore a hooded brown terry cloth robe that Maj had made. I looked like a monk. I'd also fasted for a couple of days as recommended by Larry. I swallowed a tab, sat back in the living room, and waited for something to happen.

Without warning, I felt a buzz just below my navel. I thought this must be what they talked about—vibrations. Boy, was it ever!

Suddenly, I saw the entrance to a cave across the room It was guarded by octopuslike creatures with long writhing tentacles. There were also two other creatures that looked like lions with feathers. Then I turned and saw my grandmother, who'd died when I was 12. She was to my left, hovering about eight feet above me. She sat in the same position I was in, and wore the same robe. She didn't speak or motion. She simply looked at me with a wonderful, comforting smile and told me not to worry about it.

"All of this is just a natural thing," she said. "You're at the gate of all-new experiences. The guards at the gate are to keep you from going in. But don't worry about it. If something tries to pull you, don't resist. Go with it. If you feel pushed, don't fight it. Just go with the flow."

All of a sudden, I got it. I thought about some of the

passages I'd read in *The Joyous Cosmology* and the *Tibetan Book of the Dead*, and they all said basically the same thing that my grandma had just told me

I headed for the cave. As soon as I got to the doorway, BOOM, I was sucked inside and down a tunnel at incredible speed. At the end, I saw a light. As I came out of the tunnel, I was in a place where I was surrounded by bright and diffused light. I saw a person who called out to me. I didn't know if it was a he or a she. That person didn't talk, but without speaking somehow let me know, "This is a glimpse. Where you've been, where you're going, where you are all the time."

It was too much for me to comprehend. The person seemed to understand I was having trouble making sense of it all.

"You don't have to go any further. Having seen this is enough for now."

At that point, I was pulled back out through the tunnel. The guards at the gate were asleep. I looked around for my grandmother. She was gone. I hadn't thought of her in a long time, yet she had been there when I needed her. I wanted to thank her for taking me through the entrance.

Then I got an orange from the kitchen. When I broke it open, I saw its cellular structure pulse. It looked to me like the actual cells were alternating between life and death. It all seemed perfectly natural.

I was studying the orange while standing in front of a mirror. When I looked up and saw my face, it was doing the same thing. The cells were pulsing. Some were dying and some were in the process of being reborn. It was an intricate picture. Every molecule was in constant motion. I don't know how long I stared at my face, but after a while I realized I was a constant flow of energy.

Grandmother, Juanita
Presley Martin.

Mother, Mary Martin,
at twelve years old as
a butterfly (1925).

Father, Benjamin
Hagman.

Above. Left to right: Grandfather, Preston Martin; cousin, Robert Andrews; Juanita Martin; Larry Hagman.

Below left. Larry and Mary Martin—accompanying Mother on one of her movie sets.

Below right. Larry in his Black Fox Military Institute uniform, Hollywood.

Above left. Left to right: Richard, Mary, Larry, and Heller en route to London for *South Pacific.*

Above right. Larry playing Valentine, with Jan Foley, Bard College, 1950.

Below. Larry with Mary Martin after the premiere of *South Pacific* in London.

Right. Larry and Maj Axelsson in England before they were married. (Stephen Cox Collection)

Middle. Maj and Larry on their wedding day, December 1954.

Bottom. Preston Hagman on the set of *I Dream of Jeannie* with his father.

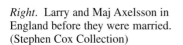

Above. Larry and Maj in their Malibu home.

Below. Left to right: Larry, Heidi, Preston, Mary Martin, and Maj.

The cast of *I Dream of Jeannie*—left to right: Bill Daily, Barbara Eden, Larry Hagman, and Hayden Rorke.

TV Guide cover.

Top. Larry Hagman and Mary Martin with the Queen Mother at the Palladium, where Larry blew his lines in a song.

Middle. Larry and Maj in Malibu.

Left. Larry Hagman on Mary Martin's lap. (Photo by John Engstead/MPTV)

Opposite page.

Above. The cast of *Dallas*, 1987. (*Dallas* © 1987 Lorimar Productions, Inc.)

Below. Filming *Dallas* in Moscow—left to right: Patrick Duffy, Sheree North, Cathy Podewell, and Larry Hagman. (*Dallas* © 1989 Lorimar Productions, Inc.)

Right. People magazine cover. Note the fingers.

Below. Billboard in Bucharest.

Opposite page.

Top. Larry with Leonard Katzman, the genius behind *Dallas*.

Middle. Larry with Burgess Meredith.

Bottom. Larry at Royal Ascot, June 17, 1980.

Right. Heaven's jester.

Below. Maj and Larry with Nancy Reagan at the White House. December 18, 1985.

Above. Going home from Cedars-Sinai after the liver transplant operation.

Below. Larry at the U.S. Transplant Games. (Photo by Jay LaPrete)

Left. Larry with Carroll O'Connor.

Below. Removing the stitches at Carroll O'Connor's home.

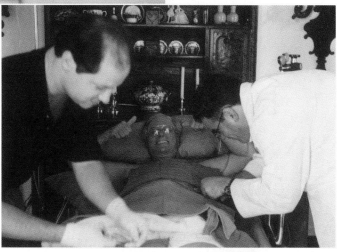

Larry's sister, Heller Halliday.

Top. Larry with Barbara Eden at the
I Dream of Jeannie thirty-fifth anniversary.

Middle. Larry and Linda Gray in Vienna on
their triumphant tour—standing ovations
for two weeks.

Bottom. Larry and Peter Fonda at
Love Ride II.

Above. The Hagman family at Christmastime.

Below. Heaven in Ojai.

Maj and Larry Hagman.

Everything was.

I was part of everything, and everything was part of me. Everything was living, dying, and being reborn.

I started playing with a sixteen-millimetre movie camera Larry had. He drove us into Beverly Hills, where we explored the different streets while staring at all the big old homes. They had beautiful gardens in front. All the colors jumped out at me. I looked at everything through the camera. As we drove along Sunset Boulevard, heading into Hollywood, I looked at people waiting at bus stops, exiting stores, and sitting in coffee shops. I used the camera to zoom in on them until I could look directly into their eyes. I saw their cells changing too.

The experience was extremely unsettling but just about the best thing that had ever happened to me. It changed my way of looking at people. I saw much deeper into their emotions. In those hours, I learned how to read body and facial language at a much more profound level. More than anything else the experience changed my way of looking at life and death.

I concluded death was just another stage of our development and that we go on to different levels of existence.

We don't disappear when we "die." We become part of a curtain of energy. In almost every religion I knew about, they say, "As it was in the beginning, is now, and ever shall be." I had an understanding of God consciousness. It was so clear. The LSD experience took the fear of death from me, the fear of manmade heaven and hell. With that out of the way, I quit worrying.

The amazing thing about this whole experience was that it was so familar. I'd been there before, done that before, and it was so, so familar.

* * *

As for the rest of my LSD, I gave most of it away. Then about a year later Maj tried it. One of the reasons the two of us are still married is that we've always shared. LSD was no different. I drove her in the hills above Malibu and we hiked through a pretty little canyon. I kept a film camera on her almost the entire time. Her experience was different from mine, since her issues were different. Her upbringing hadn't been as tumultuous, but she'd had polio when she was 21, and in fact her face was still slightly paralyzed when we started going out.

She dealt with this as she went through her LSD journey. She became her mother, her daughter, and herself, and finally, toward the end, she turned to me and declared, "But I'm beautiful."

"I've been trying to tell you that for years," I said.

LSD was profound for both of us. Maj came out cleansed, just as I'd come out of my trip full of new insights. I think our relationship was better for it. We'd glimpsed some of the answers. But that didn't mean we had quit working at learning how to deal with life.

There was a lot to deal with at the time. The Vietnam War was going on and I was unpopularly against it. I'd been asked to tour the bases in Vietnam with Barbara. I turned down the request because I didn't want to lend any credence to the war, though I sympathized with the kids who went there. But even the most patriotic of them were demoralized by the futility of the war.

At home, there were daily demonstrations at what was seen by many as a racist war conducted by a country that thought it was superior to the "yellow people." Then Martin Luther King was assassinated, and that tragic event brought home yet another instance of racial hatred. I was watching television in our little house on West Channel Road, when the bulletin came on saying he'd been assassinated.

I burst into tears. Maj cried too. I thought we'd been making progress, but looking back, I was naive. After Bobby Kennedy was shot, I didn't know what to think. I didn't know if the government was involved. I didn't know who was involved. I suspected the government was involved in all of it. Rather than distrust everyone, I felt like I had to do something myself.

For two years, I volunteered at the Watts Workshop, a storefront writing-and-acting school in the heart of L.A.'s black community. I taught acting and directing and hired several of the students to be in *I Dream of Jeannie*. One of my students, Artist Thornton, went on to start a similar workshop in South Dallas, the Artist and Elaine Thornton Foundation for the Arts, and I support him to this day.

In the late 1960s, most people I knew were trying to find answers, or at least bring up the right questions. I remember Peter Fonda asking me to a screening of *Easy Rider*. I didn't know if I could make it because I'd taken another hit of acid a few hours earlier. According to him, that made it more imperative I see his movie. He was right. I saw *Easy Rider* in a little private screening room, and afterward I glanced at the friends Peter had invited, maybe a half dozen people, and all of us had the same wild, dazed, breathless, awed look of having watched something genuinely incredible.

I left itching to get on the highway myself. Since we traveled with the family, I sent away to the U.S. Department of the Interior for a guide to thermal springs around the

world. I figured the family that bathes together stays together. We went to Canada and toured the northern United
States. Along the way we came to Boulder, Montana, site
of geothermal hot springs, the turn-of-the-century training
camp for boxer Gentleman Jim Corbett, and the historic
Diamond S Ranch, a sprawling hotel that was originally
built by a group of San Francisco millionaires so they could
frolic with their mistresses.

We checked into the Diamond S, the grand old hotel
with onion-domed towers and a ballroom at the foothills
of the Elkhorn Mountains. We were given a tour of the
Western-style building from Jim Sandal, the hotel's manager, who'd previously headed the local school and hospital
for the developmentally disabled, which was nearby.

As he showed us around, our conversation was drowned
out by a thunderous noise outside the hotel that was so
loud everything shook We ran to the front porch and saw
six army helicopters land on the front lawn. Then about
30 uniformed soldiers walked through the lobby and into
the restaurant. They were from a National Guard unit celebrating the end of their yearly training.

Lunch was exceptional, especially the service. Every time
I took a sip of water, the busboy literally ran over to refill
my glass. It was like that at every table. The waiters and
busboys took orders, brought food, refilled drinks, and
cleared dishes with unusual dispatch. They fixed their eyes
on each table, intensely studying every single movement,
waiting to do their job. There were about 15 waiters and
busboys, and something about them was different.

"What's with the waiters?" I asked Jim.

"They're from the school," he explained. "I get the ones
I've known for a long time, train 'em, and they're real

good workers. They stay here for five days, then go back for two days."

"They get the weekend off?"

"No, it might be the middle of the week. Might be the weekend. It doesn't matter to them."

Jim was proud of his staff. They did their jobs well and he gave them the best life possible. They were mostly in their 30s and 40s, and Jim was like a father to them.

We enjoyed the baths. We soaked several times a day for the five days we were there. The indoor and outdoor pools were filled with natural mineral water coming out of the ground at a constant 104 degrees. A hundred years earlier, Indian tribes that were often at one another's throats observed a truce on these sacred grounds, which they called Peace Valley. The pools were therapeutic, and so was the conversation with the people we met in the pools.

Every afternoon I wandered into Al's Bar for a toddy and a poker game with some of the locals. We also visited nearby radon mines, deep, dark caverns known as "healthy mines." Years later it was discovered that radon is a deadly gas; in fact, now we test our home for it. But then people with terrible arthritis and rheumatism would sit in those mines for hours, swearing the cool radioactive air gave them relief.

Getting to see the country on trips like this gave my family a broader and open-minded view of America and the different ways people live. And Boulder, which couldn't have been friendlier, would play an oddly significant role in my life years later.

17

There was always a fascination with how we managed the special effects on *Jeannie*. Television was very low-tech in those days. Whenever Jeannie used her special powers to pop something new into the scene, we would shoot up to a certain point, the direct would yell, "Freeze," and we would literally hold that position until the camera was cut a few moments later. Then they'd make whatever change was necessary and we'd resume shooting.

One time Barbara and I were doing a scene in which Jeannie popped in an elephant. After the director told us to freeze, they brought in a live elephant, except they brought him in backward, so his ass was to the camera. We couldn't turn him around. He wouldn't budge. The director said, "We'll just have to live with it, let's resume." After he rolled camera, I first showed my astonishment and then resumed my conversation with Jeannie. As I protested at the elephant being there—he was right next to me—he lifted his tail and broke wind, literally all over me. Perhaps that's what the elephant thought of my acting.

Somehow we managed to hold ourselves together and continue on till the end of the scene. Once the director called "Cut," I burst into laughter and quickly rushed offstage to shower and change my clothes. It was probably the most mortifying moment of my career. But there were plenty of great moments, too, especially working with guest stars like Sammy Davis Jr., Don Rickles, and Chuck Yeager, who'd broken the sound barrier. We had fun.

In the midst of all this, Maj and I managed to save up the incredible sum of $15,000. We lived frugally. Hell, we didn't have time to do anything lavish, I worked so often. One day my accountant suggested I should think about buying a house. He also suggested we look in Beverly Hills. But Maj's dream had been to live in Malibu, so we looked there and found a big, pink, asbestos-sided house we liked on the beach in the Colony. It cost $115,000, and we put down $15,000—the largest expenditure we'd ever made.

Maj was thrilled.

I didn't know what to think.

"Woman, you're going to ruin me," I said before going to bed for the next three days, feeling like I'd never get out from underneath the $100,000 mortgage.

Maj oversaw the move to Malibu. After I managed to get out of bed, I joined Maj and the kids in our new home. We had our first candlelight dinner, on the floor—a bucket of Kentucky Fried Chicken on paper plates. We rebuilt that home twice over 30 years, but Malibu felt like home from that first day we moved in.

A few weeks later, Carroll and Nancy O'Connor came to visit with their little son, Hugh. Carroll and I were sitting on the bulkhead, watching our two boys play on the sand. Hugh and Preston were about six years old, separated in age by three days. They played with their Tonka trucks. I'd just remarked how we were so fortunate to live in such a safe community when Carroll and I stared in horror as a single-engine, open-cockpit, pre-World War II plane made an emergency landing on the beach, missing our children by not more than five feet. It came so close the boys were sprayed with wet sand from the wheels.

The two of us ran down the beach and saw the plane buried nose-first in the sand. The pilot was climbing out of the open cockpit, uninjured. As soon as he saw us, he began yelling that he could've made a perfect landing if he hadn't had to pull up and bounce over "the two little bastards playing in the sand." I had to physically restrain Carroll from attacking the guy and beating him into a bloody pulp.

Malibu was the perfect place for us. By now we'd enjoyed thermal springs all over the world and Maj had promised to copy that soothing environment when we settled down. For Christmas, Maj designed and supervised the building of a large hot tub. It was one of the few, maybe even the first, of its kind. In researching it, she spoke with one of the Jacuzzi brothers, manufacturers of the original water pump, and discovered that he'd invented a head that mixed water and air to help alleviate the suffering of his own paraplegic son. She used those special heads in our tub, putting them at varying heights so they'd massage different parts of the body—neck, elbow, back, leg. She also made it deep in parts, so we could stand and get a full-body massage. We could also lie down in it. We became the most popular house on the beach because of it, and within a few years she'd built six for friends who lived in Malibu. They marveled at her creativity and would ask how she came up with her ideas. They came naturally. Her father had been an inventor. And just as naturally those hot tubs helped to define life in Malibu.

Our house was located at the end of the street. For a few years, Maj held sway over the Colony's egg-dyeing event the day before Easter. All the children in the Colony brought their eggs to our house. One year Jennifer Grant came walking in with her father, Cary, in tow. He was carrying a carton of eggs, ready to be dyed. He looked at Maj, offered his eggs, and asked, "Should I have boiled them?"

My wife, a lifelong fan of Cary Grant, said, "For you, Cary, I'll boil them." She would've boiled a hundred dozen if he'd asked.

We took our civic duties seriously. I judged the annual chili cook-off, led impromptu flag-waving parades up and down the beach while dressed in a flowing caftan, and shopped at the grocery store in a yellow chicken suit. My behavior earned me the nickname the Mad Monk of Malibu.

Living up to it came naturally. I remember when President Nixon froze workers' wages but not income from investments in the stock market. I was outraged by what struck me as a fine on the working class. I thought labor should've protested. They didn't, but I couldn't ignore it. On Labor Day, my family and friends and I built a giant 10-foot-tall chicken out of chicken wire and yellow tissue paper and then paraded it up and down the beach in protest of Nixon's policy, but mostly because of the chicken-heartedness of the labor unions. As it happened, a *New York Times* reporter was in one of the homes on the beach and reported the story, which got national play but not a word from labor.

Then I also had my silent Sundays when I didn't utter a single word. These silent Sundays actually started on a Friday after I'd spent two straight days taping rodeo scenes for an episode of *Jeannie* titled "Ride 'Em Astronaut." When I woke up Saturday morning I couldn't utter a sound. My doctor said I'd strained my voice and advised me not to talk until Monday.

Since I didn't have to work until Wednesday, I spent four whole days without speaking and I rather enjoyed it. On the next Sunday, I decided not to speak again. By Monday, I felt rested and refreshed. Not everyone liked it, though. My daughter, Heidi, then 12, left me a note that I found when I went to work.

"Daddy, as you know, I love you very much. But yesterday you were a big shit."

Maybe so, but I continued not talking on Sundays for 25 years, and all of us learned to adapt. A mystique developed around my silence. People thought it was a religious or mystical thing. I never explained, because the truth was not as interesting as the myth. It allowed me to have some fun, too. At one fund-raiser for the summer lifeguards, I posted a sign on the outside of my van that said "Hagmananda Listens." For five cents a minute people could come inside and talk to me about anything for exactly five minutes.

They found me dressed in colorful robes and surrounded by flowers, candles, and incense. Before anyone said a word, I handed them a card, warning that I would not speak, or give them absolution or advice. All I promised to do was listen. I also promised not to divulge anything they told me. And boy, did they tell me. Often I got more than I bargained for.

One man came in with his son and asked if he really

could tell me *anything*. I nodded. He introduced his boy, who was 12, then explained that he was married and that he loved his wife very much. But one day he and his son returned a day early from a camping trip and found his wife in bed with his best friend.

As soon as he got those words out, he burst into tears. His son sobbed just as hard. It was very emotional and difficult for me not to comfort them. Then my little egg timer went off, signifying their five minutes were up. When he asked if he could buy another five minutes, I vigorously shook my head no and they left.

I was wondering how I was going to recover from that ordeal when the guy stuck his head back in and thanked me. He said he'd never told anyone about that and just talking about it made him feel better. He said he still loved his wife and was going to make it work. It turned out to be one of the nicest moments.

By *Jeannie*'s fourth season, the show's ratings had dropped and there was talk about cancellation. I didn't want to see it end. I liked the show. But either way it didn't seem like I'd be out of work. The studio wanted to sign me to a deal that would keep me in their future projects. While *Jeannie* might have been struggling, they still saw me as a draw. Jackie Cooper, the production chief at Screen Gems, called me in for a meeting. As a child, Jackie had been in the Little Rascals and starred with Wallace Beery in *The Champ*, one of the most moving films I'd ever seen. He'd also starred in his own successful series, called *Hennesey*. I liked him very much, but most important, I trusted him.

He wanted to make a deal that would keep me with the studio. He said it could be lucrative.

"Just give me better scripts for *Jeannie*," I said.

Jackie took a deep breath.

"Larry, I can't give you better scripts. It's the nature of the game that if you find the right formula you stick with it."

"It's not working, though. Better writers could help."

"Look, kid, I've been there. I know what you're talking about and I sympathize with you. I can't give you any better scripts. I would if I could. The show will likely be dropped from next season. All I can give you right now is more money."

I finally saw the light.

"Okay, Jackie, that's a good idea," I said resignedly.

Jackie said for me to talk with Chuck Fries, the studio's chief financial officer, and ask for $5,000 a week. It was a large sum for those days, but he assured me I'd get it. Before I left his office, he had me write two words on the palm of my left hand: SHUT UP. Whatever happened, he implored, I was to let Chuck do the talking, and if I felt like saying anything, especially something that would piss off the man who controlled the studio's purse strings, I was to look down at my hand and do what it said.

So I went in and talked to Chuck, who initially offered me a five-hundred-dollar-a-week raise, not anywhere close to what Jackie had told me to ask for, and I wanted to tell him that he was full of shit. But I opened my hand, looked at those two words, SHUT UP, and I did just that. As much as it killed me, I didn't say a word. A few weeks later, though, I got the raise just as Jackie had promised, plus a $100,000 bonus, which at that time was a serious bit of dough. Best of all, *Jeannie* was unexpectedly picked up for a fifth season.

18

At the start of the fifth season, the network forced Sidney to finally have Jeannie and Tony get married. Everyone associated with the series knew such a made-for-TV event would counter the show's poor ratings, at least in the short term. But as for *Jeannie*'s future, it spelled the end. I knew that if Jeannie and Tony wed, the the sexual tension that kept the show interesting would be gone. All of us waged a bitter fight against the decision, particularly Sidney and me.

But the wedding episode aired December 2, 1969, amid much publicity and the highest ratings the show had enjoyed for years. I felt like a groom who walked down the aisle with a shotgun at his back. When we wrapped the final episode at the end of January 1970 (the last original show aired May 26) and said good-bye, none of us knew the show's fate.

I went straight into a movie-of-the-week for Screen Gems called *Three's a Crowd*. It costarred Jessica Walter, who

I'd worked with in *The Group*, and E. J. Peaker. It was quick and fun but no earthshaker. Then I took Maj and the kids on vacation. We spent a week visiting a friend who owned an island in the Caribbean, and then we surprised mother and Richard on the Copacabana in Brazil. Seeming genuinely delighted to see us, they invited us to the ranch in Anápolis. We went thinking we'd all matured, but Richard was as miserable as ever.

Upon returning to L.A. at the end of the summer, I drove to Screen Gems to visit Claudio, who was still editing some of *Jeannie*'s last episodes. At the gate, which I'd driven through for five years, the guard told me that I needed a pass. When I asked why, he informed me that I wasn't working at the studio anymore. I made it inside, and then Claudio told me that *Jeannie* had been canceled while I was in Brazil. We didn't get the trade papers in Brazil and my agent hadn't bothered to call me.

I was more relieved than upset. *Jeannie* might've run its course creatively, but I'd achieved my goal. From the beginning I'd wanted to make a memorable comedy, a show that children could watch with their grandparents, and time has proven *I Dream of Jeannie* one of the best and most enduring sitcoms ever. It's still on the air every day somewhere around the world.

Meanwhile I had a deal with Screen Gems. I focused on finding a quality script. I was amazed, disappointed, and ultimately frustrated by how many bad scripts were out there. I turned down three, but eventually time ran out on my deal and I simply said to myself, Do the best of the lot and try to make it work.

That turned out to be *The Good Life*, a half-hour sitcom about a husband and wife who abandon their boring middle-class lives and go to work as a cook and a butler for a wealthy couple without revealing their lack of experience. Like *Jeannie*, the premise rested on keeping a secret. It also paired me with another gorgeous blond leading lady, Donna Mills. She'd done a lot of soap operas in New York City but was a newcomer to Hollywood. I rounded out the cast with my old buddy David Wayne and Hermione Baddeley, who I'd known in London. It was a very talented group.

Claudio was the producer and one of the directors. We made sure the actors had fun, felt creatively involved, and stayed loose with a supply of champagne that one writer noted was compulsory. The set was like an extended family, and on weekend my cast mates dropped by the house to add their input to the stories. Sadly, *The Good Life* didn't last long. NBC put us on opposite *All in the Family*, and we were trounced in the ratings by my good friend Carroll O'Connor. *The Good Life* disappeared after 13 episodes, and *All in the Family* went on to make history. If you're going to be shot down, it might as well be by the best.

Knowing I had free time, Peter Fonda asked me to play a sheriff in *The Hired Hand*, a Western that he was starring in and directing. Peter had assembled a first-rate cast that included Warren Oates and my friend Severn Darden. There wasn't a bad card in the deck. We shot the movie in Santa Fe, and I fell in love with the countryside. When I got a few days off between scenes, I rented a Plymouth convertible and drove to Taos to visit Dennis Hopper, who'd been a friend of mine in New York City. We'd often gone up for the same parts.

He was living in a beautiful old home once owned by Mabel Dodge Luhan. Without exact directions, I stopped in the main square of Taos and asked around until I found someone who knew where Dennis lived. An old Indian perched on a wooden rail outside a restaurant offered to show me if, as he said, I'd "buy an old Indian a glass of wine."

I needed lunch, so I went in and had a delicious Southwestern-style meal with this old chap, whose name was Telles Goodmorning. After a couple glasses of wine, he was absolutely shit-faced, but he still remembered the way to Dennis's place. I left Telles Goodmorning asleep in the backseat and went inside.

We drank some wine and tequila, and Dennis showed a cut of a film he'd done in Peru called *The Last Movie*. I remember he had an extended scene of himself screwing a beautiful Indian girl underneath a waterfall. As it went on and on, I got kind of bored and started to say good night, but Dennis persuaded me to stay at his place instead of driving back to Santa Fe at night.

Then I remembered Telles Goodmorning was still in my car. I went out to take him back to his pueblo and saw there'd been a passing cloudburst that had dropped a whole lot of rain in my open car. I found Telles in the backseat with his blanket around him, sopping wet.

He asked, "Why you leave an old Indian in back of car?"

"I'm really sorry, Telles. I forgot you were out here."

When I opened the car door about two feet of water gushed out. The Plymouth was trashed inside. It was only a five-mile drive to Telles Goodmorning's pueblo. After dropping him off, I somehow found my way back to Dennis's and had dinner.

The next thing I remember is waking up at five in the morning with a dreadful hangover and seeing Telles

Goodmorning sitting at the foot of my bed holding a pair of moccasins. He said his wife had made them. I could tell they were special. The beadwork was spectacular.

"This is for my brother who drove an old Indian home last night," he said.

In exchange I gave him a whale's tooth I had on a leather string around my neck. I'd bought a keg of about 300 of them for twenty bucks in a New York surplus store and gave them away as talismans. Telles Goodmorning solemnly touched it to his forehead, heart, liver, and kidneys, explaining that these were the body's sacred points. (Later I'd find out just how sacred the liver was.) Then he solemnly hung the tooth around his neck, looked up, and smiled.

"We are brothers," he said. "Maybe you'd buy an old Indian a glass of wine?"

We went into the kitchen and I found him some vodka and orange juice. I had one myself, of course. A couple of those and he was out of it again. By midmorning, I deposited him back home in the same condition as I did the night before. His wife was not too happy with him or me, but she was thankful I'd brought Telles back home again. Her expression darkened when she looked down at my feet and saw I was wearing those beautiful moccasins. I feebly gestured my apologies to her. I knew I was in deep shit and made a speedy exit.

Over the next few days, I shot a couple of scenes and had a few days off. I was thinking about going back home until I was needed on the set again when Telles Goodmorning showed up at my hotel. I invited him in. He asked if I knew anything about peyote. No, but that didn't mean I wasn't curious, and I wound up invited to a ceremony later that night.

I don't know how I found my way to the designated spot, a small Quonset hut in the middle of the desert, but somehow I managed. Inside, I met Telles and eight teenage Indian boys who looked like alkies chasing a new high besides sniffing gasoline. But I gave them the benefit of the doubt. Maybe they were going through their own rite of passage. I just had to worry about myself.

Telles gave a brief but solemn talk about peyote. Then he gave us each three coffee cans. One was empty, one was full of water, and one contained peyote buttons. I soon found out what the empty coffee can was for. It wasn't long after we chewed the peyote buttons that we started vomiting into our empty cans and drinking water from the third can.

After a while, I had no perception of time. The unpleasantness passed and I started having my dreams. I felt myself sprout wings. Then I saw featherlike hair covering my legs. And I watched in amazement as my feet turned into hawk's claws.

Strangely, I wasn't anxious or frightened by the transformation. In fact, when it was complete, I took off and flew around the hut. Once I grew accustomed to my wings, I somehow broke through the walls and flew above the Quonset hut and up into the mountains. It was spectacular, and during my flight I was given my song, which I use to calm myself when I'm anxious.

Meanwhile, the Indian boys had a rough go of it. They cried and screamed. The mind is full of phantasmagoria and demons, and peyote unlocks everything up there. If you aren't feeling good about yourself, I can imagine it'd be pretty scary. My head was in a good space and I enjoyed myself. Maybe I wouldn't have been so carefree if I'd known Peter was going to cut me out of the movie. But when it played on television years later, after *Dallas* had made me famous, the network put me back in.

19

Every time I went in front of the camera, I had the same thought: What the heck, it's only my career. At 40, I had no illusions about myself. I was an actor, plain and simple. I wanted to earn a living, get exposure, find good parts. That meant for the next few years I played a variety of characters, traveled far and wide, and tried to save a couple bucks from what I got paid. I enjoyed every minute of it.

The 1971 TV movie-of-week *A Howling in the Woods* reteamed me with Barbara Eden, and we had a great time working together again. Next came *Getting Away from It All*, another made-for-TV movie, in Morro Bay, a beautiful spot along the coast south of San Francisco. Then an opportunity came along to do more than show up and collect a paycheck. Jack Harris, my next-door neighbor, had produced *The Blob*, the 1950s horror movie that gave Steve McQueen his first starring role. We were taking a soak together in my Jacuzzi when he said his son and a friend had written a sequel called *Beware! The Blob*.

"You aren't doing anything," he said. "You want to direct it?"

I jumped at the chance. I also agreed to act and to help rewrite the script. I liked the idea of working in a genre where nothing is too far-fetched or too silly to put on the screen. My biggest challenge became finding recognizable names who'd agree to be in the movie for scale. I auditioned all kinds of people, but I ended up just stopping people I knew on the beach. Like Carol Lynley. She was was walking along and I got her attention by yelling, "Hey, you want to be in *The Blob*?"

"The what?" she asked.

"It's the movie I'm directing."

"What do I have to do?"

"Get eaten by the Blob."

This seemed to pique her interest, and she signed on. I promised to do the same if she ever did a movie. Godfrey Cambridge, who'd been in Ted Flicker's Compass Theater, an extemporaneous theater in New York, came on board when I snared him walking down the beach too. I also cast Richard Webb, radio's original Captain Midnight, Shelley Berman, Dick Van Patten, Cindy Williams, my assistant John Houser, my 10-year-old son, and even my other next-door neighbor, Margie Adleman, who later sold her home, with some finagling from Maj, to Burgess Meredith, another of the Blob's victims. To get the job, all you had to do was agree to be eaten by the Blob.

This turned into one of the most fun projects of my career. The picture started with a shot of a cute little pussycat playing on the lawn outside a house. Then it cut inside, where Godfrey puts down a canister he'd brought back from the tundra in the Arctic, planning to examine it in his lab. But the can warms in his kitchen as he watches TV in the next room, the contents thaw, the top pops off, and the fun begins.

First a fly sets down on the can's rim, and *slup*, it's eaten. Then the darling kitty comes into the kitchen and paws the red goop in the can. *Gulp!* Finally, the Blob eats Godfrey, who was a mouthful since he weighed about three hundred pounds. I wrote myself in as an addled deaf-mute, and like everybody in the film, I too was ingested.

Beware! The Blob wasn't everyone's taste. Though the original film had been a cult classic that made lots of money, *Beware! The Blob* disappeared from theaters almost as quickly as that cute kitty. Reviewers didn't think too highly of it either, but I had the last laugh when it was rereleased in 1982 as "the movie J.R. shot." But it's really good, clean, silly fun for the whole family.

The projects I did in the 1970s taught me that actors don't care whether they're on TV or the big screen, they just like to work. I got a chance to work with so many great actors. When I made *The Alpha Caper* in 1973, I got a second chance to work with Hank Fonda, who made acting look so easy. Leonard Nimoy, James McEachin, and Elena Verdugo were also in that picture about ex-cons who rob an armored car.

Then I was in *Blood Sport*, a father-son sports drama with Ben Johnson and Gary Busey, who displayed an abundance of raw energy and ability as a high school quarterback. I played his coach and drew from the guys I remembered from my brief stint on the football team in high school. I remember thinking Gary was someone who had the chance to make it big, and he's done very well.

In *What Are Best Friends For?*—my third movie of the year—I worked with Lee Grant and Barbara Feldon as well as talented actors like Nita Talbot, Ted Bessell, and George Furth.

I worked my ass off to capitalize on my name after *Jeannie*, but the juice didn't last more than a couple years, and neither did the money. My career was a constant hustle for parts. An actor's life is not always mansions and hot tubs. Despite three TV movies, I was broke. At one point, we rented our house out for a month and slept on mattresses in Peter Fonda's office. Awhile later I took the family skiing in Big Bear and had just $60 on me. I figured on staying in our van for a week or so, but on the way up I stopped for gas and I checked with my answering service and picked up a message from my agent.

When I called him back, he asked if I wanted to do a show with Lauren Bacall.

"When?" I asked.

"In three days," he said.

"What's the money?"

"How much do you have now?"

"Sixty bucks."

"It's a lot more than that."

I turned the camper around, and three days later we were in London to make a TV movie of the musical *Applause*. Lauren was in the midst of a triumphant production of *Applause* onstage there. I heard that she'd been sent pictures of a number of leading-men types to star opposite her in the TV adaptation and that her nine-year-old son had picked mine from the pile and said, "Look, there's the guy in *I Dream of Jeannie*." When Lauren asked how I was, her son had said something like, "Gee whiz, he's great," and then I got the part. She's denied the story, but I believe it—mainly because it makes a good tale.

I was thrilled to get a chance to work with her. My God, when she was 19 and going with Bogie, she was gorgeous, and years later she still had the looks, voice, and presence of a great star. Her aura was intimidating. *Applause* was one of the most daunting roles I'd undertaken, and the greatest task was Betty Bacall herself.

I rehearsed for over a week with her understudy before I even met her. I was warned by producers that she didn't like to be touched. I have no idea if that was true or if she even knew this was said about her. But when it was finally time for our proper introduction, I was extremely nervous. I was led into a room where she was seated in the center like royalty. I understood why everyone was in such awe of her. She was an imposing figure. "Larry," she said, gracefully extending her hand. "How nice to meet you."

Rather than lightly shake her hand, the equivalent of an air kiss, I ran my tongue from her wrist to her elbow, an impulsive, immature piece of behavior that to this day I can't explain. But I did it and afterward I waited for something horrible to happen. I vaguely recall her laughing tensely and then I got the hell out of there.

I'm sure she asked the producers who I thought I was. I'm sure they had no idea what to tell her. Fortunately, she didn't have me fired.

She was a sexy and charming woman. As we taped, she was friendly and gracious. I would wait for my cue and each day, as I walked from our place in Kensington to the rehearsal hall in Soho, I'd think, I'm out of my league. What am I doing here? I was so uptight about working with her that I lost a pound a day during the shoot.

Once the taping ended, I needed time to recover. I took Maj and the kids to Wales. We stayed in an old Norman castle that was in ruins except for a modern little cottage in the center. Ravens perched on top of the stone walls, watching every move we made, which terrified and delighted the children. One day, I got a call from Ben Washer, my mother's secretary and confidant. He told us that Richard had died. I paused for a moment, then turned and told Maj and the kids the news. I felt sorry for Mother and sent my regrets, simple and sincere.

Next, Claudio Guzmán invited me do a movie with him in Chile, his homeland. His enthusiasm alone appealed to my readiness for adventure. Claudio said *Antonio* was a comedy, but the real fun would be staying at his parents' house. It sounded wonderful. There was a downside, though. He couldn't afford to pay me much, if any, money. I laid out the offer to Maj, who insisted that I get at least $10,000.

"You know Claudio's doing it on a shoestring," I said.

"I know," she said. "But we need to live too. Ten thousand dollars."

After that was straightened out, we went down to Chile. My daughter, Heidi, spoke some Spanish and got us around pretty well for an eighth-grader. The movie was cute. Claudio had created it around Trini Lopez, who was a fellow graduate of Weatherford High School. We got along well and had fun, though all through the shoot there was tension in the country that made us uneasy.

We didn't know what was going on at the start. Nothing worked the way it was supposd to. Deliveries were late if they happened at all. Telephones were unreliable. Locations weren't blocked out the way we'd contracted. Equipment didn't arrive. There was no hot water in the hotel. It was little everyday stuff that didn't work, and I kept wondering why.

The country ran on bribery. Everyone was on the take. Which is fine with me if that's what keeps things running smoothly. Hell, it works in cities like New York and New Orleans. Eventually I found out from some of the local crew that the people smelled revolution in the air, and they were afraid to take the normal bribes for fear of recrimination by the new regime. So the whole system stopped.

Not everything stopped. We took a train down to the southern tip of Chile. During the trip, Preston suddenly got my attention.

"Dad, the locomotive has left us!"

I looked out the window and sure enough, the engine was nowhere to be seen and our car was slowly rolling backward. Preston and I rushed to the rear of the car, found a huge wheel, and figured it was the brake. We kept turning it until we came to a shuddering stop. Awhile later, the locomotive returned, hooked up, and we continued on the journey. There was never an explanation, and needless to say, Maj and I didn't sleep that night.

Once we arrived, we loved it down there. The food was delicious, the music was great, and the air was intoxicating. It was like California, only upside down: the north was hot and the south was cool. After shooting finished, we ventured into the mountains and found a couple of hot springs that were in our book on thermal hot springs worldwide. The hotel we found there was first class. The owner was a ham radio operator and had a shortwave radio set up in one of the rooms. I think this somehow attracted some of Allende's soldiers. As we watched them tromp through the hotel with their machine guns ready, our family vacation suddenly felt a little dicey. We went back to Santiago and flew home. Two months later, Allende was overthrown, and perhaps murdered, which changed the fate of Chile forever.

My name must've had some value, because my agent got me into *Here We Go Again*, a new sitcom about a newly married couple who move into a home near their ex-spouses. I liked the premise. It seemed as if there would be endless possibilities. The cast included pros like Dick Gautier, Diane Baker, and Nita Talbot. I thought it was going to run forever, but for a series to be a hit so many ingredients need to come together perfectly, and this didn't have it.

The cast would read through a script, give their input, agree on changes with the writers and director, and then the producer would arbitrarily ignore those fixes. On the second show, I came onto the set looking for pajamas I was supposed to wear for the scene I'd just prepared for. I asked the costume man where they were. He told me that the producer had cut the gag.

"Without telling me?" I asked.

"He said he didn't want you to wear pajamas."

I was not used to being cut out of creative decisions. I expected to be involved with the writing and directing. But the producer wasn't a team player. He didn't feel he had to consult with anyone about the changes. Neither did he feel like he had to be courteous or sensitive to the actors. In rehearsals he'd whisper comments or shake his head and mutter, "Jesus Christ."

"Look," I said during a run-through, "I'm open to suggestions."

"Okay," the producer said. "I don't like what you're doing."

"If you don't like something, make a suggestion. But don't demoralize the actors."

Finally I barred him from the set. I told him he could criticize as much as he liked but he had to do it out of our sight. He argued that I couldn't do that to the producer. I said fine, then I wouldn't work whenever he was present. The other actors supported me, and we had ourselves a regular palace revolution.

Unfortunately, the tension between the production team, the writing team, and the acting team never improved. After 13 episodes, the network put the series out of its misery. It was the only show I've ever been happy to see end.

The next project I did was *Sidekicks*, a made-for-television Western costarring Lou Gossett Jr., Blythe Danner, and Jack Elam, one of the best character actors in the business. I got to be real good friends with Jack. Playing scenes with him was a joy until you went to dailies. Jack would be standing behind me during scenes and then I'd notice nobody was listening to my lines. They were all looking at Jack. It wasn't his fault—it's just that he had one wandering eye. You never knew which way he was looking.

That was a lesson to be learned: never let Jack stand behind you. There was a second lesson too: never play poker with him. We played liar's poker with dollar bills every day. I got 30 bucks per diem, and our poker playing got to the point where I just handed Jack my thirty as soon as I saw him. He was going to win it anyway. But he hated that.

"Don't do that, kid," he said. "Let's have a good game. That's half the fun."

"Half the fun for you," I said. "I know I'm not going to win, and I can't take the ignominy of losing to you every time."

I wasn't kidding. But Jack told me not to feel bad.

"Everybody loses to me."

20

It was 1974, and I'd finished a couple of made-for-TV movies when my agent called and said, "Larry, what are you doing?"

I had a feeling he never knew what was going on in my career. But he put me into *Stardust*, a feature film that chronicled the rise and fall of a sixties rock band called the Stray Cats. The starring role was being played by real-life British rocker David Essex, and Adam Faith, another musician and a terrific natural actor, had a supporting role. It was shooting in London. Martin Balsam was supposed to have had my part, but when a conflict forced him to bow out at the last moment my agent sent me the script and asked if I could get there within the week.

Originally the part was that of a Harvard mobster, a guy with a Boston accent. On the way to England, I worked on the character and developed a combination Boston-Italian accent, which was a stretch for me. The day I arrived I met director Michael Apted and the writer at an Italian restaurant in Soho. I wore a pinstriped suit and gave them my whole act, including the thick accent. When I finished, Michael quietly asked where I was from. I said Weatherford, Texas. He politely asked if it would be possible for me to play the part with a Texas accent. I lit up and in a thick Texas accent said that was a great idea.

"What name should we give you?" Michael wondered.

The name Porter jumped out first. Porter was the middle name of my dad's fishing buddy, James Porter McFarland. I needed a last name. I thought of the capital of Texas. Austin. Michael liked it, but he said that he wanted the character to have one of those two-name names.

"Porter Lee Austin," I blurted, thinking of Lee Marvin.

Michael approved and we got along swimmingly from then on. Michael's one of the best directors I've ever worked with, and I've been blessed with more than a few. The movie was complicated because it was really about drug addiction and how young rock groups were taken advantage of by their managers and the record industry and discarded when they were of no more use, and Michael had a complete and clear vision from the get-go.

Of course, it didn't hurt to have David Puttnam as a producer. Puttnam was an absolutely brilliant producer.

My character, as I look back on him, was an early version of J. R. Ewing, a fast-talking businessman who was going to fleece the Stray Cats and love every minute of it.

Keith Moon, the drummer for the legendary rock band The Who, was in the movie. He loved *I Dream of Jeannie*. He was a huge fan, and we became instant friends one bitterly chilly day when we sat together in his Rolls-Royce, drinking champagne, while shooting at Gatwick Airport. From then on that became our routine during production, drinking and bullshitting. He was a sweet guy who had a gift for impersonations. He was hysterically funny. He felt a kinship to me because his girlfriend was Swedish and so was Maj.

After *Stardust* we went our separate ways, me back to Malibu and Keith back to the madness of rock stardom. But he promised to stay in touch.

Everyone says that, and I didn't hear from him for a long time. Then one Saturday I was upstairs in bed studying lines for a movie. It was a gorgeous day. The sun was shining through the window. I was stark naked. Suddenly, from downstairs, I heard Maj yell, "Larry! Larry!" in the tone of voice I knew from experience was trouble.

I dashed down the circular staircase, and at the bottom stood a Nazi SS officer. "Yes, can I help you?" I said in a most polite voice, as if Nazi officers came around regularly.

"It's me, Keith," he said. "Keith Moon. Your buddy. Your mate."

I didn't recognize him in the uniform. Who would? Maj didn't place him at first either. Who knows why Keith was in that uniform? He never offered an explanation. Keith had bought a house in Malibu, and he wanted us to see it. He had a white stretch limo waiting in the street.

On the way over to his new home, we passed a house whose garage was open and we saw a kid playing the drums. Keith told the driver to stop. He jumped out, moved the kid over, performed a 10-minute riff that blew our minds, especially the kid's. Then he handed the drumsticks back, said, "Thank you, mate," and we took off. I could imagine that kid trying to convince his friends that Keith Moon had dropped by and played his drums.

Cut to my house a few months later. It was morning, and I got a call from Keith's girlfriend. Her voice had an alarmed tone. She said Mr. Moon—she always called him

Mr. Moon—was having a terrible fit and she wondered if I could hurry over. I pulled on my Levi's and a sweatshirt, then sped to his house.

Keith had moved from Malibu to a smaller rental house in the hills above the San Fernando Valley. I walked in and saw it was a disaster. There were holes in the doors, the mirrors in the living room were broken, and everything was covered with shit. Keith was lying in the middle, face-down.

Slowly, he looked up at me.

"Hello, mate," he said. "Good to see you, Larry. What brings you?"

I'd heard that he was having a little trouble. With a slight, somewhat comical nod of his head, he acknowledged the mess—the overturned furniture, the broken glass, everything. He propped himself up on an elbow, surveyed the damage, and explained what'd happened. His dog, an enormous Great Dane puppy, had rooted into his stash of black beauties and lapped up God knows how many. At least it had been enough for him to have had a shit fit all over the house.

After a night of clubbing, Keith had walked in and caught the dog in the middle of the rampage. As Keith explained it to me, he'd thought the dog was having too much fun by himself and joined in, trashing whatever had been over-looked.

"What do you think, Keith?" I said. "Shall we go to Saint John's Hospital? My sister-in-law works there. They also have a great detox facility."

"Yeah? Sounds like a great idea."

I went back home and cleaned up and then came back and got him. He was very calm. He'd done this before. On the way to the hospital, we took his dog, now more or less comatose, to the veternarian so he could detox too. Then we got to Saint John's. Before Keith was allowd into detox, he had to be checked out by an internist. The doctor, a young man, was in awe of Keith the rock star, but he was more amazed when Keith described his daily regimen.

"I always wake up around six o'clock and I have some eggs, bangers, and mash," he said. "And I have, um, a bottle of Dom Pérignon and a half a bottle of Courvoisier, and then I take a couple of downers because I take my nap at ten until about six."

"Uh-ah," the doctor responded and nodded, wide-eyed.

"Then I get up and have another half a bottle of Courvoisier, finish off the Dom Pérignon if there's any left, drop some black beauties, and then we go out on the town. Usually we go out to dinner, then we go to a couple of the clubs. I'll drop a few more black beauties and drink some more Courvoisier and, uh, then get in around, say, two or three o'clock in the morning, sleep till six, and start all over again."

Keith described this as if it were a rather well-balanced day. By the time he finished, the doctor had put down his notes and was just listening. He'd never heard anyone describe a routine like Keith's. Few people who had such daily habits live long enough to describe them.

Next, the doctor checked Keith's heart and blood pressure. Afterward he looked stunned.

"Everything seems to be fine," he said.

Having passed the tests, Keith was allowed to enter the detox ward. He said good-bye as if going on vacation. While I waited for some of his paperwork to go through, I asked the doc to check me out too. As long as I was there, I said, "Why not give me a little exam? Listen to my heart, look at my blood pressure."

After he completed the checkup, the doc asked if I had a private physician.

"Yes. Why?"

"You better go see him. You're blood pressure's out of sight."

Both Keith and I pulled through. But on September 7, 1978, Keith's lifestyle caught up with him when he died of too much . . . hard living. I still had another 17 years before my bad habits nearly did me in too.

There was no shortage of characters with colorful stories to tell, and many of them got told in our hot tub. I found that people always talk more freely and openly when they strip off their clothes and relax in the water. Roger Vadim, the filmmaker who'd married Jane Fonda and lived down the beach from us, was one of those people. One day, as the two of us soaked prior to his and Jane's divorce, he confided, "My greatest mistake in our marriage was to teach Jane how to read a newspaper."

Roger told numerous stories about his love affairs with Catherine Deneuve, Brigitte Bardot, and Jane, and his worldly travels, but the one story he told that's stuck over the years was how he lost his virginity. He was in his mid-teens when his parents sent him to stay with relatives in the country to spare him from the bombing they believed was headed toward Paris.

One night his cousin, a beautiful girl—as is always the case in stories told by the French—invited him into her bedroom. As he climaxed, Roger heard explosions, a constant stream of them. The walls shook, the ground quaked, and the nighttime sky seemed to be on fire.

"It was my first orgasm, and I've never had one like that since," he said.

Of course, it was D-Day, the invasion of Normandy.

During this time, we arranged for Burgess Meredith to buy the house next door to ours on the beach. He got a very good deal, and to celebrate his moving in, Maj built him a Jacuzzi. Sometimes he was a great neighbor, sometimes he was a pain in the ass. It depended on his mood. But we loved him anyhow—and there were some big anyhows. A few years later, we remodeled our house in a Santa Fe style, but when we finished Burgess claimed that we'd built two inches above the roof line and sued us for blocking out *his* sun.

I remember telling my friend Bob Wynn that Burgess was suing me. He said, "Larry, I have a prayer session ever Thursday night. About twenty-five of us get together and read the Bible. If you're having trouble with Burgess, we'll just pray that old fucker dead."

I saw no need to go to that extreme. But I spent a considerable amount of money fighting the suit and eventually I won it. By then Burgess (who'd played the Penguin on the hit TV series *Batman*) and I no longer spoke to each other. The next time he gave a big party, of course I was not invited, but I thought it was a good opportunity to get his goat for all the trouble the lawsuit caused.

I knew that Burgess hated playing the Penguin. Even though it was one of his most famous roles, he was offended that someone with such memorable radio, stage, and screen credits should be reduced to waddling around in a tux and quacking like a penguin on what he considered a lowly TV show.

Knowing this, I had Michael Woolbrech make 50 silk flags with penguins on them, and then on the day of the party I flew them up on the top of the offending roof. I also made a loop tape of Burgess quacking like the Penguin and blasted it on my stereo all day long. Maj made me take the flags down and turn off the stereo when she looked over and saw that Burgess was on the verge of apoplexy. It was one of the meanest—and funniest—pranks I ever played.

That summer Peter Sellers rented our house for six weeks. It was right after a big storm. We'd lost part of our beach and were having it and our house repaired. I warned Peter that we had to have some work done. Burgess was also replacing his sea wall. I emphasized it wasn't going to be idyllic.

"I don't care," he said. "I love the house."

"It's twenty thousand a month."

"Money's no object."

Good, because I was broke and needed the money. So Maj, the kids, our three cats, two dogs, and turtle moved into a spare room in Peter Fonda's office on Melrose and Seward. The next day the pile driver set out right outside Peter Sellers's bedroom and started hammering. Peter thought it was going to last for a few days, but the work spanned six weeks. He was livid.

"I'd like my money back," he said.

"I can't do that," I said. "I spent it. I paid off bills."

Though his lawyers threatened to sue, he stayed the entire time. In the midst of that, Peter Fonda celebrated his thirty-fifth birthday with a giant party at his office. He had about a hundred people, including his dad and sister. I put on my magenta gorilla suit and stood by the door, making sure that only invited guests came inside. I had a great time and around 2 A.M. I went to sleep on the lawn. In the morning, I woke up with a terrible hang-over and got on a rickety old bike I saw and started pedaling toward a nearby stand that made the world's greatest milk shakes.

It was one of those still mornings. There wasn't a car on the road. But on the way, I crashed my bike—the front tire slipped into a drainage grating. I injured my knee and was lying dazed in the road. The next thing I knew, two cops were staring down at me.

"Are you all right?" one of the cops asked.

"Yeah," I said.

"Good. I don't know what I could book you for—impersonating a gorilla on a Sunday morning—but just do whatever you have to do and get the hell off the street."

My next offer was much better. Paul Mazursky asked me to be in *Harry and Tonto*, his memorable film starring Art Carney as an old man who, after losing his New York City apartment, sets off on a cross-country journey, visiting his children and friends, and living life as he's never done before. Art was brilliant. I played his son, a real loser who begged his dad to move in with him and share the rent. Every one of my scenes was with Art and I had a delicious time working with him.

But for every film like *Harry and Tonto*, I did five on a par with *The Big Rip-Off*, a TV movie that was forgettable—with three exceptions. One was Tony Curtis, the star, who was so much fun. He was the best cribber I've ever worked with. You'd never know he had tiny slips of paper with his lines written down pasted everywhere. He's a master. We did one scene in a car where I held a flashlight so he could see his lines.

The second exception was meeting Brenda Vaccaro, a fabulous babe.

And the third exception? My hair. Before shooting began, Maj had said, "Let's try perming your hair." I'll just say two words: big mistake.

In 1975, I played Linda Blair's father in the made-for-TV movie *Sarah T.—Portrait of a Teenage Alcoholic*, but otherwise I barely worked the whole year. I started off the next year by making *The Return of the World's Greatest Detective*, a TV movie about an L.A. cop whose motorcycle falls on him while he's lying down reading a Sherlock Holmes novel during his lunch break. He wakes up believing he's Sherlock Holmes. The movie was intended as a pilot for a weekly series, but it didn't go.

I'd put a lot of creativity and energy into that project, and it took a while before the disappointment faded.

Fortunately, I stayed busy. I made *The Big Bus*, a parody of disaster films directed by James Frawley, another friend from New York days. He put together an unusually strong cast, including Joseph Bologna, Stockard Channing, Ned Beatty, Ruth Gordon, Lynn Redgrave, and about 25 other terrific actors. Next, I took a part in *The Eagle Has Landed*, a World War II epic about Nazi soldiers who plot to kidnap Winston Churchill. It shot in London during the hottest summer they'd had in 50 years, and I took the family with me so they could have a vacation.

The movie featured another stellar group of actors: Michael Caine, Donald Sutherland, Robert Duvall, and Anthony Quayle, the very beautiful and talented actress Jenny Agutter, and Treat Williams, who was beginning his movie career. The film's director, John Sturges, had made classic movies like *Gunfight at the OK Corral*, *The Magnificent Seven*, and *The Great Escape*.

He was brusque. He barked orders like an old-fashioned

movie director. A few times I fell into his crosshairs. Like the scene when I had the muzzle of my carbine pointed down. He wanted it up. But it was raining.

"I don't want water going down the barrel," I said. "When it rains, you sling it down."

I could almost hear him thinking: Youngsters today. But he said, "That makes sense. If that's what you want, go ahead."

I shot my final scene with Jean Marsh, who'd been a friend of mine in London when I did *South Pacific*. In the movie, she played a German spy and I barged into her cottage, prepared to throw a hand grenade into her room. Suddenly she opened the door and shot me in the forehead. Blood was supposed to splatter everywhere as I tumbled backward down the stairs.

It was a great scene.

We did it without a hitch and shooting was over for me.

I took Maj and the kids to Ireland, where we stayed at a historic castle with Kevin McClory, who had produced a James Bond picture. The castle looked like something out of an Irish fairy tale. We played croquet on the expansive lawn and servants brought out champagne. I felt very civilized. I also went to the horse races at the Curragh, Ireland's oldest and most beautiful racetrack. My friend Bob Sangster owned horses that ran there every day. Through him, I got in tight with the trainers and made a few bucks at the window. I also lost some too.

One day while I was playing croquet I got a call from *The Eagle Has Landed*'s production manager. Almost two weeks had passed since my last scene. He explained that when they viewed the dailies, they discovered the summer's heat had dried out the blood in the capsule that was supposed to have burst on my forehead and they needed to reshoot that little portion showing the bullet going between my eyes.

"This time, hopefully, you'll bleed," he said.

I returned for a few days, shot the scene, and got paid an extra week's salary, which I really needed after the horse races in Ireland.

Next, I landed a part in *Mother, Jugs and Speed*, a big-budget comedy about rival ambulance companies that starred Raquel Welch. Raquel had a reputation for being difficult, but I found her perfectly wonderful. She was also perfectly wonderful to look at. The movie, which also starred Bill Cosby and Harvey Keitel, started out funny, but the second half was loaded with stupid killings that confused moviegoers, who didn't know if it was a comedy or an action picture.

Next I worked on *The Rhinemann Exchange*, a 1977 miniseries that shot in Mexico City, which wasn't a great experience, but then I had a wonderful time making *The Checkered Flag*, a racing movie that shot on location in the Philippines, with Joe Don Baker and Susan Sarandon. Susan was a sensational person, as she's repeatedly proved over the years. I also became friendly with racing great Parnelli Jones, who had a small part as himself and served as the technical adviser.

Retired from driving, he owned a car that was running in the Indianapolis 500 just a few weeks later. When he finished his work on the film, he asked if I wanted to be his guest at the race and serve as the grand marshal. Yeah, I jumped at the chance. I loved parades, and this would be the biggest one I'd ever been in. But it meant finishing the movie, flying to L.A. just long enough to pack, then catching a flight to Indianapolis. Immediately after the race,

I'd have to fly to London, where I was supposed to start a movie. Maj planned to meet me in London with the kids. It was a lot of travel, but it was worth it.

Needless to say, I landed in Indianapolis jet-lagged out of my mind. It was the day before the race. I rode in the parade, waving to thousands of people from my perch on the back of a convertible. Afterward, I rode around on a Kawasaki minibike in the pit area, meeting hundreds of people associated with the different cars and their sponsors. I was having a great time. But according to Parnelli, the best part was what happened in the infield, the grassy area inside the raceway.

"It starts at six o'clock in the morning," he said. "They open the gates, shoot off a cannon, and everybody races to stake out a spot on the infield. What they do is get a coupla guys with motorcycles and they race ahead to claim territory for their RVs, the place they're going to spend the next 18 hours. It's like the Oklahoma Breaks, where everyone is racing to stake out land. Only instead of building a home and planting a farm, they're setting up an RV and getting shit-faced."

"I'd like to see that," I said, "but it's past midnight and I'm so tired I just don't think I can make it."

"You really have to see it," another guy chimed in.

"Then I have to stay up all night, otherwise I'll never wake up that early."

Some guy overhearing the conversation offered me one of Keith Moon's favorite pills. But it was a first for me.

Pretty soon, sleep was a non-issue.

At 6 A.M. I was standing in the infield, surveying a long green straightaway covered by a low-lying fog, and I was absolutely wired. Suddenly there was a boom and through the mist I saw a line of RVs and motorcycles racing toward me. Realizing I would get creamed if I stayed in that spot, I kick-started my minibike and took off in front of them.

I'd never seen anything as wild, but it got wilder once people began to drink—or whatever. I spent the rest of the morning riding around, saying hi to people, accepting beers, and having a blast. There was no slowing down. At one point, I encountered a circle of RVs that was set up like a wagon train. They were end to end and you couldn't get in unless you went through one of them. Naturally, that made me curious.

Nosing around, I spotted a gorgeous young woman and said hello to her. When she realized I was Larry Hagman from *I Dream of Jeannie*, she invited me inside.

Well, right in the middle of this grand American spectacle, I walked into a major orgy. There must've been 30 to 40 people fornicating in every conceivable position known. I felt out of my depths and returned to the pits for the race. Parnelli had been right, though. The 500 was exciting, but the real thrill was what happens in the infield.

21

I was fortunate I had enough of a name to get TV movies like *Intimate Strangers* and *Cry for Justice*, which allowed us to maintain our lifestyle, but just barely.

In fact, I was broke again when I bumped into Richard Donner, a friend from my earliest days in Los Angeles who was about to establish himself as one of Hollywood's top filmmakers. When we saw each other, he'd just cast Christopher Reeves and Marlon Brando in *Superman*, his latest movie, and was about to leave on location.

"Hag, you want a job?" he asked.

"Does a bear shit in the woods?" I replied.

"I just saw you in *The Eagle Has Landed*, and it'll be a snap for you. You'll pick up some good dough. We're going to be on location in Banff for about a month or two, and I suspect I'll need you up there for probably three or four days."

Those three or four days turned into about two weeks because of bad weather. But if I was going to be rained in, I picked an entertaining group of people to be marooned with. I wasn't around Christopher Reeve or Marlon Brando, which was too bad, though I can still boast of having been in a film with both of them. And also Glenn Ford, Trevor Howard, and my old Screen Gems boss Jackie Cooper; they were all part of the action. So was Margot Kidder. After the movie, she moved out to Malibu and I got a call from her, asking if I knew a good doctor.

"What's the matter, honey?" I asked.

"I was riding a horse with a Western saddle," she said. "It bucked me up and I landed on the saddle horn. I think I broke my clitoris."

"Oh honey, I know just what to do," I said and made a few calls before finding a doctor who fixed her up.

I was a hero to her and advised her to ride English saddle from then on.

The next Saturday night was like most weekend nights. There was a party for the cast and crew on the hotel's expansive balcony overlooking the grand Banff scenery. I filled some plastic bags with powdered sugar and taped them up so they looked like another powdery substance. They had the heft of a pound each. When I arrived at the party, I waved them around like tins of caviar and said, "Hey, everyone, look what I just got in the mail!"

People froze and stared, completely rapt and amazed. I specifically offered them to Dick Donner, who ran in the opposite direction, and all I heard was him saying, "Uh, no, no, no thanks."

I gave chase, but then, in front of the whole company, I did one of those phony *I Dream of Jeannie* trips and let go of the bags. They flew over the parapet and exploded at the bottom, about 20 feet below. The hundred or so people there rushed to the railing and saw the ground blanketed with white powder. There were gasps and groans and cries of "Oh my God!"

This first *Superman* was the classic story of the alien orphan sent to Earth from his dying planet. He grows up and uses his superpowers to destroy evil. I played an army colonel in charge of soldiers who were escorting an atomic-tipped missile. My scene revolved around the gorgeous Valerie Perrine faking a car accident in order to distract the military guards, thereby creating a diversion that would allow her people to steal the missile.

One of my men spotted her lying in the road unconscious but nonetheless provocatively.

"There's been an accident, sir," he told me.

I assessed the situation myself and said, "I think she needs mouth-to-mouth resuscitation and vigorous chest massage."

With that, all the soldiers started to jump on her.

I called the men to attention, ordered them to do an about-face, and pompously said, "I'm not going to have my men do anything I'm not prepared to do myself."

Then *I* jumped on her.

We printed the first take, did the coverage except for my close-up, and then it started to rain. It kept raining for five straight days. A week went by before Dick was able to shoot outside again, which provided me with a desperately needed additional week's pay.

Finally I did my close-up and finished my part of the movie. I was ready to go home. But a Canadian air controllers' strike made it impossible to fly out of Canada. Valerie and two of her girlfriends were in the same situation. I persuaded the production company to furnish us with an RV and a driver to take the four of us to the airport in Great Falls, Montana, where we could get a plane to L.A.

We set out at eight in the morning, driving through Banff National Park and drinking champagne and enjoying the spectacular scenery. At one stop for food, I went searching through my wallet for a credit card that wasn't maxed out and a tiny little dot of blue paper fell out. All of a sudden I remembered that years earlier I'd squirreled away a tab of acid in case of an emergency. I told myself this long drive qualified as one and swallowed it.

A while later, as we were driving by a beautiful mountain stream that emptied into a large blue pool, I decided I had to go swimming. The driver stopped and I stripped down to my Skivvies and dove in. The glacial water must've been 35 degrees, but it didn't make any difference to me because I was generating my own heat. I swam around as if I were in a heated pool. I saw the girls and a bunch of other people watching me from the bank and asking, "What the hell is that guy doing in there?"

I was talking to the trout.

Eventually I got back in the van and I continued having a great time on the road. Mileage markers flew by, but when it got dark the driver said he needed to sleep before we got in an accident. After he stopped, the wind started whistling through the RV. It was freezing cold. The driver worried about carbon monoxide buildup and wouldn't leave the motor on to provide heat. We didn't have any blankets. The girls pulled their sweaters on, wrapped up in the curtains, and were fine. I was traveling light and didn't have much other than what I had on. In addition, I was coming down off my acid trip.

Nobody offered to let me curl up with them and I decided

to lie down on the floor. A few hours later, with the night-time temperature near freezing, I couldn't stand it any longer. I woke Valerie and asked if I could share her curtain with her. She turned me down. Desperate, my teeth chattering, I turned to one of her girlfriends and asked, "C-c-c-c-can I-I-I g-g-g-get in with you?"

She moved over and I curled up. Sex didn't enter my mind. I just wanted to get warm.

The next morning the ground was covered with snow. Forgetting the fact that I'd nearly frozen to death the night before, I was the first one to jump out and make snow angels. Valerie laughed at my impulsiveness, then joined me, as did the other girls, in making snow angels.

Finally, we made it to Great Falls. As we boarded the plane, I spotted a large Indian chief headdress in a store. It cost $100. I was down to my last $125 travel per diem. I had them hold the plane while I debated whether or not to spend money I couldn't afford to spend. I looked at that headdress and couldn't resist.

Back in L.A., Maj was vaguely amused as I marched into the terminal wearing my new headdress.

"I figured you'd come back in a hat like that," she said.

It wasn't much after that, just before Christmas 1977, that Maj and I went to see Mother and Ethel Merman costar in a once-in-a-lifetime musical benefit for the New York Public Library. We settled into a friend's apartment on Central Park West. Lorimar had sent over two scripts for me to look at. One was a sitcom, the other was a drama. Before we got dressed for the theater, I started reading *The Waverly Wonders*, a half-hour comedy, which at that time I figured was my forte.

Maj went into another room with the second script. It

was titled *Dallas*, and it laid out the story of two warring oil families in Texas, the Ewings and the Barneses. After reading just two scenes, Maj let out a loud whoop and cried, "Larry, this is it! We found it."

She had me take a look, and after reading the first nine pages I knew she was right.

Dallas was Romeo and Juliet set among the oil fields, except there wasn't one likable character in the entire episode. Not one nice person. For television at the time, that was a real breakthrough. Mama was an old bitch. Daddy was an alcoholic asshole. My little brother was a womanizer. And my character, J. R. Ewing, was a combination of all of them.

"Mine's not the main part, but I think I can go someplace with it," I said.

"I think the show's different enough to do well," Maj said. "Everyone's an antagonist. It's fun."

Right then I called my agent and asked who else was involved. He let it slip that Barbara Bel Geddes had been signed to play the mother. When I found that out I knew the show was going to be a class act. She'd been one of my favorite actresses for what seemed like all my life. I instructed my agent to make a deal.

"The money's not very good," he warned.

"It's more than I'm making doing nothing," I said, and then more seriously added, "I'm not worried. If the show goes, the money will take care of itself."

The whole cast gathered for the first time in producer Leonard Katzman's office, where we read through the script. The first person I met was Linda Gray, who gave me a big hug. That hug was the start of a lifelong friendship. When we let go, which I did reluctantly, I was totally tongue-tied. All I could say was, "Hello, darlin'."

"Nice to meet ya, husband." She grinned.

At that moment I knew that Leonard had cast the perfect partner for me.

Patrick Duffy was a big, good-looking kid who felt like an old friend as soon as we shook hands. Both of us had worked on the 1974 TV disaster movie *Hurricane*, but in different scenes, so we never met. Ironically, I knew his father from the bar he owned in Boulder, Montana. While we were making *Hurricane*, Patrick's dad had urged him to call me.

"Larry Hagman's a big star," he'd said. "He can get you started in the business."

As it turned out, Patrick did all right on his own, starring on ABC's popular series *Man from Atlantis*. From his perspective, *Dallas* was already better.

"There's no chlorine burning my eyes," he said. "And I don't have to act with webbed fingers."

I loved the whole group. Barbara Bel Geddes, a former *Life* magazine cover girl who'd starred as the original Maggie in Tennessee Williams's *Cat on a Hot Tin Roof*, impressed me as a kindred spirit. When asked what about the role of Miss Ellie interested her, she said, "I needed the job." Jim Davis was a rugged, handsome, taciturn, perfect Daddy. Victoria Principal struck me as absolutely gorgeous. And talk about fate: it turned out that years earlier, when I enlisted in the air force at Bushy Park, her father was stationed on that base and she went to the American School there. Charlene Tilton was the most adorable teenager I'd ever met. She had all the qualities of a ripe Texas tomato—and sweet beyond belief. Steve Kanaly, who'd eventually play my bastard brother, was a real cowboy. He looked it, talked it—and was. Ken

Kercheval was the perfect choice to play my nemesis. He was a powder keg of unpredictability that made his work so charged, and it always came out riveting.

Then there was Leonard Katzman, the true genius behind the show. The man wrote, directed, produced, and served as the real head of the family. Without Leonard, *Dallas* wouldn't have been an eighth as successful. When I first met him in his office that day, I thought he was a real Hollywood producer, a kind of stereotype, and he turned out to be anything but that. He was a real human being, psychiatrist, rabbi, priest, ally, friend . . . and conniver.

When it came to making a TV show work, he knew every trick in the book, including the politics of dealing with the network. He was the man.

God knows what they all thought of me.

I arrived for that meeting in a fringed buckskin jacket and a big old cowboy hat. I also carried a leather saddlebag crammed with bottles of perfectly chilled champagne, which I set on the table with an authoritative *clank*. The folks seated around the table traded looks that said, "What've we got here?"

I made a toast.

"I just hope we all have a real good time," I said, flashing the first of J.R.'s memorable shit-eating grins.

And boy howdy, did we!

Back home, Maj asked how everything had gone at the reading. I told her that I loved the cast and thought the script would work, although the writers didn't know shit about Texas. The plan, as Leonard had outlined it, was to to shoot the initial five episodes in Dallas and go on the air in April as a midseason replacement. Everything sounded good, though I'd heard talk that Lorimar's top executives, Merv Adelson and Lee Rich, didn't believe *Dallas* would go beyond the original order.

"So I don't know," I said. "At least I'll get paid through those five. And while we're shooting, I take a trip to Weatherford and see Juanie."

"Not to worry. It's going to be a hit," Maj said confidently. "I feel it."

22

In the beginning Southfork was quiet. The mansion was virgin territory. The halls were silent and still, not yet haunted by years of scandal, family fighting, and backstabbing. Daddy hadn't died, Mama hadn't departed, Bobby hadn't stepped out of the shower, and J.R. hadn't been shot. We had no idea we were destined to spend the next 13 years together. As Patrick said to me a few weeks after we began taping, "I hope they let us know what's going on with the series early enough. I just rented a house and if this isn't picked up, I've got to get another job."

My concerns were more immediate. When we began taping in late January 1978, Dallas was gripped by one of the coldest winters on record. It snowed like crazy. My old bread van, which I'd driven out from L.A., provided the only warmth at the different locations where we worked. In the absence of fancy dressing trailers, it was the cast's unofficial headquarters. I stocked it with champagne and whatever else people wanted. We jelled as a group from all the time we spent in there.

We made nightly trips in my van to Western dancing bars such as Whiskey River, where I discovered great acts like Vince Vance and the Valiants, an outrageous group that plays 40s, 50s, and 60s music. I'm their unofficial mascot and stand in on keyboard or bass guitar whenever I hear they're playing nearby. My instrument is always unplugged, but I've learned to make it look legit.

At each bar, I went straight to the hostess and said, "Hello darlin', 'member me, Major Nelson from *I Dream of Jeannie*? I wonder if you have a table for all of us?"

Patrick and I hit it off from the get-go. On one of the first shows we taped, we had a dramatic confrontation after I exposed his betrothed's relationship with the ranch hand Ray Krebbs. Pissed off, Bobby grabbed my shoulders, spun me around, and was about to hit me. But as I turned, he saw I had drool running down my chin. He cracked up.

"Here I am acting my life out and you're drooling," he said.

I glanced toward Victoria, who was by the fire, wearing as little as we could get away with on network television.

"If you were looking at her, wouldn't you drool too?" I asked.

I think we were destined to be best buddies. One night as I drove a bunch of us to a restaurant, Patrick was drinking champagne and watching the world pass through the plastic bubble on the roof of my van when he suddenly exclaimed, "Hey, that's my hometown."

I had a photo from my family trip to Boulder, Montana, taped on the wall, and it had caught Patrick's attention. In it, Maj and I were standing in front of Gamble's Hardware.

"That's my hometown," Patrick said.

Talk about being blown away. I told him about our trips to the nearby hot springs and the many afternoons I'd spent in the bar there.

"Holy shit, Larry!" he said. "My dad owned that bar!"

I told him that was one of my favorite pictures, and Boulder was one of my favorite little towns.

Since I'd been to his hometown, I decided I had to show Patrick Weatherford, my little hometown. I promised to take him quail hunting. Early one Sunday morning we loaded my van with a couple cases of wine and a case of Tom Moore whiskey—Juanita's favorite—and we took off to introduce Patrick to my step-mother. We didn't sober up all weekend. Patrick kept up pretty good for not being a big drinker. But when I poured bourbon over my corn-flakes for breakfast, he drew the line.

"I know I'm in training," he said, "but I'm not quite up to your speed."

Patrick was pale and suffering when we pulled up to the set early on Monday morning. Jim Davis took one look at him and said, "Where the hell have you been, boy?"

"I went over to Weatherford to meet Larry's step-mother," he groaned.

He also met some of my high school buddies. As a matter of fact, later that day I got a call from the husband of a friend of mine, looking for Patrick. He was irate.

"Where is that son of a bitch, Duffy?" he asked.

"Why?"

"He was drinking champagne out of my wife's shoe."

"Yeah, and he wasted a good bottle of champagne. Your wife was wearing open-toed shoes."

For these first five episodes, the cast was put up at the North Park Inn, a crumbling motel amid barren fields on the north edge of Dallas. It wasn't the classiest joint. Patrick's bedroom floor had a crack in it so large that if he dropped his watch he'd have to go downstairs to get it back. I personalized my surroundings by hanging Indian batik bedspreads on the walls, setting up a toy railroad set around the perimeter, and lighting dozens of candles. There wasn't a mini bar, so I filled the tub with ice and champagne bottles.

One night Patrick, Jim, and I got together and listened to Jim tell us about all the cowboy films he'd made. God, he must've made a thousand of them. We also had a few drinks while he talked. After a few hours, Patrick and I took Jim back to his room and when we returned to mine, there were three fire trucks parked outside. My room was filled with smoke. Apparently, while we were gone, a candle had melted the phone and the smoke had set off the fire alarm.

I apologized and offered to pay for the smoke damage. Fortunately it wasn't as bad as it looked. After we'd washed the bedspreads, you couldn't tell there'd been a fire except that the ceiling didn't match the other rooms. It didn't matter, though. Soon after we left, they tore the place down and built a huge shopping mall that is now in the center of Dallas, which shows how much the city has spread out since then.

Meanwhile, we were working long, hard days on the show. Veteran TV writer David Jacobs created *Dallas* as a classic drama about a poor girl who marries into a wealthy family that could as easily have been set against the steel business in Pennsylvania or the textile mills in New England. But putting it in Dallas exposed a whole new part of the country that nobody had exploited, at the exact moment in time the city itself was expanding as a center of prosperity and power.

The Dallas Cowboys were the hottest team in America—and make no mistake, football rules.

Leonard Katzman insisted on shooting the first five shows on location in Dallas, not the backlots of Hollywood. He wanted the authenticity of the real thing, but more important he knew how essential it was to work where the suits couldn't constantly look over his shoulder and second-guess him.

A lot of elements contributed to the show's success. Many a master's degree has been earned with a scholarly dissertation about *Dallas*. The country needed a diversion from a terrible recession. People couldn't spend money for movies, dinner, and a baby-sitter, so they stayed home, turned on the TV, and watched guess what? A television show that revolved around greed, power, and sex and gave them something to talk about all week.

The world of corporate finance in Dallas is much more complex and devious than any of the story lines we ever devised for the show. In truth, *Dallas* was a simplistic view of what people imagined Texas oil families were like. We simply indulged that stereotype and made greed, treachery, and blackmail seem like good, sexy, all-American fun. As J.R. said, "Once you get rid of integrity, the rest is a piece of cake."

I couldn't have been more ready to step into J.R.'s boots. I'd been working on his character for years, particularly in *Stardust*. I grew up in Texas and knew all those good old boys. I knew the vernacular. I knew people who really were like J.R.—one in particular. I always said J.R. was a composite of people, and in a way he was. But I have to admit when it came to creating J.R., I reached back into my past and called on the memory of Jess Hall Jr., the man I'd worked for as a teenager at Antelope Tool Company. He was a respected pillar of the community. But he also once drove his Jeep up the front steps of my dad's house at 2 A.M. and left it on the porch for a week.

I'd known him for 30 years. I never told Jess I'd used him as the model for J.R. I worried he'd be offended. After he retired from business, Jess made a special seasoned salt for cooking in his garage as a hobby. The salt was tasty, but I warned him it wasn't healthy in heavy doses.

"It can lead to a heart attack," I said.

"Bullshit, Larry," he replied. "The body needs salt. It's the best thing in the world."

Well, he had a massive heart attack and his doctors took him completely off salt. True to form, he kept making the seasoning product, without the salt, using just the herbs. He still did well with it and it tasted great.

The first *Dallas* episode, titled "Digger's Daughter," premiered on Sunday, April 2, 1978, in the 10 P.M. slot that had been home to the *Carol Burnett Show*. Not since *Peyton Place* had TV viewers been treated to a family as dysfunctional as the Ewings. When Bobby delivered the shocking announcement that he'd married Pamela Barnes, daughter of Jock Ewing's bitter enemy Digger Barnes, played by my old friend David Wayne, prime time was forever changed.

But that was just the tip. It was also revealed that Pamela had played around with the ranch hand, Ray Krebbs, who was involved with J.R.'s niece Lucy. J.R. offered Pamela a fistful of cash to leave his brother and tried to ensure his own control of the family's millions by having a child with his wife, Sue Ellen. Worst of all for J.R., Bobby was finished with being a roving ambassador and wanted to play a bigger part in the family business. There wasn't anything mellow in this melodrama.

As Cecil Smith wrote in the *L.A. Times* review, "The scene is set for some very steamy drama to come on the arid Texas plain."

Ratings for the first episode didn't seem to indicate a hit, but the numbers grew steadily, and by the fifth episode, "The Bar-B-Que," *Dallas* was red hot. The episode—in which Pamela tragically miscarried after a fall during a struggle with J.R. in the hayloft—finished twelfth. CBS ordered 13 more episodes for the next season, and we were on our way.

All of us stopped looking for new jobs and returned to Dallas that summer to start the new season. We got a chilly reception from the locals. The city was still reeling from being the site of President Kennedy's assassination and was sensitive about its portrayal on the show. Dallas was rebuilding civic pride through the Dallas Cowboys football team and their cheerleaders, so at the start our depiction of Dallas as the home of greed and villainy didn't make us a lot of friends.

I remember being asked by an acquaintance to watch a football game at the Dallas Country Club, which was a bastion of old Dallas money. My friend introduced me to the men at the bar, budding real-life J.R.s in their 30s and 40s. It was a nice afternoon, and when the game ended, I bid them so long.

"Glad to meet you boys," I said.

But as I reached for the door, one of them said, "Good to meet you . . . *boy*." A chill went up my spine.

That sentiment stayed with me and gave me food for thought.

My concern was just how bad could I make this bad boy and still keep him lovable.

But remember that when *Dallas* began, J.R. was not the main character. Bobby and Pamela were the centerpieces. J.R. gradually grew through conversations Linda and I had in the background. While Patrick and Victoria played out the main focus of a scene, we made up our own show. I'd ad-lib something like, "Honey, I put this shirt on this morning and a button's missing. Now what the hell is this all about?" And she'd say, "Well, J.R., I tried finding a button, but I just couldn't." Then I'd go, "Here's a hundred dollars. You better buy yourself a bunch of buttons and fix all my shirts."

Eventually Katzman started paying closer attention to us when he watched the dailies and finally he asked, "What are you two doing back there?"

"Having fun," I said. "We were deepening our characters."

"Well, that stuff's good."

We found our characters about the time the network ordered another 10 episodes. That was a full season. It gave Katzman and the writers time to more fully develop the characters, especially J.R., who hadn't been allowed to blossom into his full nastiness. It allowed me to really shape J.R. to match the picture I had of him in my head. I added phrases and nuances that made J.R. my own, which is my modus operandi as an actor. I just do it. If they pick up on it, I know they're paying attention.

They had to pay attention as we shot the seventeenth episode. Irving Moore, a good friend of Katzman's, was directing that show, which featured a terrific guest-starring appearance by Brian Dennehy as a bad guy who, along with his partner, holds the whole family hostage during a hurricane—as if a hurricane would ever get as far as Dallas. That showed how much the writers knew about Texas.

Anyway, he had us in the living room and made Sue Ellen sing the song "People."

People, people who need people . . .

Tears streamed down her face as she sang.

She was a knockout.

Finally Charlene, playing my niece Lucy, got up and said, "I've had enough of this. I'm going upstairs to bed." Dennehy kindheartedly let her go, though only because he knew his partner planned on following her and raping her. As this sexually ripe 17-year-old walked across the room, there was a close-up on me, and I followed her with my eyes, revealing lascivious thoughts.

Irving yelled, "Cut."

"Larry, that's you're niece!" he said. "You can't look at her like that."

"Wait a minute," I said. "She's a woman. She's good looking. This is Texas."

"But Larry—"

"Okay, Irving. Fine. Let's do it again."

The next take I gave Charlene an even more lecherous look and Irving printed it. From then on, they knew J.R. was capable of anything, and it gave them an idea of the direction they could take him.

I did my part offscreen, too. When the cast guested on *Dinah's Place* with Dinah Shore, our first big national talk show, I ensured it would be a memorable appearance. Before our entrance, I opened some champagne backstage and Jim got shit-faced. Then I gave the whole cast hats to wear and flags to carry, and led them in a parade through the audience and onto the stage.

While being introduced to Dinah, Jim accidentally knocked off his London Bobby's hat. It struck Dinah's bad knee, causing her to gasp in pain. Jim immediately bent down and apologetically began kissing her knee. As he did, his hand moved up her legs and everything got wonderfully chaotic.

The lesson became more and more clear. As J.R. went, so did *Dallas*. The correlation was indisputable. By the end of the season, *Dallas* was firmly situated among the 20 top-rated shows and J.R. had emerged from the background, having driven Sue Ellen to drink and infidelity, so that finally, while eight months pregnant, she was sent away into a sanatorium. What fun!

For the end of the first full season, Katzman came up with the idea of keeping viewers hooked over the summer by cooking up a season-ending cliffhanger. In the finale, which epitomized *L.A. Times* TV critic Howard Rosenberg's description of *Dallas* as "terrific trash," Sue Ellen escaped from the loony bin, narrowly survived a car wreck that left her in a coma, and gave birth to her baby prematurely. Bobby and J.R. bonded in the hospital over the tragedy. Ratings soared.

This was good television, but what went on behind the scenes was even better. None of us could ever forget shooting that scene in Sue Ellen's hospital room. As Bobby and I gazed down at my comatose wife, who was connected to numerous life-supporting tubes, I talked about how beautiful she was, even in the dark light of tragdy. Bobby put his arm around me. It was a rare and touching moment of brotherly affection. The crew was enthralled, the set perfectly still. Everybody knew it was one of those special moments.

"Shall we sing the old song we sang when we were boys?" Patrick asked.

"Yeah, that'd be nice," I said.

Then we started:

"Do your balls hang low? Do they swing to and fro? Do they itch like a bitch when you drag 'em in a ditch? Can you throw them over your shoulder like a continental soldier? Do your balls hang low?"

By the time we finished, there wasn't a dry eye on the set. Of course, the tears were from laughter.

I thought Linda was going to kill us.

23

As the second full season began, I didn't have to worry about success going to my head, but my stomach was another matter. Over the past year, I'd gained close to 30 pounds by indulging in the good life, and when we went back to work none of my clothes fit. On New Year's, Maj and I went on the Optifast diet. We also jogged two miles daily. Within two months, I'd dropped 35 pounds. Maj took off 27. I felt and looked the best I had since *Jeannie*.

My timing couldn't have been better, as my life was about to take on a whole new shape. Though we'd almost finished shooting for the year, CBS made a last-minute request for four additional episodes, something practically unheard of so late in the year. But *Dallas* was the sixth-highest-rated show. The network wanted to keep up the momentum and take advantage of more advertising income.

Mr. Katzman and his writing staff plotted out the new

shows, and as the story goes, when they began discussing the cliffhanger, now a part of the *Dallas* formula, someone said, "Why don't we just shoot the bastard?"

The buildup was vintage J.R. Besides nearly losing the Ewing fortune and cheating family and friends with bogus Asian oil leases, he'd driven Bobby from Southfork, humiliated Pamela, planned to send Sue Ellen back to the nuthouse (upon discovering this she quietly slipped a pearl-handle pistol into her purse), and accused his ex-mistress and sister-in-law, Kristin, of prostitution (after which she hissed, "I'll kill him"). In other words, J.R. had been very busy.

Yet in the final episode, J.R. ended up very much alone, collapsed on the floor of his office after being shot by an unseen assailant.

That show aired on March 21, 1980. I watched at home, as I did every episode. By morning, though, it was clear this one wasn't like any of the others. *Dallas* had been seen by nearly 50 million people in the U.S., more than any show except the Super Bowl. *Dallas* finished number one in the ratings for the first time. Total viewership was estimated at 300 million in 57 countries around the world. It was a phenomenon, bigger than anyone ever imagined. Ronald Reagan was campaigning against Jimmy Carter, American hostages were being held in Iran, Polish shipyard workers were on strike, and all anyone wanted to know was, who shot J.R.?

My mother quipped, "How could I have raised such a rotten kid?"

I also realized it was the opportunity of a lifetime. As the world asked who shot J.R., I posed my own question— was the network willing to pay me more money to come back to the next season? Overnight, it seemed, J.R. was everywhere. There were J.R. T-shirts, coffee mugs, bumper stickers, and buttons. J.R. hats were for sale. An English rock group scored a hit with the single "I Love J.R." and the flip side "I Hate J.R." I knew CBS and Lorimar were making a mint. Everyone was making a windfall from J.R. except me.

As I saw it, it was also my turn to cash in. I had my agents tell Lorimar that I wanted to renegotiate my contract or else I was walking away from the show.

This was a gamble—the gamble of my life.

Friends called asking if I'd lost my mind. They warned that if I didn't pull it off, I'd never work in Hollywood again. My mother was incensed. To her a contract was sacred. "You don't go back on a contract," she scolded. But because of that ethic, which I'd observed, she'd made hundreds of dollars on the stage while the producers of hits like *South Pacific* and *The Sound of Music* had made millions.

"I know the risks I'm taking," I said.

And they were big. I was almost 50, and I wanted to make the move from hired hand to participant. If I blew it, I figured I could survive for a couple years. In reality, they easily could've written me out of the show. J.R. could've been killed. The show would've survived. It was hot. But I knew Katzman's sensibility. He was too intelligent to let J.R. die. Even as the studio played hardball by floating rumors about possible new J.R.s, I believed everything would work out.

In a way, it already had. I had a house, a wife I loved, great children. Everything I'd ever wanted.

What was I really asking for? CBS and Lorimar were making more money than they'd ever, ever expected. Many

many millions more. I just wanted what was fair.

Which was the instruction I gave to my agents. I let them handle the negotiations and then turned to my publicist, Richard Grant, for a strategy on how to handle myself and use public opinion to my advantage. Good PR would make me more important and Richard knew how to execute that.

He knew a lot more than that. He understood what was important to build a career and put himself between me and the stuff that wasn't necessary, the thousands who phoned daily with interview requests ranging from what J.R. would do if he were president to would Larry/J.R. endorse a new line of cat food. He knew how to capitalize on the J.R. mystique. He was brilliant.

"First you need to leave the country," he said. "This is bigger than anyone at CBS or Lorimar can comprehend. We're talking the world. Then, wherever you go, you must be highly visible. I want them to see the whole world is obsessed with J.R. Finally, I will be the only person who will know how to get in touch with you. Not your agents or lawyers. It all goes through me."

I made only one addition to the plan. Before Maj and I left, I sent Richard, my agents, and my lawyer white Stetson cowboy hats. I stipulated that they wear them anytime they went in to CBS. As I reminded them, the good guys always wore white hats.

When negotiations began, in June, Maj and I flew to London and rented an apartment near our friend Henri Kleiman's place. Nobody other than Henri and Richard knew where we had holed up. But except for that bit of privacy, I attempted to make my whereabouts as public as possible by partying at Annabel's, the exclusive nightclub, creating photo ops with female police officers, and shopping at Harrods. I didn't have any problem attracting attention.

Great Britain—no, the entire U.K.—was obsessed by *Dallas*. The BBC figured one out of three Britons watched the show, and when reruns began after the cliffhanger, the *Daily Express* ran a humorous editorial warning, "Withdrawal symptoms are bound to set in to such an extent that Britain could clearly be facing its darkest hour." The same was true in Greece, France, Germany, Italy, Turkey, countries as unlikely as Zambia and Zimbabwe, and even the Eastern bloc countries, like Poland and Hungary. Only the Soviet Union kept the show out, yet tapes were still smuggled in.

"Keep going out," Richard advised when I checked in with him, as I did my agents, every day. "Every photo and bit of TV footage shows up over here, and the more they see, the sooner they'll start to see this is an international phenomenon."

Visibility wasn't a problem. Old friend Kevin McClory took us to Royal Ascot, one of the grandest of horse racing's spectacles. Dress was festive and formal—top hats and morning suits for the men, and summer frocks and outrageous hats for the ladies. Drink was the same—champagne and Pimm's cups. The proper decorum also mattered. As Kevin and I walked across the paddock to inspect a horse that was being run by a good friend of his, people started chanting, "J.R.! J.R.! J.R.!"

Not an unpleasant situation for one looking for attention.

But Kevin was worried my enthusiasm for being center stage might run afoul of protocol.

The queen was inspecting a horse that she was running

that day. She was right across the paddock from us.

"Whatever you do, don't respond," he warned. "It'll seem as if you're trying to upstage the queen, and that would put us in a bad light."

I was on my best behavior.

Still, the queen still sent her equerry to inquire about the commotion. He was a pleasant man in his fifties, perfect for the job, and he asked Kevin to identify the person responsible for causing the disturbance. Kevin said it was J.R. The man didn't believe him and stepped sideways to obtain a better look at me.

"Oh my God, *it is J.R.!*" he exclaimed and rushed back to report to Her Majesty.

The queen never sent for us, but soon there were thousands of people surrounding the paddock, chanting, "J.R." I was always flattered by that kind of reaction. Just as I was reaching the gate to exit the paddock, I turned and tipped my hat to the people, and they went bonkers, cheering like I'd single-handedly won the European football cup for them. That angered Kevin.

"Now you've done it," he said. "We're on the queen's shit list."

"As if you give a damn," I said. "You're Irish!"

When *Dallas* went back into production, in July, we were still at the negotiating table. There wasn't a deal, but we were close. CBS and Lorimar had agreed to let me direct at least four episodes per season, develop made-for-TV-movies through my own company, and take a piece of the merchandising that continued expanding to include games, Stetsons, dart boards, books, cologne, and even a beer called J. R. Ewing's Private Stock. (More than five hundred thousand cases were preordered.) But they thought I was being unrealistic by asking for $100,000 per episode. I argued that was fair market value for an international star.

"We've come in under budget every season," I told my agents. "There's plenty of money."

Even when Lorimar leaked word that they might let J.R. die or replace me with another actor, I didn't get nervous. Nor did I feel a twinge of panic when they started shooting with a double, his head swathed in bandages. I couldn't understand that, as I'd been shot in the stomach. If negotiations fell through, they were supposedly going to hire another actor and explain that J.R. had undergone plastic surgery after the shooting. I never believed a word. Never felt the first drop of sweat.

Once negotiations were focused solely on salary, I knew I was in. The mood was different. In preparation, Kevin took Maj and me to his place in the Bahamas so I'd be close enough to Dallas to get to the set within hours of consummating a deal. We were getting exciting about going back to Dallas. I was on the verge of winning!

The phone rang every few hours. Between calls, we swam, ate, drank, and wondered when we were going to get on a plane. We spent one afternoon with actor Richard Harris, who lived nearby, and then made plans to party at the casino that night. As I dressed for the evening—Maj didn't go—sipping champagne, we got the phone call. We had an agreement.

All I had to do was show up for work in Dallas the next day and my holdout would be officially over.

I kissed Maj and we toasted each other's success. It truly was as much her success as mine.

"Don't stay out late," she said. "We have a 10 o'clock plane tomorrow morning."

*   *   *

But an early night with Richard Harris? Impossible. We celebrated my good fortune by singing songs and drinking vintage champagne all night. I stumbled into bed around 4 A.M. and had been asleep for about three hours when Maj got me up and moving. I'd hardly say I moved very fast. I was blown out. We had an even tougher time rousing Kevin, who was essential to our departure because we'd locked $10,000 in cash and our passports in his private safe and we needed him to open it.

Kevin's first 10 attempts failed. Pained, embarrassed, and deeply hungover, he swore he couldn't remember the right combination.

We suspected our host didn't want to remember.

Time was running out before our plane was scheduled to take off. Maj's patience was running out too. I saw her irritation build as she checked the clock. Then like a bomb she exploded: "Kevin, open the fucking safe or I'll have Larry beat the shit out of you!"

I was astounded. I'd never seen Maj so angry. Also, I hadn't been in a fight since the Golden Gloves. Nor did I want to fight my old friend. But like a good husband I pretended to be in synch with the plan. I didn't want to harm Kevin, and besides, he was in pretty good shape.

But apparently the look on Maj's face persuaded him to cooperate. With his forehead covered in sweat, he managed to get the safe open.

We grabbed our cash and passports and jumped in Kevin's vintage Cadillac, a boat of a car with shark fins on the back. There was a palpable sense of escape, relief, and excitement as Kevin gunned the engine, but while speeding out of the gates he ran over the curb and tore off the muffler, so there was a horrendous noise and a sheet of sparks behind us all the way to the airport. Shades of West Point. I always seem to be arriving at important occasions with great cacophony.

Luckily this was the Bahamas, and the plane was an hour late taking off, which allowed us to make the connecting flight in Miami. Once in Dallas, we were whisked by a waiting helicopter directly to Southfork. After circling, the chopper made a spectacular touchdown by the pool. The cast and crew were glad to see me arrive. None of us had spoken throughout my renegotiation, but they told me that they always expected me to return. They were also well aware that my victory opened the door to raises for all of them as well.

Nowadays I look at the salaries that are being paid to top TV actors, people like Kelsey Grammer, Drew Carey, and the cast of *Friends*, and I think, Good for them. I also think they should give me a little nod for blazing the trail for episodic television.

Once I was back at work, the big question still remained to be answered. Who shot J.R.?

A newspaper syndicate with papers in London, South Africa, and Holland offered a quarter million dollars if I'd reveal it to them exclusively. For a moment I considered telling them the wrong information and then saying I was tricked by the producers, but I decided not to be so like J.R. in real life. Everyone asked me. In truth, I didn't know who shot J.R. None of us did until we finally filmed the episode.

Actually, I didn't even know then. Katzman kept everyone in the dark by handing out scripts with key pages missing and filming J.R. being shot by practically everyone on the set, including several guys on the crew. He jokingly suggested that after editing the show he'd lock everyone in a motel until it aired.

There was a time when the network feared that viewers might lose interest in the mystery over the summer, but they solved that concern with clever programming that kept the "who done it" episode from airing until the fourth week of the new season. The delay, which included Cliff Barnes, Sue Ellen, and Alan Beam getting arrested as suspects, rekindled the buildup around the world.

Just three days before the secret was unveiled, I performed with my mother in London at a gala 80th-birthday celebration for the Queen Mother, who I learned was addicted to *Dallas*. A while earlier, I'd set out to capitalize on my fame by putting out a record, which was not very successful. Nonetheless, I was requested to sing it at the royal command performance. Henry Mancini conducted a huge orchestra, which included a choir. I walked onstage as they played the theme from *Dallas* and received a wonderful ovation. I started the song with great confidence, but halfway through I went totally blank. I turned to Mr. Mancini and motioned for him to stop. He asked, "Do you want to begin again?"

"Yes," I said.

There was deathly silence in the audience. Two thousand five hundred sphincters were puckered. Henry started the orchestra again, and I proceeded until I got to the same place. I motioned Henry to stop again, turned to the royal box, and said, "Sorry, ma'am. If you're going to blow it, blow it big."

I got a huge laugh among some hoots and whistles. I wasn't mortified. I simply introduced my mother. She sang a medley of songs she'd made famous onstage in London, and we ended in a duet of "Honey Bun" from *South Pacific*, which I'd done with her at the Drury Lane so many years earlier. It actually turned into quite an affectionate moment.

Afterward, I sheepishly walked through the receiving line to meet the Queen Mother and Prince Charles.

"You really were a bomb out there tonight, weren't you?" Prince Charles said truthfully but jokingly.

"A stinker," I said.

Then I got to the Queen Mother, who said, "Now I want you to tell me, young man, who shot J.R.?"

"Not even for you, ma'am," I said.

By then I'd seen the final cut and knew the shooter's identity. It was Sue Ellen's sister, Kristin, played by Mary Crosby. Mary was a sweet little girl when she came on the show, hardly past 18, and gorgeous. Her father, Bing Crosby, had given my mother one of her earliest breaks by having her sing on his radio show as a regular. But I didn't let family connections interfere with business. When Mary started on the show, one of our first scenes involved J.R. seducing her. Irving Moore was directing and was a stickler for realism. He was particularly hard on ingenues. For some reason, we couldn't get the scene right for him. In the scene, Mary wore a sexy dress with spaghetti straps, which I was supposed to remove one strap at a time while kissing her. After a couple tries, she whispered, "Larry, don't push me away because there's nothing holding my top up."

I respected that. After each take I held her close while the director said, "Cut, let's do another one." I don't even remember what kept going wrong. Finally, after the eighteenth take, which we knew had been right on, I thrust her at arm's length and her whole top fell off as the director yelled, "That's perfect." Then I quickly pulled her close and we waltzed off the set. Neither of us has ever forgotten that scene.

Fans of the show say the same thing about the show that aired on November 21, 1980. They say they'll always remember where they were the night they found out who shot J.R. That Friday's show drew more viewers than any show in television history, a 53.3 rating, or an estimated 83 million people—more than had voted in the presidential election three weeks earlier and a record that stood until the final episode of M*A*S*H in 1983. The final tally worldwide was 380 million!

People have asked how that made me feel, being at the center of all that, but the numbers are so huge I never completely comprehended them—and never will.

I simply enjoyed it. I'd sign autographs for anyone who asked, provided they told me a poem, a prayer, or a song in return. A lot of people balked at this, but I always thought that if I gave my signature away people didn't place any value on it. But if they had to work for it, and essentially pay for it, they got an experience they never would've gotten if I'd signed and we'd never interacted. Both of us walked away with something memorable.

I got some marvelous poems and songs. If people said they didn't know any songs, as many did, I asked them to sing me "Happy Birthday". If they said they didn't know any prayers, I asked them to repeat with me, "Now I lay me down to sleep . . ." Then I'd ask them to bless their loved ones and me. Often that led to further discussions, and autograph sessions could last for hours. But I got to know a lot of people. It was wonderful, and then I'd give them my "money."

There were only so many autographs I could sign when crowds swelled into the hundreds or more. It took so much time. So I came up with the idea of handing out funny money I had printed up—thousand-dollar bills with my picture and the slogan "In Hagman We Trust." On the first batch of ten thousand, I put my Malibu P.O. box on the back and told people to send a stamped self-addressed envelope and I'd return it with a personally autographed picture. But after a few months, the post office complained that I was jamming them up and suggested I find another method of responding to the public. I eventually discontinued giving out my address because there just wasn't enough time in the day to sign all the requests. Now the back says, "This is printed on recycled paper. Why not recycle yourself? To receive an organ donor card, please call (800) 622-9010." The response has been very satisfying. I can amuse people and maybe save lives.

At the peak of J.R. craziness, my mother also helped keep it all in perspective. I remember one weekend in particular when we met her in Las Vegas to see my friend Joel Grey perform. After cocktails, we waited for a couple of taxis, but there was just one in front of the hotel, and once the driver spotted me, he yelled, "Hey, J.R., get in!"

I tried convincing Mother and her companion/secretary, Ben Washer, to take the cab, but she insisted I get in. While we stood there debating, the driver settled it by saying, "I don't want the lady. I want J.R." Mother insisted that I go first. Just then another cab arrived. Before we pulled away, I rolled down the window and grinned, "That's show business, Mom!"

Cut to the theater. Midway through the show, Joel announced that he had some special guests in the audience. First, he introduced me, "my dear friend Larry Hagman, who plays J. R. Ewing on the number-one-rated show, *Dallas*." The crowd gave me an enthusiastic ovation. Then Joel introduced my mother, or, as he said, "a woman who's better known as Peter Pan!"

As she rose and waved, people went nuts. They stood, with some climbing on their chairs for a better look, and clapped so long the house lights went up. Despite Mother's efforts to quiet the house, the applause wouldn't quit. It was literally a showstopper.

Finally, after blowing kisses to all sides, she sat down. Then I felt a tap on my knee. There was Mother, leaning toward me. With a twinkle in her eye, she said, "And that's show business too, baby!"

24

The more successful *Dallas* became, the more fun I had, and there was no end to the enticements that came my way. There were opportunities for commercials, endorsements, travel, and every other imaginable opportunity. I frequently said no. Specifically, I'm thinking of a night when Patrick and I were having a beer at a cowboy bar and I was approached by a twenty-something knockout who asked if I wanted a Texas sandwich. I asked her what she meant by a Texas sandwich.

"Me, you, and my sister," she said.

When I still said no thanks, she said, "Well, okay, you want a Bud Lite?"

J.R. wouldn't have hesitated, but that was him. I knew in general it was best to say no and avoid potential trouble. Like the time I opened a Western store in Oklahoma City. I flew there, signed autographs, and stumbled back into my hotel about 1 A.M. My buddy, stand-in, and bodyguard, Tim O'Connor, and I had a two-storey apartment in the motel. After saying good night to Tim, I went upstairs and there was a drop-dead gorgeous thirty-something blonde in my bed. She'd turned the lights low and a bottle of Dom Pérignon was open on the side table.

"Hi, J.R.," she purred. "My husband's away for the weekend and I thought we could get to know each other."

What a waste, I thought. What bad timing. I sat down and told her how much I appreciated her offer, but she'd missed my window of availability by 30 years. Besides, I had to get up early in the morning to go to church. Still, we had a glass of champagne before Tim made sure that she left without a story to tell . . . or sell.

Sex wasn't the only thing I said no to. Tobacco was also high on my list of forbiddens. For much of the 1980s, as America was accepting the deadly truth about cigarettes, I was the most famous antismoker. Instead of trying to work with the dozens of charities that asked for some of my time, my publicist, Richard, suggested I focus on one thing, so I chose the American Cancer Society. Nationally, I helped launch their Great American Smokeout Campaign. So did Mother and my daughter. Closer to home, I waged a protest when a billboard for Marlboro cigarettes went up behind my house along Pacific Coast Highway. For 10 years, I took the work seriously and I think made a difference.

But my passion for getting people to quit killing themselves didn't always make me popular on the *Dallas* set, especially with Barbara Bel Geddes, who smoked in the makeup room every morning. It was stinking up the place and was just plain unhealthy for everybody in the room.

"So," she said.

"So cut it out, please," I said.

She kept on smoking.

After she had a heart attack, her heart surgeon told her that she had to quit or die. She quit.

About a third of the show's cast and crew also smoked, including Mr. Katzman. If they lit up around me, I'd pull out my pocket-sized portable fan and blow the smoke back toward them. All that secondhand cigarette smoke took a toll on my voice. Finally one afternoon, my throat hurt so much I was forced to deliver an ultimatum. If we allowed smoking on the set, then I wanted to stop production for 10 minutes every hour to air out the soundstage by opening the giant doors.

"No way," one of the producers said. "You're talking about stopping work for at least 80 minutes a day. That'll cost us between ten and twenty thousand dollars a day. Times five days a week. That's a hundred grand a week. Every week. Larry, you're out of your mind!"

"Then why don't we just ban smoking on the set?" I suggested.

"We can't ask people to stop smoking."

"Then we'll take a 10-minute break and ask them to go outside."

"That's still a hundred thousand a week downtime!" they raged.

No one took me seriously. Then one day I stopped production because my throat was so dry and irritated. I insisted on taking a break while the soundstage was aired out. The doors were opened, blowers brought in, and the air was cleared. Then I returned to work. After several days of doing that, smoking on the set was banned. Yet my victory resulted in complaints. A few guys from the crew said I was discriminating against smokers and a couple guys on the crew threatened to quit. My response? "Good, let 'em."

Jim Davis was my toughest case. I got him to temporarily quit his five-pack-a-day habit after I grew tired of hearing him clear his throat before every take. The disgusting noise he made sounded like *goomba*, which is how we fondly referred to him. Goomba. But he started up again after being diagnosed with inoperable cancer. None of us including Jim himself knew he was sick until the summer of 1980.

We were shooting a scene in the woods. Fittingly, it was me, Bobby, and Daddy. The three of us were on a hunting trip, a passion all of us shared in real life. As written, we were supposed to be roughing it in sleeping bags by the campfire. But the day we shot the scene, I brought a cot, an ice chest, a comfy chair, and mosquito netting—but only for me.

"Larry, this is supposed to be roughing it," the director said.

"This is the way J.R. roughs it," I replied.

He acquiesced.

All of us had fun. But as the day wore on, the temperature rose and took a toll on Jim. At first, he had difficulty remembering his lines. Then his memory left him altogether. He didn't know where he was. Neither was he too sure about me or Patrick. "Where the hell are we?" he asked. Texas, I said. "What the hell are we doing here?"

The second time it happened Patrick and I took him aside and asked questions to test his memory. Do you know your name? "Jim." Do you know where you are? "No." Do you know you're making a television series right now? "A television series? I'm working?"

The moment Mr. Katzman realized the problem he stopped shooting and sent us back in a car. Initially we thought he had heatstroke, but soon Jim broke the sad news that doctors had found cancer. When I saw him with a cigarette, he said he'd started smoking again, explaining, "Why the hell not?" Despite aggressive chemotherapy, which made him so weak he couldn't get up from a chair without assistance and which caused his hair to fall out, Jim worked until a month before he died, in 1981.

I directed his final episode, which was terribly sad because all of us knew he was in his last days. We left on hiatus, wondering if we'd see him again. Maj and I were touring the Scottish countryside when Jim passed away. I heard the news from a Scottish reporter from a local paper who was waiting for me to walk downstairs at the quaint inn where we were staying.

"Jock died this morning," he said. "How do you feel about it?"

I felt sad, I said, but I'd been expecting the inevitable.

"But aren't you upset?" he asked.

Yes, definitely, I said—"but only because of the way you broke the news to me."

I sent a wreath to the funeral that said, "Good-bye, Goomba." Of course, I still see him every day. The first thing you see when you enter my home is the oil painting of Jim that hung in the living room at Southfork.

In 1981, *Dallas* hit number one. So much energy went into the show, but real life didn't stop for any of us. Whether it was Linda's divorce, Victoria's breakup with Andy Gibb, or Charlene giving birth, we all went through something. Including me. I was hit hard when I got word that my mother had been in a horrific car accident that left one friend dead and another critically injured.

It was the Sunday of Labor Day weekend in San Francisco. She was with Ben Washer, her dear friend Janet

Gaynor, and Janet's husband, producer Paul Gregory. The four of them were on their way to dinner in Chinatown when their cab was struck by a van that ran a red light. The van's driver was drunk. Ben died instantly. Janet was critically injured. Paul escaped with broken ribs and minor kidney damage. Mother, unable to remember anything about the crash, suffered two broken ribs, a broken pelvis, and severe heartache over Ben.

Maj and I flew to be with her immediately. I was distraught and more upset than I realized. I had no patience for the reporters and paparazzi who were camped outside San Francisco General Hospital, waiting for me. We decided to go through the emergency door in the back. There was no way I wanted to give an interview or pose for pictures. But in the hallway we ran into one guy who'd anticipated our move. He was after the big bucks the tabloids would pay for a photo of me looking upset, and I was in the frame of mind that gets celebrities in trouble. The more film he snapped, the closer I got to snapping myself.

I demanded he turn over his film. When he refused, I grabbed his camera, stripped the film out of it, and dropped the camera on the floor. He threatened to sue, but I never heard from him again.

Mother was able to leave the hospital after nine days. As we helped her out of the hospital, she was complaining about having to use a "dadburn walker." Then we heard a noise from up above. We looked up and saw doctors and nurses hanging out the window, crowing, mimicking Peter's Pan's famous cry: "Er-er-er-errrrrrh! Good-bye, Peter!" they called. Mother lost it. All of us did. The tears gushed out as much for the sentiment as for knowing what could've been except for fate and modern medicine.

A year later Mother sang at my daughter's wedding, and in October 1984, she did a benefit for San Francisco General Hospital's Trauma Center, where she'd been treated. At age 70, she fit into the same Peter Pan costume she'd worn nearly 30 years earlier on Broadway and soared over the audience singing, "I've Got to Crow." She also dedicated "The Way You Look Tonight" to Janet, who'd died several weeks earlier of complications stemming from the accident.

It was a great way to say thank you.

By then, Mother and I had learned to appreciate each other in ways that had been impossible when we were younger. In fact, her name was brought up once, maybe twice in connection to joining *Dallas*, but the closest she got was a press party for the show that was held at our home in Malibu. It was a sensational party, too. CBS had brought in all the TV critics from around the country, maybe two hundred people. Sushi, just coming into fashion, was served by beautiful girls in kimonos. Everyone from *Dallas* was there and being interviewed in different parts of the house.

After everyone had been spoken to, the reporters converged on my mother. One young girl gushed to mother, "Miss Martin, what's it like to have an icon for a son?"

My mother gazed benignly down upon her and quietly said, "My dear, my son is a star. I am an icon."

That's what I loved about mother—her truthfulness.

I was upset when Barbara Bel Geddes left the show in 1983. We had a relationship like the one I had with Jim. No one including Barbara ever told me that she had complaints. Afterward, I learned she felt like she was being worked too hard and wanted more money. None of those problems was unsolvable. I could've helped to work out a compromise. But Barbara was following the advice of a business manager, one of those guys who helped her out of a job, and her departure was a done deal by the time I heard about it.

Donna Reed was brought in to replace Barbara. I'd admired her in *From Here to Eternity* and dozens of other films, as well as *The Donna Reed Show*. If we had to replace Mama, I thought, she was an excellent choice. She definitely brought a different take to the character. I first noticed it in her very first scene. She'd gotten off a plane and was running up the ramp toward Bobby and me. I remember thinking running was something Mama would never do. By this time, viewers knew the character as well as we did, and as much as I adored Donna, she didn't have the strength or edge that Barbara had given Mama.

Barbara decided to return the next season. Several weeks before she made the decision, I had lunch with her in New York and said that I wanted her back. I was unaware that talks were already going on. Obviously, her return made me happy, but I was quite upset at how the news reached Donna.

Donna found out she wasn't being asked back from a French reporter as she got off a plane in Paris. I was stunned when I heard how she'd been informed. I had no idea. Her agent, the producers, Lorimar, CBS—no one had told her. That was cold, callous, unthinking, and unforgivable. Nothing we said could ever have made amends to Donna, who died of cancer two years later with her trust in the business shattered, and rightfully so. I wish we could've dumped the way that was handled into what we called the Black Hole of Calcutta.

*   *   *

The Black Hole of Calcutta was a passageway on the studio lot that ran from one street to another. It was lined with tiny portable dressing rooms on wheels that had been made in the 1930s. Despite all the hundreds of millions of dollars *Dallas* generated, we used them the entire time we shot the series. They were universally loathed by the cast. During the summer there was no air, and in the winter months the wind whistled through like the North Pole.

One year I got so fed up I asked the Lorimar honchos for my own motor home on the set, one of those luxury palaces on wheels outfitted with a bedroom, kitchen, phone, radio, TV, and various items that would make it a comfortable retreat. They said no, arguing if they gave one to me, they'd have to give one to all the principals at a cost they estimated at $5 million. They also said paying the Teamsters would be about another $1 million a year. Seeing their point, I made a point of my own.

"I'll tell you what," I said. "Give me fifty thousand dollars a year and I won't ask for an RV."

Done deal. They thought they'd gotten away with a big saving, but the series lasted another 10 years, making me half a million dollars for just keeping my mouth closed. I laughed about it every year.

But that didn't solve another problem we had. The bathrooms. I don't know about the women's, but the men's room was an absolute pit. For the first five years, we didn't even have hot water. Then L.A. health officials forced that issue as well as a reconfiguration of the toilets to make room for a handicapped stall.

That made the stalls so narrow it was impossible to shut the door without banging your knees. A situation that called for comfort was untenable, so we used the handicapped stall. No one who needed it was ever there.

Then one day I was sitting on the toilet when I was interrupted by a sharp bang on the door, followed by a contemptuous voice demanding to know, "Who's in there?"

I replied that I was.

"Who are you?"

Not recognizing the questioner's voice, I said it was none of his business.

"Well, what are you doing?"

I was doing what people do when they sit on the toilet, I explained.

"Don't you know this is for handicapped people?" he asked.

"Yes, I do."

"I'm handicapped. I'm in a wheelchair, and I need to get in there right away."

"I'm really sorry," I said. "But I'm right in the middle of what I'm doing, so you're going to have to wait."

He didn't care.

"I'm going to call security," he said.

"Fine," I said.

It wasn't like I tried to take a long time, and when I finished, I opened the door and saw an incredibly frustrated, pissed-off guy in a wheelchair was parked directly outside. He was plainly handicapped. He was also incredibly angry. Somehow he had no idea who I was and told me that security was on their way.

I started to walk out.

"Hey, asshole," he said, "what's your name?"

"Patrick Duffy," I replied. "And go fuck yourself."

25

On set and off, Patrick Duffy was the perfect companion for me. He was almost as good looking as me, almost as talented, almost as funny, and almost as smart. We were kindred spirits who liked to hunt, fish, and play practical jokes. Early in the show, David Wayne and I took him salmon fishing in Vancouver. On the plane we sat in first class telling fishing stories while being served drinks and hors d'oeuvres. By Patrick's eighth vodka, I looked at David and said, "I didn't know this guy was such a drinker."

"Yeah, he's really tossing 'em back," David agreed.

Indeed, Patrick got drunker and drunker. Before landing, he made a pass at the flight attendant. At that point, I thought his joking had crossed the line from funny to obnoxious. Even after I said something to him, Patrick kept slugging back the drinks. David and I worried how we were going to get him through customs. Once the plane landed, though, Patrick changed. All of a sudden he was perfectly sober. Grinning, he confessed that he'd enlisted the flight attendant's aid and had her fill his vodka bottles with water.

Patrick was also very spiritual. Introduced to Buddhism by his wife, Carlyn, he would rise at 4 A.M. to chant for an hour and chanted for another hour at night with Carlyn and their children. One day I asked what he chanted for. Patrick cocked his head to the side and smiled. "Money."

"No shit?" I said.

"It's working, ain't it?"

At the end of the 1984 season, Patrick left the show. At 37, he wanted to see if he could make it even bigger in movies. He also had a sense of being underappreciated. After talking it over with his wife, he broke the news to me. I told him that he was making a mistake and gave him the same lecture Hayden Rorke had given me almost 20 years earlier when I wanted to leave *I Dream of Jeannie*. I said if you leave a show when it's number one, people will think you're nuts.

Patrick left anyway. In the finale of the 1984 season, he saved his wife, Pamela, from being run down by her crazy half sister, but was struck himself. He died in the hospital a few hours later. Though the series was nudged out of first place in the overall ratings by *Dynasty*, we continued our roll.

But the next year was dismal for both the show and me. Not only did Patrick leave, Leonard Katzman resigned too, a result of his constant clashes with the other executive producer, who took over. Under his guidance, our happy family fell apart. The new guy in charge was the antithesis of Leonard. He wasn't a creative person. All he created was anxiety. He berated line people, pinched pennies, and undermined eight years of success by trying to inject the show with glitz. It wasn't *Dallas*.

One day I received an audiotape from Patrick that reminded me just how grim the situation had become. I popped it into my tape player. On it, Bobby was being buried, and Patrick was saying, "Larry, help! I'm six feet under. Let me out! Let me come back. Please! Let me come back. I'm sorry. I made a mistake."

It was a joke. When Patrick left, he had no intention of ever coming back. He said he was making more money than he had on the show. I was on my own, and it forced me into a confrontation, something I hate. But I told Lorimar chief Lee Rich that he had to replace the producer. His reply was an impossibly frustrating look that said, "You're an actor. What do you know about this stuff?"

I said he could take $1million out of my salary and give it to him if he'd leave. Lee didn't pay attention. So I said, okay, make it $2 million, just get rid of him. He still refused. I had one more meeting, and there I made my final proposal. The producer had to go or I wasn't coming back the next season.

"You're going to walk away from that kind of money?" he asked.

"If he stays there won't be any money, because there won't be any show," I said.

Television executives aren't stupid. At the end of their day, they make decisions based solely on numbers. They look at ratings and profits. When they studied *Dallas*'s slumping ratings and considered the fate of the series without Patrick *and* me, they saw the producer might be most costly than imagined, and soon he resigned for reasons he said were personal.

Katzman signed back on. Both of us knew that if *Dallas*

was going to come back, we needed Patrick. We immediately started plotting to bring him back. First, I called Patrick and had a long talk, basically explaining that no matter the circumstances of his departure, we could write him back into the show. Forget being rational. We'd find a way. Money was no problem either. If he wanted a raise, which he did, we'd make sure he got it.

"How'd it go?" Katzman asked.

"I think he realizes it's cold out there," I said.

Before the season ended, Patrick worked out terms that brought him back. Then I had him out to the house for a celebratory afternoon. After a long, relaxing Jacuzzi, we went to our local watering hole for lunch, the Baja Cantina. On the way, Patrick reminded me, as Katzman regularly did too, that his return was top secret. Katzman hadn't even worked out the story line introducing his return in the season's finale. Fine, I understood. But when the waitress came to take our lunch order, she said, "Hi, Patrick. I hear you're back on *Dallas*." Our jaws hit the table. We were shocked.

"Where'd you hear that?" Patrick asked.

"On the radio as I came into work," the girl chirped.

It shows you how tough it is to keep a secret in Hollywood.

A good attitude is vital to a healthy, happy life, and my attitude improved simply by watching the 1985 season's cliffhanger when Pamela woke from a dream and saw her dead husband, Bobby, step from the shower and say, "Good morning." Ratings rose. Viewers were confused, amazed, and thrilled. The buzz returned. And most important, my best friend was back on the show.

When the next season premiered, Patrick's resurrection

was explained by casting the entire previous year as a nightmare, which it had been for us. When the three of us reunited in Dallas to start shooting, the old zest returned as if on cue. As did the jokes and partying. While on location, Maj and I, Linda, Barbara, and Priscilla Presley stayed at Caroline Hunt's luxurious Mansion on Turtle Creek Hotel, which is one of the three best hotels I've ever been in my life (the other two are the Lanesborough in London, which Caroline's company also manages, and the Oriental in Bangkok). The rooms are gorgeous, the service is unparalleled, and the food superb. My suite alone set the production company back $21,000 a month.

I kept my room stocked with champagne. I usually had a five-pound tin of caviar, which I acquired in bulk from a Russian film director friend in exchange for VCRs and videotapes of *Dallas* that he dispersed in the Soviet Union. If people in the Soviet Union enjoyed watching our show as much as Linda, Sheree Wilson, Priscilla, Barbara, and Maj and I enjoyed eating beluga, then the commies were in trouble.

We were still in Texas, though. That was its own reality. One day I was having lunch at the Mansion when I was spotted by an old lady. I felt like a deer caught in headlights the moment I saw the spark of recognition in her eyes. She struggled up from her chair, grabbed her walker, and started across the room. It must've taken her three minutes to inch across the dining room. "Here comes an old lady wanting my autograph," I said to Maj.

As soon as she got next to me, she said, "Take this, you rascal," and then hit me upside the head with her handbag and knocked me right out of my chair. I literally saw stars. Then she chuckled a tad remorsefully. "Oh my goodness,

Mr. Hagman, I'm so sorry. My husband is dead, and before he died, he gave me a .38 revolver. I always carry it with me and I forgot it was in my handbag."

"That's all right, ma'am," I said, rubbing the bump that had risen on the side of my head.

"I'm really sorry. But you are such a rascal."

Speaking of pistols, Nancy Hammond, a friend we made while in Dallas, owned the penthouse in the towers at the Mansion. Her husband, Jake, who'd passed away, had left her wealthier than some countries. But nothing thrilled Nancy like a good bargain. One day she told us about how she drove her Cadillac to Costco to pick up some Dom Pérignon that was on sale for some ridiculous price like $60 a bottle. She bought three cases, arranged for them to be delivered to her apartment, and walked back to her car.

"And then you know what happened, Larry?" she said. "I got there and there were two men sitting in my car."

"Really?"

"Yes," she said. "I walked over and pulled out my gun—the one Jake gave me before he died—and I said, 'You bastards, get out of my car or I'll blow your heads off!' They ran across the parking lot. Then I put the key in the ignition and do you know what? It wasn't my car."

Another time Maj and I were having lunch with Nancy at the Ritz-Carlton in Washington, D.C. She walked in and, after we kissed and hugged, asked if I wanted to see her new diamond ring. I admired her enormous rock, but I couldn't help notice something was wrong with her finger. I asked what had happened.

"I was making some salad dressing and I stuck my finger too far into the blender. It took the finger right off," she explained. "Zip. Right like that."

As a result, she had a fake finger made and attached the diamond ring.

"But I keep having to send it back because the older I get, the more wrinkled I get, and the damn finger doesn't wrinkle at all."

Then she removed her finger and handed it to me.

"Take a look, Larry."

I couldn't think of anything to do with her finger. But just then the water served my Bloody Mary, so I stirred it with Nancy's finger.

"That's the most disgusting thing I've ever seen anybody do," she said, before bursting out in laughter. "That's why I love you."

Only one dark cloud marred the 1985–86 season. The week before Thanksgiving, Patrick's parents were shot to death at their bar in Boulder. Two 19-year-old guys, who'd been looking for money, were arrested later the same day, the murder weapon, a shotgun, still on them. Patrick's belief in the continuum of life helped him handle the tragic news better than the rest of us on the set that day. He got to Montana aboard Lorimar chairman Merv Adelson's private jet and buried his mom and dad in a Buddhist cemetery in Japan.

In 1987, I knew the series had begun a slow curve downward. Victoria left, with Pamela dying in a fiery car crash. She was at an age where the move made sense, and I knew better than to try talking her out of it. Dack Rambo, who spent two seasons playing J.R.'s cousin, was also written out of the show. Openly bisexual and outspoken about having AIDS, Dack accused me of getting rid of him because I was homophobic. Until then, I liked Dack, but his charge was so far-fetched it wasn't worth arguing in the press.

My philosophy about people on the show was made clear years earlier when we had problems with one of the actresses showing up chronically late. It screwed up everyone's schedule, from hair to makeup, which created tension, delayed production, cost money, and so on. None of which did anyone any good. So I asked Leonard to change her call time to 4 A.M. from 6. She quickly got the point. In show business you can be a drunk, a drug addict, or psychologically screwed up, but you cannot be late. It's the only thing you can't be.

In 1988, the show's tenth season, Priscilla continued the exodus when she left to take over the operation of Graceland. A few years earlier, she'd thought about leaving and asked me to lunch to get my input. After talking over all the angles, including how chilly it had gotten for Patrick, I said that whatever she decided was fine, but the bottom line was that, selfishly, I liked having her around. Priscilla stayed that time. When she finally did leave, it was for the right reasons and things turned out great for her.

26

Midway through 1989, Linda announced she was leaving. Sue Ellen and J.R. had been divorced, and she felt her character wasn't being developed in a way that challenged her after so many years. Katzman controlled the story lines, and he kept writing Sue Ellen as a beleagured woman. He wasn't going to change. She got sick and tired of it, and rightly so. Still, I don't know how many dinner parties I had where I begged her not to go. I would've used every bit of my clout if she wanted to stay, but in the end I reluctantly understood.

At least Linda was with us when we shot several episodes on location in Europe. It was a Katzman extravaganza designed to inject new interest in the show. The professional terminology is "ratings stunt." But in reality, viewers don't care about locales no matter how exotic. It's similar to why they never bothered to analyze why J.R., a guy worth a couple of hundred million, still shared a home with his parents. People want to turn on their sets and forget what happened at work that day.

But none of us argued against a European itinerary that included Salzburg, Vienna, and Moscow. *Dallas* epitomized American capitalism, and taking it to the center of communism only nine months before the Berlin Wall came down was a bold stroke that signaled the good guys had won.

We had a terrific time in Salzburg and Vienna, two magnificent cities, but Moscow left a lot to be desired. Maj and I had been to Moscow a few years earlier as part of a tour through Japan, China, and the Soviet Union. Like most Americans, I'd spent all my life fearful of the Soviet Union. But that fear vanished after we'd spent time there. Nothing worked, nothing could be fixed. I knew if they ever pushed the button to send up their missiles, they'd most likely blow themselves to kingdom come.

So when we went with *Dallas*, I told everyone to bring oranges, cheese, cookies, toilet paper, and anything else they might want or need because they sure as hell wouldn't find it over there. If any of my cast mates had thoughts about checking into a comfortable hotel, they vanished when we were let off in front of a plain four-storey building and told we'd have to carry our luggage up four flights to our rooms. Hearing that, I went straight to the concierge, who told me the elevators hadn't worked for three years.

"But we have parts coming from Czechoslovakia," he said. "They will be here in two years."

I had five bags, containing all my costumes. An older man who looked to be in his eighties spent about an hour and a half carrying them up to our room. By his third trip, he was panting, sweating, and looking like he might have a heart attack before he finished. But I was so pissed off about our accommodations that I let him suffer the first round because I was sure my turn was next. Sheree's fiancé, Paul Rubio, walked around the lobby waving his American Express card while asking, "Where can we find a hotel that works?"

"There isn't one," the concierge said.

"What about one where we can get a drink?"

"I can help you out there," I said.

I'd stayed at the National Hotel and knew they had a bar that served alcohol, the choice being Heineken or straight shots of vodka. Without hesitating, the whole group piled into our bus and I treated drinks at the bar. Then everybody spread out to look for better places to stay. Despite the effort, our conditions didn't improve.

One of the producers we hired locally to grease the palms of Soviet officials invited us to his home, a *dacha* outside the city. One look at it confirmed my suspicion—he had to be Russian mafia. In Moscow, the poor people, meaning just about everyone, lived in run-down apartment buildings, and the few rich people had apartments only slightly less run-down. When a neurosurgeon earns only slightly more than a street cleaner, there's no incentive to do anything.

But our local producer was proof that crime paid. He owned a two-storey modern home that looked straight out of California. It was furnished with new appliances, televisions, VCRs, and enough champagne and caviar to make us feel we were back at the Mansion in Dallas.

Because the only way anyone in the country could've seen *Dallas* was on black-market videotapes, I walked around the city unrecognized. It felt great to be anonymous again. I walked leisurely through museums and churches without being stopped once for an autograph. All of us actors remarked on a similar experience. But then we ran into a group of East German tourists who picked up television signals from West Germany, and they were fanatical *Dallas* fans. Our guide, a pretty little girl, had no idea why four hundred people suddenly went nuts seeing us. She asked them to stop, but they ignored her.

"That's J.R.!" they screamed. "J.R., we love you!"

Our guide didn't understand and called for security.

"But you're just an actor," she kept saying.

I couldn't begin to explain the reach of television to someone who'd never seen it the way we knew it in America, and as for a phenomenon like *Dallas*, forget it. She couldn't have understood.

Nine months later, I watched CNN's coverage of the Berlin Wall being torn down and realized that *Dallas* had impacted that side of the world. Pop music also had an effect, but ideas combined with pictures were even more powerful. Every time people in Hungary, Poland, and East Germany watched *Dallas*, they saw what they didn't have—the beautiful clothes, the big homes, the abundant food, and the lifestyle. Eventually, enough people began say, "Wait a minute, I want that stuff too! And why don't we have it?"

I honestly believe that as *Dallas* crossed the borders into Soviet-controlled countries, it played a big part in the downfall of the Soviet empire. When the people from the Eastern bloc countries saw what they were missing, they realized what a farce communism was.

My mother, happily retired for years in Palm Springs, never complained about her aches and pains, even after her car accident. But in 1989 she suffered from back pain so severe she didn't have to complain. It was obvious. We took her to a renowned sports doctor in L.A. After a series of tests, including X rays, he asked if she had an internist. Maj and I exchanged looks. Clearly his question meant her problem was more serious than a backache, and it was.

Upon further examination, Mother was diagnosed with colon cancer. She checked into Cedars-Sinai Medical Center, where Dr. Leonard Makowka performed a three-hour surgery. It was his first operation at the renowned hospital. Five years later, purely by fate, I'd be his last operation there.

Meanwhile, despite the surgery, Mother's prognosis wasn't good. Dr. Makowka found the cancer had metastasized. I visited daily, until she returned home to Palm Springs. Then we did what we could for as long as we could. She spent her final days at Eisenhower Memorial in Rancho Mirage.

The last time I saw Mother was on a Sunday, the day of the week when I didn't utter a sound. Mother was used to that habit of mine. Fortunately, the important stuff between us had already been said years before. She'd let us know she was grateful that her children had given her a second chance to be close to them, and she knew that we felt the same way about her.

When I walked into her hospital room a prominent television pastor was sitting on her bed, holding her hand and praying for her. His regular visits had started to concern me. Call me cynical. I'm from the South, and every pastor I'd ever met while growing up made deathbed visits in an effort to get their church "remembered." I made sure Mother didn't remember his church at all.

After he left, we had a wonderful visit. She'd never liked Bach, yet she knew I enjoyed whistling Bach inventions. So she started whistling one of my favorites. I did counterpoint. We whistled while holding hands until she grew too tired. I sat for a while longer, then kissed her good-bye.

She passed away the next day. That was on a Monday. I arranged to have her cremated, told Maj that I would pick up the ashes at the Palm Springs mortuary, and we planned a burial on Saturday in the family plot in Weatherford.

Meanwhile, that week I was directing an episode of *Dallas* on the Irvine ranch a couple hours south of L.A. It was a complicated week. I had a herd of a thousand head of cattle to move around as we shot. There were also horses, wranglers, a chuck wagon, and all the parapher- nalia of a roundup. Plus I was acting in every scene. Then on Thursday night, at the last minute, the shooting schedule was changed and I was handed 10 pages of additional dialogue I had to learn by the next morning.

Exhausted, I stripped naked and walked around my hotel room with all the windows open to keep myself awake while studying the script. I made it until sunrise. The tele- phone rang. It was Maj, who was in a panic because she hadn't received the ashes. I was supposed to have had them sent to Malibu. But I'd forgotten. I'd also left the note with the mortuary's address and phone number on my desk in Malibu, and I was afraid to ask Maj to get them. We were leaving the next day for Weatherford.

"Where are the ashes, Larry?"

I calmly said I'd call the mortuary and have them deliv- ered to me on location and bring them to Malibu myself.

There was a knock on the door just in time.

It was Patrick, telling me it was time to go to work. I turned to him and he saw the fear in my eyes.

"Hey, you've got to help me on this thing," I said.

Both of us phoned mortuaries in Palm Springs until I

found the right one. I'll never forget saying, "Hello . . . Larry Hagman here. Do you have my mother's ashes there?" Neither will I forgot the man's response. "Yes, as a matter of fact Mr. Weasel is just walking out the door with them. He's going to mail them to you."

I suddenly recalled a plan to mail them, which I obviously screwed up. But something else got my attention.

"Who's going to mail them?" I asked.

"Mr. Weasel."

I started to laugh. Punch-drunk from sleep deprivation and anxiety, I thought that was the funniest thing in the world. I turned to Patrick and told him that Mr. Weasel had my mother's ashes. He cracked up too. Then Mr. Weasel got on the phone. I said, "Mr. Weasel, do you have my mother's ashes?" That put both of us on the floor. "Yes, I do," he said, unaware there were two men on the other end writhing in hysterical laughter.

"I was waiting for instructions on what to do with them and decided I better mail them to you."

I was laughing so hard I couldn't speak. He thought I was crying.

"I'm sorry you're taking this so hard," he said.

"I'll be all right," I said.

We arranged for a *Dallas* company car to pick them up and they reached the set about 4 P.M. I took them to Malibu without telling Maj about my lapse in memory or revealing the different scenarios that had run through my head if I hadn't been able to get them, including using the ashes from the chuck wagon fire on the set and then sneaking back to Weatherford to bury Mother properly without anyone knowing the truth. Fortunately none of that had to happen.

Early the next morning we flew to Weatherford. The whole family, including Heller and her husband, Bromley,

and all her kids, met there and we had a tearful good-bye.
Many of Mother's old friends spoke. We put pictures of
the family in her ashes. I included a photo of Linda Gray,
who Mother adored. And I added a miniature bottle of
Kahlúa, her favorite drink. It was a fitting memorial to a
life well lived.

That experience started me thinking about my own
burial. I want to be ground up in one of those chippers,
the kind they used in the movie *Fargo*, and spread across
a field and plowed under. Then I want the field planted
with wheat that would be made into flour and used to
bake a huge cake. A year after my passing, my friends
would be invited to a big party and they'd get a piece of
me. And every year I'd come back again.

Early in 1991 I took Patrick up to a fishing camp a friend
of mine owned outside of Medford, Oregon. It was a classic
old lodge on 162 wooded acres along the Rogue River.
Maj and I had been going there two or three times a year
for 10 years, fishing for salmon and steelhead.

The first time I'd taken Patrick there we'd limited out.
It was unbelievable fishing. Just as we were about to take
the boat out of the river, he'd reeled in a fourteen-and-a-
half-pounder. None of the fish we caught had been under
eight pounds.

This was another special trip. While we were there, my
friend who owned the camp called and mentioned that he
was interested in selling the place. He wanted slightly more
than a million dollars. I knew *Dallas* was likely to be
canceled at the end of the season and didn't want to spend
that kind of money when I had other expenses. It took me
about two seconds to convince Patrick to buy it. I figured
I'd sponge off him anyway.

After Patrick and his family moved in, I asked him to send me the rod and tackle I kept there. I needed it for a trip. I told him exactly where I kept it.

"The one in the closet?" he asked.

"Yeah, that's it."

"Oh, it came with the house," he said.

Actually, it came from starring on a series that ran on prime time longer than any other except for *Gunsmoke* (and most of them were half-hour shows). If not for *Dallas*, Patrick wouldn't have purchased a spectacular fishing camp and I wouldn't have been building a magnificent mountaintop villa in Ojai, 70 miles outside of L.A. Neither of us would've been wealthy beyond our dreams. Neither of us would've had the roles of a lifetime. Neither of us would've had the fun or the friendships. But after 13 years and 356 episodes, *Dallas* came to an end. Only three of us were left from the original cast: Patrick, Ken Kercheval, and me.

Poor old J.R. had proven his mettle when it came to scandal, bribery, blackmail, philandering, and family infighting, but poor ratings were beyond even his skill for manipulating a situation to his advantage. But it was time. There wasn't much left that the show—or J.R.—hadn't done. By the time Katzman put the finishing touches to the last script, I betcha J.R.—who everyone thought was so smart—had lost Ewing Oil and about a billion dollars.

The final episode, a two-hour special, provided a fitting send-off. J.R. had lost everything important to him—Ewing Oil, Southfork, his family and friends. Drunk and angry, he went upstairs and pulled out an old Colt Peacemaker that had once belonged to his daddy. He was about to contemplate blowing himself to smithereens when a guardian angel, played by my friend Joel Grey, showed him what life at Southfork would've been like if he'd never existed. We filmed the last scene February 8, 1991, and it was a bittersweet farewell.

At the end-of-season wrap party at the Marina Yacht Club in Marina del Rey, all of us sensed the show probably wouldn't be back. There hadn't been an official announcement by the network. But everyone talked about it. Patrick and I didn't expect to be back. Others, not understanding the economics behind such decisions, hoped for the best, pointing out that our ratings were still better than at least half the shows on the air. Only Katzman, in a reserved mood all night, knew the reality but he didn't want to tell anyone the news and ruin the party.

Three days later Leonard called and filled me in. He said it almost like it was an afterthought. By the way, Larry, we've been canceled.

"Well, there you go," I said.

It was neither a whimper nor a bang. Just the end of a natural life span. Reagan left office, so did J.R. He had a good run. But there was a bright side. A few days after Katzman had given me the official word, Maj and I attended the screening of a movie and then went to a party afterward. Normally I would've turned in early because I had to wake up at 5 A.M. But no more. As I told Maj, I was unemployed. I could party till the sun came up if I felt like it.

27

One day long after the last episode of *Dallas* had been filmed, I was showing a friend around Malibu. The beach community's signature was still its surfers, but it had otherwise gone through dramatic changes over the 25 years we'd lived there. Property prices had increased sixtyfold. Shacks that had once lined the beach had been replaced by multimillion-dollar architectural masterpieces. All the old people had either died out or sold out.

Maj and I weren't planning to sell out, but we were building our dream house on top of a twenty-three-hundred-foot high mountain overlooking the ocean and Oxnard plain. I had no complaints. At 60, I was having too much fun traveling between our other homes, in New York and Santa Fe, fishing, hunting, or just tooling around behind the wheel of my Rolls-Royce or on my Harley-Davidson.

One day I got a call from Linda Gray, who said she'd

been approached to do the play *Love Letters* at the Cannon Theater in Beverly Hills. She asked if I'd like to do it with her. I said, "Go back onstage? There's no way in the world you're going to get me to go back onstage! It's too much work."

"Oh come, Larry," she said. "You'll love being in front of an audience again."

"As you know, Linda, I adore you," I said, "but you can just forget it."

Three days later we started rehearsals, and a week after that we opened to a sellout crowd. Every night for the next two weeks also sold out, with standing ovations. Linda was right as usual. I loved it.

Then we accepted an offer to do the play at the English-speaking theater in Vienna, Austria. Opening night was a resounding success. The audience stood and cheered through five-minute curtain calls. The line of people waiting outside for us to sign their programs was literally a block long. Tables were set up in the stage door alley and police had to be brought in to keep the queue in order. It took two hours to take pictures and sign autographs.

At a party afterward, we were eating dinner with the company, friends, and everyone involved, and the theater manager gave Linda and me a toast, declaring, "I'm so thrilled by the quality and success of the show, if my life ended tonight I'd die happy."

The next morning his wife called to say that he'd passed away in his sleep. Thinking back to his toast, Maj and I and Linda were dumbstruck. It was very strange. The mood for the second performance was somber at the beginning of the show, but at the end we still got our standing ovation. From this, we got offers to tour Switzerland and Germany. A few months later, we returned to Switzerland, where we continued to be a success. But as soon as we crossed into Germany, it turned into a disaster.

The promotor's idea of publicity was a small, half-inch squib in the general entertainment paper. If you blinked, you missed the notice. There were very few press interviews and practically no radio or TV interviews. We played Stuttgart in a twenty-five-hundred-seat auditorium with 18 people present—two in the balcony, four in the mezzanine, and the rest scattered throughout the orchestra. One of them was Maj, who laughed alone at all the right places and stood and clapped at the end.

That turned out to be the model for the rest of the tour.

At first it was funny, and then less amusing, and then totally demoralizing. Then it became funny again when we realized there was nothing we could do to change the situation. We were playing in English to a German audience in working-class communities where most of the playgoers were Turkish. The language barrier itself was probably insurmountable. The people who did buy tickets were very enthusiastic, but it was hard to tell becuase their laughter took a while to travel from the cheap seats to the stage.

There was an upside—we didn't have to spend two hours afterward signing autographs. To say the least, it was a humbling experience that brought home the vagaries of an actor's life, from the pinnacle of international stardom to the tortured obscurity of a provincial actor. Miss Gray and I had carved a close friendship in our 13 years on *Dallas*, but there's nothing like sharing a disaster to deepen those bonds.

We performed *Love Letters* one more time, for a week at the Rubicon Theatre in Ventura, California, and got back our full houses and standing ovations, so I know we didn't cause the debacle. However, let me say this: if Linda ever wanted me to play Hamburg with her again, I'd be right there with her.

Carroll O'Connor had seen us do *Love Letters* at the Cannon Theater and absolutely loved it. He came backstage with tears in his eyes. He understood every nuance of the play. As we talked, he asked if I wanted to direct *In the Heat of the Night*, his successful CBS series. He had made the transition from Archie Bunker to a southern sheriff, an almost impossible feat given the indelible impression he'd made on audiences as Archie. But that he did it was a tribute to his enormous talent as an actor.

I directed several of the one-hour shows, plus one of *Heat*'s two-hour movies-of-the-week at the end of its run. In fact, as it would turn out, I was in Georgia in early 1992 directing Carroll when I first noticed my energy was kind of low. I didn't think much of it until months later. Nor did Maj, who attributed my sluggishness to having put on a few extra pounds. So I instructed my personal trainer, Taylor Obre, my Princess of Pain, to work me out a little harder. By May I'd dropped a few pounds and felt better.

But one day during my workout, Taylor and I got into a conversation about medicine and health-related topics.

"Have you had a checkup recently?" she asked.

"No, not for at least a year, and maybe longer."

Taylor shook her head disapprovingly and wrote down the name of her internist. Several days later I watched Dr. Paul Rudnick draw what looked like two gallons of blood from my arm. He also took a chest X ray, gave me an EKG, and prodded the middle regions of my body. It was the most thorough medical exam I'd had in my life. You would've thought he was looking for a loophole that would get me out of the draft all over again.

On June 3, shortly before Maj and I sat down for dinner, Dr. Rudnick called. He said results from my blood workup were back and they showed a life-threatening situation. I had no idea what he was talking about. I'd worked out early that day. I felt great. But here he was, telling me I was sick. The test results indicated I had cirrhosis of the liver. He said, "If you keep drinking, I don't think you'll be around in six months. If you quit, you have a chance of living a normal life."

At the time of the call, I was holding a glass filled with vodka and orange juice. I usually had a few before dinner, then switched to wine.

I immediately put the drink down the drain and checked my watch. It was 6:15 P.M., June 3, 1992.

That was when I quit drinking.

Despite a report in one of the tabloids that I was sick, I never felt ill. I wouldn't have even gone to the doctor if it hadn't been for Taylor. Though I'd averaged about four bottles of champagne a day for the past 15 years, I never got drunk. I drank just enough to keep that click going, that soft, comforting high that playwright Tennessee Williams wrote about in *Cat on a Hot Tin Roof*.

But I gave it up that moment without any problem. It was the same way I'd quit smoking 30 years earlier. I'm lucky. I seem to have the kind of self-control that allows me to stop without suffering withdrawals, DT shakes, falling-down episodes, headaches, or any of the other side effects of such a drastic change in lifestyle.

A second, more thorough exam by Dr. John Vierling, medical director of the Liver Transplant Program at Cedars-Sinai Medical Center, confirmed my liver's tissue was scarred and deteriorating, He described it as a textbook case of advanced cirrhosis, the eighth-leading cause of death from disease in the United States. According to Dr. Vierling, I fortunately wasn't in need of a transplant, not yet anyway, but my blood required testing every three months to check for tumors, which commonly grew in diseased livers. Otherwise, I could do as I pleased.

And I did. I went with Peter Fonda and Willie G. Davidson, the grandson of Harley Davidson, on our long-planned ride to Sturgis, South Dakota, the biggest motorcycle rally in the world. It meant missing a wedding in New York, which Maj and Linda Gray went to without me. Our Malibu neighbor Burgess Meredith was also invited. We happened to be on speaking terms at that time. Actually, he typically called Maj three times a day for advice. He called so often that he referred to her as his "rent-a-wife."

Anyway, Burgess was staying at the Ritz-Carlton, next door to our New York apartment. On the night before the wedding, we were all at a party at "21," where Burgess gave the bride and groom his private stash of Petrus wine, which he conveniently stored at "21." The next morning the bride and groom called up Maj and asked her to check in on Burgess, who they said had had an accident after the party. When Maj got there Burgess was sitting on his bed in his skivvies, being checked out by paramedics who had been called by the hotel's doctor. An ambulance was on its way. Burgess didn't seem too upset. When he saw Maj, he nonchalantly said, "Oh hi, what are you doing here?"

"Going to the hospital with you," Maj said calmly.

"Would you grab my address book and medicines?" he asked as he was being loaded on the gurney.

The ambulance took them to the hospital. Several hours

later, the doctor found Maj and asked how well she knew Mr. Meredith.

"Thirty-five or forty years," Maj said.

The doctor was puzzled by the bruises he'd found on Burgess.

"What do you think is wrong with him?" he asked Maj.

There was a rumor going round that Sharon Stone had taken Burgess back to the hotel after the party and he'd made a pass at her and fallen down the stairs. But Maj didn't tell that to the doctor. She simply said, "I think he suffered an attack of Petrus," and let the doctor figure that out by himself.

A few weeks later, Burgess came back to Malibu and thanked Maj for saving his life. He sent over a tree stump that had been painted with beautiful tulips by our mutual friend Margie Adleman. And Burgess regarded us as the best of friends again—at least for a while.

Over the next two years, I didn't have any major complications or complaints. I kept up my workouts with Taylor and stayed in pretty good condition, except I noticed a steady loss of energy. I also had persistent nosebleeds, which I ignored, even though later on I'd learn they were signs of liver malfunction.

The really big event in our lives was moving into our home in Ojai. It had taken five years to build. Maj had designed it and supervised every facet of construction. She made daily trips from Malibu to Ojai, 170 miles round trip, five days a week. Her attention to detail and decorating, which included importing one-hundred-year-old roof tiles from Provence, France, ensured the home that materialized lived up to her vision, which it has and beyond.

She earned my complete admiration. I don't know how she did it without killing anyone. When the carpenter doesn't show up, the electrician can't do his job; when the electrician can't do his job, the plumber can't do his job; and when the plumber can't do his job, the gardener can't do his job, and so on. Maj stepped in when our first contractor didn't work out, and she stood tall. Having heard remodeling or construction is a surefire way to break up a relationship if both partners are involved, I stayed out of the way and contented myself with earning the money and letting Maj indulge her remarkable talents.

She's made our home a showplace that we enjoy and use for fund-raisers for politicians, be they Republican, Democrat, or independent, and causes we believe in. We also host charity events for the Ventura County Museum of History & Art, the Ojai Music Festival, Ventura's Rubicon Theatre Company, among many. We believe that when you live in a community, you have to support it, help it grow, and in the case of a unique little town like Ojai and the surrounding environs, protect the quality of life.

We knew the site of our home was special. Not a day went by when I didn't stop at the gate and admire the view of the house, to say nothing of what I saw when I stood on the terrace looking across the Oxnard plain to the oceans and the Channel Islands beyond. Our house is situated on an escarpment twenty-three hundred feet above sea level. About two hundred yards from the terrace, it drops almost a thousand feet straight down. When the sea breezes hit that, they're pushed upward in a giant wave of air. In the afternoons, sometime after one, we can look out and see buzzards, hawks, crows, and occasionally, when we're lucky, half a dozen condors all circling and playing some kind of game with the wind that only they know. It's a magnificent sight.

One day while Maj and I were watching this phenomenon, I asked her what we should name our home. I suggested Hagmans' Hideaway and Hagmans' Haven. After a long pause, mesmerized by the circling birds, Maj quietly whispered, "Why don't we call it Heaven?"

I thought about it for a couple of minutes and said, "Maj, that's a fantastic name. And I think it's the closest I'm ever going to get."

So, Heaven it is. I'm Heaven's keeper and Maj is the abbess.

Shortly after staking our claim to Heaven, we found ourselves fighting to preserve that and perhaps much more, including our lives. On the day before Thanksgiving, we awoke to find the National Weather Service pouring foundations for what we would come to know as the NEXRAD Doppler radar tower, part of what the Weather Service described as a new generation of detection systems that warned of storms, flash floods, and tornadoes. Less than a thousand yards from our property, the tower was ninety-six feet tall and topped by a 30-foot ball that loomed over the neighborhood like a science fiction monster. It was painted green to blend in with the trees. It towered about 60 feet above them.

The Weather Service never informed anybody they were going to put it in. Nor did they tell us that it would pulse 24 hours a day, every day, emitting microwave radiation, which they maintained was safe even after I pointed out their board of review didn't include a single medical professional. My neighbors and I formed a group called VCARE (Ventura Coalition Against Radiation Emissions) and commissioned a study, which found what all of us considered to be unacceptable levels of radiation. We were up in arms ("The federal government has come in and raped me," David Hedman, an environmental engineer, claimed), and after living with it for a while we were downright scared.

By March, 3, 1994, we aired our concerns on *The Montel Williams Show*. One man told about his two pet parakeets, both born after the tower went up, that were unable to grow feathers. He also had two pigeons that were born with defects; one had a giant beak, the other was a dwarf. One of my dogs miscarried, then lost a lung for no apparent reason. Another dog died suddenly of another mysterious lung disease. Hedman's children complained of headaches and earaches. And there was more that didn't get on. One woman, too ill to attend the taping, developed three tumors in her ovaries. Then a woman who lived in the shadows of the tower gave birth to a child with a hyperthyroid condition.

Then I joined the list. In early spring 1995, shortly after I finished playing a Texas millionaire in Oliver Stone's movie *Nixon*, one of my blood tests came back irregular. I had an awful, sinking feeling as I received the news, but Dr. Vierling wasn't alarmed. He ordered additional tests, including a CAT scan and MRI, and they indicated a slight growth.

"It could be the liver rejuvenating itself," he said.

"That's good news?"

"Maybe. Sometimes the nodules revivify."

"What do we do about this?" I asked.

"We watch it for now."

On June 22, I went back for another checkup. The growth had gotten a little bit larger. It wasn't good news.

Dr. Rudnick called in Dr. Leonard Makowka, Cedar-Sinai's director of transplantation services. We already knew each other from when he'd operated on my mother five years earlier. He ordered his own battery of tests. I had CAT scans, PET scans, MRIs, ready-to-eat meals—everything the hospital could throw at me.

I marveled at the machinery, the high-tech equipment that dissected my body without leaving so much as a scratch, and thanked my lucky stars I had the insurance to pay for it. Thank God for strong unions like the Screen Actors Guild and the Directors Guild. The tests revealed a small tumor, measuring 2.7 by 2.8 centimeters, about the size of a marble. Dr. Makowka couldn't tell me whether or not it was malignant without a biopsy, but he said it was situated next to a major vein in the liver, which wasn't good.

"This isn't uncommon with a cirrhotic liver," Makowka said. "They're hotbeds for tumors. Like pearls in an oyster. They love to grow in there."

I entered Cedars on a Thursday afternoon through a back entrance and checked in under an assumed name while wearing a fake mustache, as my publicist was paranoid the tabloids would find out. Dr. Makowka did the procedure early Friday morning. At three o'clock that afternoon, less than 24 hours after I'd snuck in, Maj, her sister Bebe, and my publicist, Richard Grant, smuggled me back out—but only after Makowka's chief coordinator, Michel Machuzsek, scouted the underground parking lot and reported back it was all clear.

Despite all our precautions, the following day Richard got a call from a reporter from a London tabloid asking if it was true I had been in the hospital for chemo.

"No," Richard said.

"Is J.R. dying?"

"No, he's not. That's absolutely false."

We hadn't even gotten the results.

But the story came out anyway: CAN J.R. BE SAVED?

It didn't speak highly of the security at Cedars-Sinai. Richard was livid. I was anxious to know the results.

Maj and I went to Santa Fe. Movement is always good, especially when waiting for test results. It gives you something to do. We didn't have to wait long. The telephone rang on Monday morning, and it was Dr. Makowka. He told us the tumor was malignant.

I put the phone down and looked at Maj, who up till this point had managed to keep her emotions in check. But this caused her to lose it. Not completely. But she cried and felt scared. Rightfully so. Hearing a doctor who specializes in treating terrible diseases say the words "malignant tumor" is terrifying. You're allowed to lose it. We'd been married 40 years. We were still having the time of our lives together. Maj suddenly realized that that time might be running out.

We hugged for a long time.

I reacted differently. I kind of stepped out of myself. Instead of panicking or worrying, I got very calm and asked, "What do we do about the situation?"

We flew back to L.A. and discussed the options with Makowka, who explained the tumor was positioned against a vein. If the cancer got into the vein, it could get into my bloodstream and travel throughout my body, none of which was good. He recommended a liver transplant. I got a second opinion from Dr. Don Morton, the medical director and chief surgeon of the John Wayne Cancer Institute. He brought up another method, that of freezing the tumor, though both he and Makowka agreed it was too far along and too close to the vein to seriously consider this method.

There was also a third option. I could do nothing and die.

"We don't want a remission," Dr. Makowka explained. "We want a cure, and the only cure for a bad liver in your condition is to replace it with a better one."

One thing about liver disease: it makes you lethargic, and encephalopathy sets in—in other words, you just don't think straight. I didn't. I didn't realize it, but it took me a long time to assimilate things. When Makowka and Vierling mentioned a liver transplant, I said, "Look, I've had 64 years of a fabulous life. I don't want to walk around a cripple. I'll bow out gracefully when it gets too painful or inconvenient. I'll take a pill like I intended to give my dad and shuffle off this mortal coil."

Well, this didn't set well with Maj. She called me a bunch of names and said she didn't go along with that idea and that I was going to have a liver transplant if I could find a donor no matter what I thought about it. She has always had a way of persuading me to see the light. This time she just set her foot down and said, "No way, Jose."

That spurred my interest in a liver transplant. I had several more meetings with my doctors, and they persuaded me that if I got a donor liver and took a few pills every day I could lead a normal, happy existence—you know, if I was inclined toward happiness.

When it was put like that, I said, "God knows I've always been a pretty happy person."

On July 19, my name went on a nationwide list along with five thousand other people awaiting a new, healthy liver.

The news got out and spread quickly. I got calls from friends. Baseball great Mickey Mantle had just undergone a liver transplant amid criticism that his notoriety had helped him, a lifelong alcoholic, receive a liver quicker than others. I looked up the statistics. The average wait was between 30 days and a year. Decisions on who got a liver were based on medical condition, blood type, size, and proximity to the donor organ. I had no idea why Mantle got his. Nor did I know when *or if* I'd get mine.

Richard sent out a press release. "In spite of this latest development, Mr. Hagman remains in excellent health and spirits and his prognosis for a full recovery and long life is excellent, according to his medical team."

I believed that was true. I had no reason not to.

Michel Machuzsek coordinated everything that had to go on between the patient and all the doctors. She called to ask how I was feeling, scheduled appointments, blood tests, MRIs, and all the other stuff that goes into preparing for a liver transplant. If Makowka, who performed the surgery, was God, she was the angel Gabriel tending the gates.

One day she asked me if I still drank. I said no. She asked if I was in any support program. Again I said no, explaining that I didn't feel I needed one. I'd been able to give up alcohol for the last two years and didn't miss it at all. And if it wasn't for the goddamn encephalopathy, I'd be thinking straighter than I had in 40 years.

Michel smiled as if to say, "Good for you," and then said she'd like me to meet Dallas Taylor, the original drummer for Crosby, Stills and Nash. Makowka had performed a liver transplant on him a few years earlier. Now Dallas ran a men's group of recovering alcoholics and drug addicts. I called him up and arranged to get together.

We met at the Newsroom Cafe on Robertson Boulevard, a wonderful restaurant where you can get newspapers and magazines from around the world as well as delicious food. Dallas handed me a copy of his book, *Prisoner of Woodstock*, which would show me what a simple and naive life I'd led. Over lunch, he told me about his career, the gory depths his addiction had taken him, and how Makowka had saved his life with a transplant. He also told me about the Monday night meetings and invited me to come to the next one in Beverly Hills.

Two Mondays later, he and comedian Richard Lewis picked me up and took me to a meeting. It was held at someone's home. There were about 30 guys in a room, many of whom I knew or recognized. The meeting was simple. One guy started it by reading "How It Works," or the twelve steps to sobriety, from the AA Blue Book, then said his name and described his week since the last meeting, staying within the three-minute time limit, which gave everyone a chance to speak.

"I'm glad to be here," I said when it was my turn. "Dallas dragged me in. I haven't had a drink in nearly three years and I don't plan to."

It went around the room like that until the last person had shared his story. Then all of us stood up and said the Serenity Prayer: "God grant me the serenity to accept the things I cannot change, the courage to change the things I can, and the wisdom to know the difference. Amen."

Since that day those Monday night meetings have become an essential part of my life and I've said the prayer every morning after I brush my teeth while looking at a framed photo of my liver donor, which I have courtesy of the *National Enquirer*. It's proved to be one the most important prayers I've ever known. As soon as I began meditating on it, it opened up a whole new avenue of living—compassion, strength, conviction, and wonder. And of course, at that time as I wondered whether or not I'd get a donor liver, I needed all of that and more.

28

At the hospital, I'd been given a beeper and told it would go off when a compatible liver became available. As Maj and I drove to Malibu, we made several different plans for getting to the hospital quickly when the time arrived. In lieu of having a specific date, we prepared down to the smallest details, from packing bags and writing down important phone numbers to keeping a helicopter at the Camarillo airport on call.

A few days later we drove up to Heaven. As we passed through the front gate, my beeper went off. Maj looked at me; I thought, That didn't take long. I called in immediately, but they said it wasn't them. It might've been a wrong number. Later that afternoon the beeper went off again at the same spot on the hill and I figured out it was the radar tower. The microwaves triggered the beeper. It happened often when I drove up and down that road.

As we waited, Maj and I tried to enjoy every moment. We spent time with the people we loved. Our kids and grandchildren came up to the house. Family and friends called night and day, including my sister, Heller, whose talks with Maj helped keep her strong and positive.

One day I was in the Jacuzzi with Richard and asked what his mother had been up to lately. He laughed.

"Lar, my mother died a year ago," he said. "She's having lunch with your mother today."

I knew that. It was my memory going as a result of my liver not working properly.

About two weeks after he'd diagnosed the cancer, Makowka talked to me about the possibility of performing an intermediate procedure to buy more time while we waited. There were risks, none of them pleasant. Before making a decision, I asked if I could go to Vancouver with Patrick on a fishing trip at the end of July.

"Sure, go on your fishing trip," Makowka said. "By the time you get back we'll have a recommendation."

I made arrangements in case I had to get back to L.A. in a hurry, but the private jet I had on standby throughout the four-day trip never had to budge from the tarmac. Instead I had a wonderful, relaxing time with Patrick even though I didn't catch a single fish. It was like all our previous fishing excursions—a nonstop laugh riot, only this time minus the booze.

When I got back, Makowka told me that he wanted to do the procedure. On August 5, he performed a chemo-embolization, a onetime procedure that killed the tumor with chemo and blocked the blood vessel feeding it. I came out of the hour-long operation fine. I kept a positive attitude. But it was impossible to predict how long my health would last. It was only a matter of time. As Makowka said, there was only one sure thing about my condition—I needed a new liver.

*   *   *

"The wait is hard," Dallas Taylor told me. "It's like being a condemned man on death row waiting to hear if the governor will grant a reprieve."

In 1990, Dallas had been in the same position I was in. He wore a beeper and hoped a matching donor liver could be found before it was too late. Makowka had performed his transplant surgery too. Dallas told me what to expect from the operation and was a great inspiration.

So was David Crosby, who filled me in on the details of the seven-hour transplant operation he underwent at UCLA in November 1994. I got together with David for lunch and he proudly lifted up his shirt and showed me his scar, a huge incision that indicated the surgeons split you open as wide as a frog in biology class. He also told me about the side effects, like temporary pain and discomfort, your lack of immunity, the danger of rejection, and how a buildup of fluids causes your scrotum to blow up about 10 times its normal size.

Nothing I heard during those pep talks scared me. Long after the operation was over, some people said I'd seemed frightened, but I don't remember feeling it. I didn't want to be in pain. Nor did I want to die. But the operation didn't scare me. Death isn't the end of everything. It's just another step.

"Did you have your tour yet?" Dallas asked one day.

No, that came next. About a week after the chemo-embolization, I familiarized myself with what was going to happen when I was operated on. At Makowka's suggestion, I toured the hospital's ICU ward, where I'd be taken after my surgery, and I met Leonard's entire staff, from nurses to psychiatrists. I had no idea of the number of people involved.

There was also a slender black man who stood in the background. His name was Dan Simpson. He had an air of elegance that made him seem different. I asked what he did.

"I am the harvester," he said.

"Harvester?"

"Yes, I go out and talk to the family of the potential donor and try to persuade them to let me bring back the organ."

I didn't get to know him much beyond that brief conversation, but I never forgot the profound effect meeting him had on me. Maybe because this gentle soul was the closest anyone waiting for a transplant ever got to the most important person in the whole procedure, and of course you never met that one. The donor.

It's worth emphasizing I had no idea when, or even if, I'd ever receive a suitable liver. But we continued making preparations at the hospital, like special security, ensuring Maj would have her own room while I was there, and protecting the privacy of my hospital records from the gossip rags. It's irritating we had to go to such lengths, but if not, we were sure everything from my X rays to urine samples would end up in the tabloids.

Then on April 14, my beeper went off. It was about 11 o'clock at night, and Maj and I were in bed, reading. She bolted up and somehow her sister Bebe, who was in the guest house, heard it too, and everyone started clucking around the house. I called in to the hospital.

"Sorry, Mr. Hagman. I dialed the wrong number."

"Okay, thanks," I said, shrugging at Maj.

When I told Maj it had been a wrong number, the two of us sighed almost simultaneously, clicked off the lights, and went to sleep.

Eight days later I was up early. While Maj visited with my sister, Heller, who was in from New York, I went down to shoot on the skeet range Maj had built for me down the hill near the helicopter pad. I hit my share of clay pigeons, which made it an excellent morning. Then it got even better. I was in the middle of the driveway on my way back to the house when Maj called out that Leonard Makowka was on the phone. He said he had good news and bad news.

"Oh?" I said.

"The bad news is that I'd planned to call you today to invite you to go fishing next weekend in Vancouver. I heard the salmon are running."

"I was just up there. They sure weren't running then."

"It doesn't matter. I can't invite you—not this weekend anyway."

"Why not?"

"That's the good news. We have a perfect liver for you. It's on its way. We're sending a helicopter for you. Can you be ready in half an hour?"

I'd been on the United Network for Organ Sharing (UNOS) list thirty-three days. Now I had less than 33 minutes to get to the hospital.

Right then I paused, the first of countless such pauses I've made since, to think about the person whose liver would soon be mine. You aren't permitted to know anything about that person. Nothing. Not whether they're male or female, black or white, rich or poor, happy or unhappy, and I think that's good. It's proof that we're all the same, all here to help one another if we can. I thanked that person profusely for signing their donor card.

The helicopter touched down on the landing pad beyond

the driveway. The pilot smiled and helped stow our small bags. Within two minutes, we were airborne, heading south. I'll always remember my little sister, looking so worried, standing on the driveway and waving to me as we flew toward L.A. Maj and I held hands the whole way and looked at the scenery below. It was so pretty. I turned to Maj at one point and said, "What a nice day."

Then we landed at the hospital. The entire flight had taken 26 minutes.

At that point, it was kind of like being in the theater and hearing the stage manager say, "Show time." Michel met me at the helicopter pad and took me on a roundabout way into the hospital to avoid any paparazzi who might've been tipped off that I was on my way. Then began the long process of being prepped for major surgery. Between 7:30 and 8 P.M., the helicopter landed with the harvester and his precious cargo. Maj was chatting with Michel while I talked with Richard on my cell phone when a young man came in and told me he was there to take me down to the operating room.

"I've got to go," I said. "My driver's here."

My attitude couldn't have been better. I was in a great mood, joking with Maj, not troubled by an ounce of fear. On the way to the OR, I pulled the sheet over my head so nobody could snap a picture of me. I kept wiggling my feet so they wouldn't think I was a corpse. In the OR, I was given an enema. I've heard of high colonics, but this was ridiculous. Neither Dallas nor David had mentioned it. I hoped that enema wasn't going to be my last thought. Because then I got a shot, the first round of anesthesia, and before anyone could tell me to count backward, I was out of there.

*   *   *

It was about 11 P.M. when Makowka actually began the operation. During the 16-hour surgery, much longer than originally planned, he played music to keep everyone's attention sharp. Later, he told me the first song he'd played, as he made the incision, had been the theme from *Dallas*.

Periodically Leonard or one of the other doctors left the room and gave Maj an update. It's impossible to predict what's going to happen in the operating room, but with each report he assured Maj everything was going well. The cancer hadn't spread and the new liver appeared to be a perfect match. There were a few minor complications. Leonard had to rebuild the bile duct connection to my liver, and he needed three hours to clean out gallstones. Earlier, I'd asked him to save the stones so my artist friend Barton Benes could turn them into a ring, and he happily told Maj that I'd be able to wear my ring.

Finally, late in the afternoon on August 23, Makowka came out and told Maj the operation was over. The surgery had been successful and I had been taken to recovery. But he added the cautionary words she already knew from previous discussions: I wasn't out of the woods yet. The first 48 hours after an operation like this were crucial and would indicate my chances for making it out of the hospital.

I remember opening my eyes and seeing Makowka and Maj staring down at me. The operation had finished five hours earlier. I was groggy from the anesthesia. I had a tube in my nose, one down my mouth, two in my side, one in each arm, one in my groin, a catheter on my dick, and I was on an aspirator. I was also connected to an automatic blood pressure machine. I remembered Dallas had mentioned being frustrated by his inability to speak, but

I drew on more than 20 years of not talking on Sundays and relaxed.

"You're doing great," Makowka said.

Then I connected with Maj.

"You look just like a machine," she said.

I made up some mantras and meditated on my favorite mental image, a field of mustard in flower, that wonderful bright yellow with a red rose in the middle. I concentrated on breathing. I'd take two deep breaths, then drift off into a kind of sleep. I felt in a state of limbo.

At some point they gave me a piece of paper and pen and asked me to draw a Texas star. I thought I did, but when I saw it later it looked more like an amoeba. Makowka asked if I would autograph the picture, but he was just joking. He told me I'd come through the operation with flying colors and to enjoy the rest.

I drifted through the heavily-medicated first couple of days in ICU, spending most of that hazy time focused on my celestial song. Everyone has their own unique song, an inner melody that fuses each of us to the deep, modulating, harmonious hum of the celestial orchestra that's the collective energy of everything that's ever lived and ever going to live. It's our life force. The power of the universe. Think of the aurora borealis. When I see those lights, I can't help but say, "My God, I'm part of that."

Later, when I told Dallas about that song, he said, "Oh yeah, that's your muse."

When I asked if he had experienced anything like that, he said, "Sooner or later, everybody does."

The days I spent in ICU meditating on my song gave me a feeling that was ecstatically happy and familiar—and it confirmed what I'd always suspected, that every one of us living creatures is part of a collective energy that is also ecstatically happy and familiar. The culmination of that energy is love. It's with us now, it always has been, and it always will be. Every one of us has this familiarity. We know it. The problem is, we bury it under so much apprehension and worry.

But on medication I was able to blend into the bigger picture, the way I had done on my first acid trip. I also glimpsed over the edge of this level of existence into the next, and there was that person again, welcoming me but indicating it was not yet the time to cross over. Yet I was allowed to understand there was more to life. This was not the end. There were more levels, an infinite number of levels, of existence, each one adding to the hum of the cosmic orchestra, as if we're alway spiraling upward until we reach a state of atomic bliss, like the pleasant chime of a triangle being played.

Every religion that I know of tries to figure out the same question—what's the meaning of life?—and each one offers a different path to the same answer, which is love.

The meaning of life is love.

So don't worry.

Be happy.

Feel good.

29

After two days in ICU, they took the breathing tube out of my mouth, allowing me to talk. According to Maj, who stayed by my side, I said the same thing over and over.

"I am so lucky," I said.

"Yes, you are."

"I love people," I said in a singsongy voice.

"I know you do."

I also talked about starting a rock and roll band with Crosby and Dallas. I wanted to call it the Grateful Livers and we could play my celestial song.

After two more days in ICU, I was moved to my own room, which was filled with healing crystals sent by Linda Gray. I constantly asked people to massage my aching, itching, swollen feet. Unfortunately I couldn't request the same treatment for my scrotum, which was the size of my head.

They told me I was a model patient. I let the nurses

poke me, check my pulse, and keep me clean. They started explaining the complex medications they were giving me but I was still too woozy to make any sense of what they said. The next day they got me out of bed and forced me to sit in a chair, which was really difficult because I was so weak. I wondered if that's what it felt like to be old. They wanted me to try to walk, but I didn't have the strength.

"It's going to take a lot of effort," one of the nurses said. "It's not easy."

At some point that day Maj had discovered a paparazzi dressed as a doctor in the hallway near my room. He'd gotten past the hospital's security and she recognized him. It turned out he had a small camera. My own security people got rid of him. But the incident made me feel help-less and paranoid. That night I asked Maj to sleep in my room. The nurse helped her pull a mattress in there and she slept on the floor next to my bed while holding my hand.

Later that night, well past midnight, I had the TV on and was watching Steve McQueen in the movie *The Hunter.* I'd known Steve slightly, one motorcycle guy to another. But the tenacity, strength, and will to live I saw in his performance in that movie struck a chord in me that the nurses hadn't been able to reach when they'd wanted me to walk. Inspired, I struggled out of bed and reached for my IV stand. The noise woke Maj, who said, "What the hell are you doing?"

"I'm going for a walk."

"Let me call a nurse," she said.

"No, just help me get ahold of this IV thing and open the door."

A few moments later I was out the door, walking. It was

more like an unsteady waddle with my scrotum swinging
to and fro, throwing me off balance, but at least I was out
of bed and moving into the hall.

"What's going on?" the duty nurse asked.

"I'm taking a walk," I said.

I trudged down the hall muttering to Steve, "Thanks,
buddy."

From then on, I improved daily. The only pain that got in
my way was psychic. I was overloaded by the feeling I
could read minds and control what happened on television.
I watched André Agassi play in the finals of the U.S. Open
and all the action looked to be in such slow motion that
I could actually help him think about his shots. Lots of
good it did, since he lost. The same thing happened when
I watched baseball. I could actually steer the ball where I
wanted it to go. I should've been connected to a Vegas
sports book, because I knew all the results ahead of time.

My mind generated an abundance of thoughts and ideas.
It was obviously due to having a healthy, functioning liver.
Also because I was taking massive doses of steroids. But
for the first time in years, my body wasn't full of toxins.
The blood pumping into my brain was good and pure. But
it was almost too much for me to handle. I was on the
phone all day long networking people. A friend of mine
was a master knife maker who wanted to retire but had
a two-year backlog and couldn't. So I put him in touch
with Peter Fonda's stepson, Thomas McGuane Jr., who
had a passion for making knives, and I imagined he'd want
the job. Wrong. I put a pal in Vermont who knew about
tapping sugar maple trees in contact with a guy in North
Carolina whose trees were diseased. That they were elm
trees didn't deter me. It went on like that nonstop.

I also went on a creative binge, inventing new products. I came up with a fiber-optic lamp that had 15 adjustable snake-shaped tentacles coming out of the base, each one with a lens at the tip and they could be pointed in different directions. One lamp could handle an entire room. "That'll be a thousand bucks," I told Maj, who replied, "Great idea, honey."

I also created a traveling suit. One day I asked myself, What does a businessman need when he travels? The standard blue suit. Also a blue blazer with a pair of gray slacks and white slacks. And a tuxedo. The tuxedo is always a pain in the ass because you use it only once but still have to schlepp it around the rest of the time. Then I got the idea and invented the all-purpose traveling businessman's outfit— basically the clothing version of the Swiss army knife: a light Italian wool dark blue suit with removable buttons. For the blue suit, there were blue buttons. To convert it to the blazer, you switched to gold buttons, which inserted like cuff links. For the tuxedo, you used the blue buttons and Velcroed a satin shawl onto the lapels. With a tux shirt and cummerbund, you're all set for a formal event. Now, instead of three jackets, you had to take only one.

I've since had it made, it works perfectly, and it all fits into a carry-on bag so I don't ever have to check luggage again.

I also invented shoes with different-colored outer coverings that just had to be Velcroed. I haven't been able to sell that idea to anybody, but it seemed like a great idea to me. It still does.

They told me to rest, but I kept coming up with ideas for gift packages, belts, and assorted items from orthopedic canes to coffins. Maybe all that creativity was due to having a lot of time on my hands. Of course, it could've been all the drugs they were pumping into me—the morphine, the predmisone, and the like. Anyway, it was a fun, creative time and it was clear to everyone I was doing well.

Finally, after nine days in the hospital, Makowka said I could go home. It was less than the two weeks he'd originally told me that I'd need to spend there. (Dallas had spent six weeks in ICU alone.) Ironically, though, on the day I left, Makowka admitted that during surgery he'd discovered my liver was much worse than he'd thought. Without a transplant, I probably wouldn't have lasted more than two more weeks.

Carroll O'Connor and his wife, Nancy, offered to let Maj and me stay in their Westwood home so that I could be close to the hospital in case of an emergency. We stayed there for a month. Bebe, who'd kept her nursing license current after retiring from Saint John's, was my head nurse and coordinated an around-the-clock nursing staff that included two others, Frank Horton, one of the gentlest people I've ever met, and Rene Marschke, who superbly filled out colorful and happy sweaters. It was a joy to see her walk into my room.

Linda Gray and Dallas Taylor visited almost daily. They were part of a group of friends and family that tried to keep my spirits up, which wasn't difficult because I was so happy to be alive. I had a smile on my face all the time. The hardest part was getting accustomed to the routine of taking all my medications. I was on steroids, antirejection pills, pills to counteract the pills I took—26 in all, five times a day. I had to learn how to test my blood sugar level and inject myself with the proper amounts of insulin, since a side effect of one of the medications I took was being a diabetic. I also had to be extremely careful about greeting people or shaking hands, since I had almost no immune system.

But everything went well and after about a month we moved back to Ojai, where we celebrated the holidays. I was able to attend the premiere of *Nixon*. Two months later, I got clearance to go back to work. The first order of business was a *Dallas* reunion movie for CBS. The project had been in the works for two years, but had gotten sidetracked by Patrick's busy schedule and my illness. Finally, in March, Patrick, Ken Kercheval, Linda Gray, Mr. Katzman, and I got together in Dallas. "It's just like old times," I said as I waited for the van to take us to the location.

"Older, Lar," Patrick quipped. "Take a look in the mirror. It's much older."

Until then, I hadn't seen Patrick for months.

"What have you been up to?" I asked.

"The usual," he said. "Drinking and having fun. And you?"

"Same thing," I quipped.

Linda described being back together as a happy déjà vu. Mr. Katzman said that when he wrote the script for the final episode, he thought it was the end of J.R., but greed and lust were always popular. So was the quest for ratings and money, I cracked. Indeed, the movie picked up where the series had left off, with J.R. surprising mourners at his own funeral, explaining he'd faked his own death to snatch his son's inheritance. Now the Sultan of Scandal wanted to regain control of Ewing Oil. "Are you telling me the thought of Cliff Barnes running Daddy's business doesn't make you want to puke?" he said to Bobby in the opening scene.

It was vintage *Dallas* on-screen and even more so away from the camera. I was constantly busy running my lines, while Patrick only had to glance at his script to memorize his dialogue. Eighteen years after I first saw him do that it still impressed me.

"This is such hard work," I joked.

"Especially when the check comes," Patrick said, laughing.

When we wrapped in April, all of us were ready to do it again. Linda was on board. So was Patrick. So was I. Before all of us scattered, I hosted a dinner, where I lobbied for several reunion movies a year. Especially, as I declared to proper laughter, if they paid us what we were worth—a fortune.

But a great script, not money, was the primary motive when I signed on for the new series *Orleans*, a zesty gumbo of colorful characters produced and directed by *China Beach*'s John Sacret Young. It began production in New Orleans five days after the *Dallas* reunion wrapped. Maj flew down ahead of me and settled us into the famed Claiborne Mansion in the French Quarter which we leased for the two months we were scheduled to film. The home had been the mayor's mansion prior to the Civil War and had a gated courtyard that gave us privacy from paparazzi.

I had high hopes for *Orleans*. CBS had ordered a tryout of this ensemble drama about a wealthy, politically connected New Orleans family. I played the clan's patriarch, Luther Charbonnet, a respected judge who mingled comfortably with priests, politicians, and prostitutes. I'd get laughs by telling locals he was an honest and incorruptible judge.

Though it had been only seven months since my

operation, and I still needed to build my stamina, I felt great. I took a daily three-mile walk with Allison Zuber, another gorgeous trainer, lifted weights, and gained more strength every week. I had a harder time striking the right note with my character. I spent Sundays driving around New Orleans, studying people, eavesdropping on conversations, and soaking up the atmosphere, of which God knows there was an abundance.

On the first day of shooting, the wardrobe woman was robbed at gunpoint outside her home. The next day, three people were shot across the street from our location just outside the French Quarter. I heard the shots from my trailer. Most of the crew witnessed it. People yelled, "Get down," and, "Stay inside." But of course, every one of us ran out and saw the action.

That really rattled nerves. I remember the wife of Brett Cullen, one of my costars, was so shaken that she flew back to L.A. with their infant son. I'm sure others also wanted to jump ship, but for different reasons. The show was done more like a movie, which made it labor-intensive. John Young was also a perfectionist who wasn't concerned with working overtime. Sometimes he shot till sunup, but my cutoff was midnight. I made it known that, at 64 years old, this grandfather of five was long past dying for a role. The kids had no problem working as long as required. But as Cullen explained, "We aren't as rich as Larry."

None of us got rich from *Orleans*. CBS didn't pick up the show after several midseason airings drew less than stellar audiences. It was ironic, since the series got probably the best reviews of any that I'd ever done. But critical acclaim wasn't enough to sustain a series as expensive to produce as *Orleans*.

That gave me time to start riding with my motorcycle

club, the Uglies. Peter Fonda had been an Ugly for years and he'd gotten me into the club a couple years earlier. Oliver Shokouh, the founder of the Love Ride, the biggest motorcycle charity event west of the Mississippi—it attracts twenty-five thousand riders every year and has raised millions of dollars for muscular dystrophy—had invited me to go with him and a couple others from the club to a Love Ride in Zurich, Switzerland. I was going to be the grand marshal. So Oliver, his girlfriend, Debbie, Maj and I, and five other Ugly brothers arranged to go there and then take an extended motorcyle vacation through Switzerland, France, and Monaco, where we'd stay on a yacht belonging to my friend Lars Magnuson and watch the Grand Prix car race. Lars had moored his yacht, as he had for years, on the course's most dangerous corner, so we were excited.

We arrived in Zurich on a Friday morning. That afternoon I got a call from director Mike Nichols, who I'd known in New York City years before. He asked if I'd read for a part in his new film, *Primary Colors*. I asked when, and he said, if I got the part, my scenes would start shooting on the next Wednesday.

I explained how complicated it would be to cancel all of our arrangements and how I'd be letting down the Uglies.

"What if I send you the script?" he asked. "Read it and let me know what you think."

"Fine," I said.

The next day, Saturday afternoon, his secretary from Los Angeles showed up with the script under her arm and asked me to read it. Maj and I sat down immediately and read it together. I called Mike and told him that I thought the script was wonderful and my part in particular was sensational, and that I'd love to do it. There was a long pause and he said, "Okay, you got the part."

I talked it over with the Uglies and they said they could make other plans and to go for it. After I served as the grand marshal for the Swiss Love Ride on Sunday, Maj and I flew back to L.A. on Monday. On Tuesday I met with Mike and John Travolta, both of whom seemed happy with me. I was fitted for costumes, and the next day I began shooting my part.

I shot for a few days and then had a week off. During that time I nearly ruined my chance to be in the picture when I wiped out on my Harley. I was headed from my house to the music festival in downtown Ojai. I wasn't going more than 15 miles per hour down a winding mountain road. Suddenly a car came around the corner and, I thought, drifted into my lane. For some idiotic reason, I hit the front brake, which caused my Harley to go down. The eight-hundred-pound bike landed on top of me, pinning me to the pavement.

I felt fluid dripping onto my eyes. It was a mixture of blood and gasoline leaking from the bike. I somehow found the valve and turned off the gas. If I hadn't been wearing my helmet, which I always do, I would've been a goner. The girl driving the car tried to lift my Harley, but it wouldn't budge. I told her to quickly drive up the road and get a friend of mine, John Long, who I'd just seen parking some cars for a friend's party. She brought him not more than five minute later. They both somehow got the bike off of me and Lola, John's wife, drove me to the Ojai hospital, where there were about six people in line at the emergency room. I waited over an hour in terrible pain before anyone had time to look at me. If I'd had internal injuries, I easily could have bled to death.

It turned out I had three broken ribs, which were more painful than my transplant operation. I was afraid to cough, sneeze, and especially laugh—the pain was so intense. When I showed up on the set of *Primary Colors* a few days later, my arm was in a sling. No one knew about the accident. Everything had been kept out of the news. That day was one of my biggest scenes, the one when I announced my intention to run for president in opposition to John Travolta's character. It was being shot at UCLA in an outdoor arena filled with three thousand extras, balloons and streamers, cameras, and crew. My God, it couldn't have been more crowded, and I could barely move.

Mike was in front of a monitor, watching a replay from another scene as I hobbled by on my way to makeup. He looked up, probably wondering who the cripple was. Then he did one of those double takes.

"Hi. What happened to you?" he calmly asked.

"Oh, I had a little motorcycle accident," I said blithely.

"Do you think you can do the scene today?"

"Oh yeah, absolutely," I said cheerfully.

He paused and gave me a more careful examination.

"Are you going to wear your arm in a sling?"

"No, I can move it."

Truthfully, I couldn't move it worth shit. But it didn't matter as I began to feel the euphoria that I get right before going in front of a crowd. I asked Mike if we could forgo rehearsal. I also asked if he'd mind not telling the audience that I was the actor about to come out. I wanted to ride that wave of excitement they would have when they recognized me. Mike, always ready for an idea that helped a performance, said, "Fine by me. Let's do it."

With cameras rolling, I walked onstage. The audience

had been told to cheer with enthusiastic abandon, but when they recognized me they went nuts. It was my first appearance in front of a group of people since my operation nearly a year earlier. I felt such warmth and love. It was a sublime moment. I went through the scene, gesturing and moving as if my banged and bruised body were 30 years younger. Of course I didn't even feel my broken ribs. Nothing hurts when you're in front of an audience.

30

Shakespeare was right when he said all the world is a stage. He was even more accurate when he added that all the people are playing parts. This is true wherever you go, whether it's Hollywood, New York, London, Paris . . . everywhere. But nowhere was it more evident to me than in Romania.

We'd been asked to come to Romania to help Prince Paul, grandson of King Carol II, raise money for children with AIDS. It doesn't matter how busy you are, you can't turn down a cause like that. We went to London, then to Bucharest, where, as a video crew documented our visit, we toured army bases and university campuses, helped the prince announce a shipment of more than $200,000 worth of medicine, and posed for pictures with all the local politicians. I knew there were tens of thousands of kids with AIDS, but I never saw one.

On my first day there a man approached me on the street with tears in his eyes. With wonderment in his voice, he said, "J.R., you have saved my country. You have saved Romania." He went on to explain that Nicolae Ceausescu, the country's terrible dictator, had allowed only three hours of television a day—two hours of political propaganda and one hour of *Dallas* to show the corruption and decadent morality of the United States.

Big mistake! People watched *Dallas*, and liked what they saw, and when they overthrew Ceausescu, they shot him and his wife five hundred times.

The man's story confirmed what I'd experienced in Russia a few years before.

Over the next few days, we toured the old cities of Sibiu and Transylvania, where I listened to stories about Tepes the Impaler, who'd turned back Ottoman invaders in the mid-1400s and filled a forest with twenty thousand Turkish and Bulgarian prisoners he'd impaled on stakes. The history was fascinating, but we never saw his castle.

Then we went back to Bucharest. The day before we were scheduled to leave, the producer of the video told us it was time to get his most important shot. Maj and I were eating breakfast in our hotel room when he revealed his plan.

"Now Mr. Hagman," he said, "this is the scene where you come out of a doorway, tip your hat, and say, 'Welcome to Southfork.'"

"Southfork?" I said incredulously.

"Southfork . . . Romania." He said it as if this was common knowledge. "And then we pull back to show the Southfork ranch. Just like in *Dallas*."

It turned out there was an amusement park near Slobozia, a city in southeastern Romania about an hour from Bucharest. The park was owned by Alexandru Ilie, a weatlhy entrepreneur who built a fortune on cheddar cheese, then built himself a colossal tourist attraction featuring a replica of the Eiffel Tower, a zoo, monster waterfalls, and a reproduction of Southfork smack in the center of his three-hundred-acre luxury ranch. Why Southfork? He said that *Dallas* had become a part of people's lives in Eastern Europe. Why not give them what they want?

After hearing the whole story, I looked at the producer and then turned to Maj. Suddenly I felt as if the trip might've been a setup. I didn't know what to say. Fortunately Maj did.

"No fucking way," she told the producer.

He looked stunned.

"What?"

"That's an endorsement," she said. "If Larry does the shot, we're endorsing an amusement park, and we're not doing it. Larry gets paid for that."

"But you are here—"

Maj interrupted.

"We're here for kids with AIDS. If you're going to do an endorsement, do it for kids with AIDS."

The situation got pretty tense. It turned out we hadn't been told how much of the trip hinged on this particular shot. Apparently there was a whole web of business dealings and intrigue based on it. The producer looked like he was going to have a heart attack. I urged calm and suggested that if he wanted me to endorse the amusement park he should find a way to compensate me. It was simple.

"How much do you get for endorsements, Mr. Hagman?" he asked.

I explained that I received from $100,000 to $500,000 for endorsements in the United States. Those figures disturbed him. Disregarding the fact that Mr. Ilie, the owner of the amusement park, was said to be worth over

$100 million, the producer said there wasn't that kind of money in Romania. There was no way he could raise that kind of money in such a short time. In that case, Maj advised him to forget the shot.

He asked us to give him three hours to come up with something. Meanwhile, Maj and I went on a tour of former Romanian dictator Nicolae Ceausescu's gigantic marble palace. It was the second-largest building in the world next to the Pentagon, in Washington, D.C. We walked around with our mouths open. The place contained meeting halls the size of football fields. It was impossible to reconcile the enormity and the wealth on display there with the poverty of the people whose blood had been spilled constructing the monstrous palace.

Halfway through the tour my cell phone rang. It was the producer. He'd found an oil company that he said "would be positively delighted if you would make a commercial for them." They were also willing to pay $100,000. I said, "When?" He said, "How about in 15 minutes?" I said, "Done deal."

Our limousine whisked us to a location, a very modern-looking gas station on the outskirts of Bucharest, and I taped a commercial for Luke Oil. The whole thing took maybe an hour. They also took stills for magazine ads. I signed the contracts, and then asked for the money in cash. They said it was impossible to get that kind of cash in Bucharest, which made me say to myself, There goes a hundred grand. But a week later we were back in L.A. and my bank informed me that the funds had arrived.

Three months later, a director of the Romanian film crew who'd done the commercial visited us in Santa Monica and showed us pictures of me in my Stetson, holding a bottle of Luke Oil, that was displayed on a 10-storey building in Bucharest. Apparently my picture was plastered all over the country. He explained that Luke Oil was the leading Russian oil company in Europe. It was a good omen, because my mother's nickname for me was Luke.

My life has been full of good omens. I've been blessed with a knack for finding the right person or getting a lucky break. Take my diabetes. Two of my neighbors in Ojai, Rick and Virginia Loy, have two boys who are juvenile diabetics. She's investigated probably every treatment known to medicine to try to help her children. One of the doctors who's been of significant help to them is Diana Schwartzbien. I went to her, and through her method of a low carbohydrate diet and exercise I went from taking 26 units of insulin in the morning and 16 at night to being totally insulin free. Like with everything else, including AA, it works only if you work at it.

Some of my endeavors haven't been as successful. My campaign to remove the radar tower from Sulphur Mountain is still ongoing. The tower still stands, emitting what I believe is harmful radiation, and I'm continuing to battle the bureaucracy. I'm convinced that one day it will be moved to a proper site. People continue to smoke, but to a much lesser degree than 20 years ago. The government still subsidizes tobacco while condemning it at the same time. Eventually a balance will be struck and tobacco addiction will be added to alcohol and drug addiction and perhaps a successful treatment will be found.

I don't want to sound like I'm on a soapbox, but I think I've entered a more spiritual stage of my life. As I grow older, I see myself in a period of giving back. The way the world seems headed, I feel like I have to be involved with many organizations. I am at present the National Kidney

Foundation's spokesperson for organ transplants and also involved with Habitat for Humanity and the Solar Electric Light Fund, a nonprofit that brings electricity to areas of the world where people have never seen a lightbulb. I also have been appointed to the Advisory Committee on Organ Transplantation under the U.S. Department of Health and Human Services.

I never thought I'd live this long or this far into the twenty-first century, but here I am, and I'm concerned about the world my grandchildren are inheriting.

Sure, there are advances every day. Computers go faster and drugs work miracles. But they also come with two pages of legal warnings that they might do more harm than good. The brilliant surgeon who performed my liver transplant had to quit practising because the insurance companies and accountants were telling him how to treat his patients. Politicians legislate the destruction of the environment so we can drive SUVs, and they do it without considering the effect they are having on the whole chain of life of which we're a part.

Rome fell when the lead went from their pencils into their wine and the lawyers took over society. Everything was crooked. Nothing got done and problems piled up. Finally, the barbarians came through and solved all the problems for them. They killed everyone.

But poets are still writing about love, musicians are still making music, and kids are still thinking they know how to do things better than their parents. As long as that continues, we've got a chance.

While I was writing this book, something my mother said when I was young came back to me. She didn't tell me to be a great or successful actor. Nor did she tell me to be a good human being. She said that over the passage of time, my goal should be to acquire my own wisdom. To do that, she said, I needed to gather my own experiences. She told me not to fear making mistakes. To take chances. Have fun. Live.

I've done all of that to the best of my ability. I wouldn't have been able to tell the same story without Maj by my side for nearly 50 years. We've gone through everything together. Our partnership has been the most fortunate part of my life. Our children, Heidi and Preston, have turned out well, and our grandchildren seem to be doing the same. That's a pretty great story by itself. I came from a kind of kooky, nontraditional family, yet if asked what has been the most important part of my life, I'd say family. It's family that makes success richer and sadness less painful.

Writing a book like this compels you to want to sum up your life. I'm not going to give in to that urge. Let someone else sum up my life when it's over. As far as I'm concerned, I'm still playing the game. My mother finished her autobiography at 70. She said that she'd found love was "pure gold." By coincidence, as I write this last sentence, I'm also 70 . . . and I found the only answer is love.

Don't worry.
Be happy.
Feel good.

(from top left):
Our granddaughters, "The Blondies,"
Rebecca, Nora, Tara, Kaya, Noel.

ACKNOWLEDGEMENTS

I want to thank my mother, Peter Pan, without whom I wouldn't even be here.

My grandmother, Juanita Martin, without who Mother would never have been.

My father, Ben Hagman, who taught me how to hunt and fish.

My stepmother, Juanita Hagman, who kept me in line as a teenager.

And of course my beautiful little sister, Heller Halliday, who has put up with me all these years.

Heidi Kristina Mary Hagman and Preston Benjamin Axel Hagman, my two wonderful kids who I love dearly.

The Blondies—my five granddaughters.

Berit Axelsson, my sister-in-law and a wonderful nurse who supervised all my nursing during my illness.

Shelly Greenhut, who has stood by me all these years in spite of being a brother-in-law.

My mentor and great friends, Carroll and Nancy O'Connor.

Roger and Lorelle Phillips, my oldest and staunchest friends.

Henri Kleiman, my second oldest buddy, the best man at my wedding and so much more . . .

Linda Gray for being such a loving friend and for putting up with all my s***.

Richard Grant, to whom I will always be grateful for masterminding my public relations with the press and the networks. Just being a lucky actor is not enough; you have to have stimulating and knowledgeable guidance. Richard provided more than that . . . he is also a good friend.

Sidney Sheldon, whose genius and tolerance allowed me to make my mark.

Claudia Guzman, who made working on *Jeannie* so much fun.

Leonard Katzman, the genius of *Dallas* who kept us going for thirteen years.

Dallas Taylor, who kept me on the straight and narrow in AA.

Michelle Maschuszek, who has really kept me on the straight and narrow.

My wife, Maj, and I are actively involved in numerous civic and philanthropic activities. Between 1981 and 1991, I was chairperson for the American Cancer Society's "Great American Smokeout." During those eleven years, the campaign was successful at increasing the awareness of the dangers of nicotine. I continue to support the organization and encourage people not to smoke. I have also served as national spokesperson for the National Kidney Foundation's

Transplant Games since 1996. I am the Honorary Chair of the NKF's TransAction Council, a support and advocacy group for transplant recipients. In these capacities, I have tried to generate nationwide media coverage for organ donation and the success of transplants.

I have also worked for the introduction of legalisation that would eliminate the three-year limit on Medicare coverage for anti-rejection medication that transplant recipients need to take on a daily basis. I was recently appointed by Tommy Thompson, the U.S. Secretary of Health Resources and Services, to the Advisory Committee on Organ Transplantation. I strongly urge everyone to think about how they might save lives by filling out an organ donor card.

INDEX

(LH refers to Larry Hagman)

Abbott, George 76
Actors' Equity Association 58
Adelson, Merv 200
Adleman, Margie 169, 260
Adler, Polly 92
Advisory Committee on Organ
    Transplantation 296
Agutter, Jenny 187
Aherne, Brian 118, 120–1
All in the Family 97
American Cancer Society 227
Anderson, Judith 16, 92
Apted, Michael 178–9
Arthur, Jean 20
Artist and Elaine Thornton
    Foundation for the Arts 151
Ashley, Elisabeth 127, 128
Axelsson Berit (Bebe) 75, 86, 116,
    117, 283
Axelsson, Maj 70–91, 107–8,
    114–15, 117–19, 121–2,
    134–5, 265
    Bontril (uppers) 141–2
    Brazil 82–4
    flying 143–4
    Heaven 262
    Heidi's birth 88
    Ireland 188
    Jacuzzis 156–7, 184
    LH's father, meets 80–2
    LH, marriage to 75
    LH's mother, attempt at
        rapprochement with 86–7

LH's proposal of marriage 73
Los Angeles, move to 132
LSD 150
Malibu house purchase 155
Ojai move 260–1
pregnancy and miscarriage 84
pregnancy, second 86
pregnancy, third 98–9
Preston's birth 99
Rome 122
Times Square apartment 91
Wales 173
walk-on part 76, 77

Bacall, Lauren 171–2
Baddeley, Hermione 163
Baker, Diane 175
Baker, Joe Don 189
Balsam, Martin 178
Bardot, Brigitte 183
Beatty, Ned 187
Benes, Barton 276
Bergen, Candice 140
Berman, Shelley 169
Blob, The 168
Bolmier, Bill 75
Bolmier, Shirley 75
Bologna, Joseph 187
Boulder, Montana 152–3
Boyer, Charles 133
Bradbury, Ray 143
Brando, Marlon 192
Bridges, Beau 90

Bridges, Jeff 90
Bridges, Lloyd 90
Britton, George 57, 58
Buchwald, Art 77
Burr, Aaron 85
Busey, Gary 170
Byers, Joey 26, 27

Caine, Michael 187
Cambridge, Godfrey 169–70
Carney, Art 186
Cash, Johnny 2
Castelnuovo, Nino 118
Ceausescu, Nicolae
Channing, Stockard 187
Coco, James 109
Collins, Jackie 70
Collins, Joan 70
Columbia Pictures 105–6
Compton, Fay 97
Cooper, Jackie 159–60, 193
Cosby, Bill 189
Crosby, Bing 222
Crosby, David 146–7, 272
Crosby, Mary 222
Cullen, Brett 286
Curtis, Tony 186

Dacy, Jane 86
Dailey, Dan 11
Daily, Bill 130, 137 141
Dallas 197–200
    autographs 223–4
    "Black Hole of Calcutta" 234
    Dinah's Place guesting 209–10
    end of series 252–3
    European locations 244–5
    first episode 206
    first season, end of 210
    J.R. character 205–6
    J.R. merchandise 214, 217
    location shots 205
    onset smoking ban 228
    pay negotiations 214–19
    ratings number one 213
    reunion movie 284–5
    Russia 245–7
    U.K. sojourn between series 215–6
    "who shot J.R.?" cliffhanger
        213, 220–2

    worldwide acclaim 216
    see also Chapters 22–6
Dallas Cowboys football team 205,
    207
Danner, Blythe 176
Darden, Severn 22, 40, 163
D'Auvray, Jane 88
D'Auvray, Val 9, 88
Davidson, Willie G. 259
Davis, Jim 198, 203, 204, 229–30
    death 230
Dean, James 86
Deneuve, Catherine 183
Dennehy, Brian 208–9
Dewhurst, Colleen 93–4
De Wilde, Brandon 93, 95–6
*Dr. Strangelove; or, How I Learned
    to Stop Worrying and Love the
    Bomb* 106
Donner, Richard 192, 193
Duffy, Patrick 198, 201, 202–3,
        226, 249–50, 251–2, 271, 284
    Buddhism 237
    Dallas, leaves 237
    Dallas, returns to 239–40
    parents, death of 242
    salmon-fishing trip 236–7
Duvall, Robert 187

Eckles, George *See* Terrel, St. John
Eden, Barbara 129, 136, 141, 168
Elam, Jack 176–7
Essex, David 178
Evans, Wilbur 58
Experiment in International Living
    38

Faith, Adam 178
Fanchon and Marco School of the
    Theater 6
Farentino, James 109
Feldon, Barbara 171
Flicker, Ted 41, 62, 70
    I Dream of Jeannie 140
    Nervous Set, The 100
    Once Around the Block 85–6
Fonda, Henry 105, 123, 170
Fonda, Jane 183
Fonda, Peter 146, 151, 163, 185,
    259, 287

Ford, Glenn 193
Frawley, James 187
Fries, Chuck 160
Furth, George 171

GAC agency 126
Gautier, Dick 175
Gaxton, William 11
Gaynor, Janet 82, 230–1
  death 232
Geddes, Barbara Bel 197, 198,
    227–8
  Dallas, leaves 232–3
  heart attack 228
Ghostley, Alice 102
Goodmorning, Telles 164–6
Gordon, Ruth 187
Gossett, Lou, Jr. 176
Granger, Farley 99
Grant, Cary 157
Grant, Jennifer 157
Grant, Lee 171
Grant, Richard 215, 227, 264–5
Gray, Linda 197, 254–5, 256–7,
    283, 284
  Dallas, leaves 244
Gregory, Paul 231
Grey, Joel 224–5, 253
Guzmán, Claudio 140, 163, 173

Habitat for Humanity 296
Hagman, Ben (father) 4–5, 25–31,
    34, 35, 79–82, 132
  death 139
  Martin, Mary, marriage to 5
  state senator, campaign for 27
  stroke 138–9
Hagman, Bill (uncle) 5
Hagman, Carl (uncle) 5
Hagman, Hannah (paternal grand-
    mother) 5
Hagman, Heidi (daughter) 91, 97,
    173
  birth 88
  wedding 232
Hagman, Juanita (stepmother) 80,
    132–3, 203
Hagman, Larry:
  Alcoa Hour, The 93
  alcohol 113

  poisoning 46
  quitting 258
Alpha Caper, The 170
Antelope Tool Company vii,
    32–5
Antonio 173–4
Applause 171–2
assistant stage manager 58
Axelsson, Maj:
  marriage to 75
  proposal to 73
Banff 192–4
Bard college 40–4
Beauty Part, The 101, 102–4
Beware! The Blob 169–70
Big Bus, The 187
Big Rip-Off, The 186
birth 3
Black Fox Military Institute 13
Blood Sport 170
Bontril (uppers) 141–2
boxing 26–7
Brazil 82–4
Broadway debut 92
Career 86
Cavern, The 116, 117–18,
    119–21
Checkered Flag, The 189
chicken-suit protest against
    Nixon's incomes policy 157
Chile 173–5
chorus work 54
Clarance Derwood Award 98
Cock-a-Doodle Dandy 42
Comes a Day 92
Cry for Justice 192
Dallas See Chapters 22–6 *and
    main entry*
diabetes 294
Eagle Has Landed, The 187–8,
    188–9
early life 6–34
Edge of Night, The 100–2
Ensign Pulver 107, 108–13
Fail Safe 104–6, 133
first car 32
flying 143–4
football 25–6
Getting Away from It All 168
God and Kate Murphy 97

Good Life, The 121, 162–3
Group, The 139–40
Harry and Tonto 186
Heaven 262
Here We Go Again 175–7
Hired Hand, The 163
Howling in the Woods, A 168
hunting 28–30
Hurricane 198
I Dream of Jeannie 91, 104,
    129–32, 134–7, 140–1
    canceled 162
    fifth season 160–1
    ratings, fall in 159
    special effects 154–5
In Harm's Way 122–5
In the Heat of the Night 257
Intimate Strangers 192
Ireland 188
liver 258–76
    chemoembolization 271
    cirrhosis of 258–9
    transplant ix, 276
    transplant, recovery from
        277–84
    transplant, return to work
        after 284
    tumor 264–5
Los Angeles, move to 132
Lost Angeles, move to 8–9
Love Letters 255–7
LSD 147–50, 195
Malibu house purchase 155
Margaret Webster's Shakespeare
    workshop 45
military service: 64–70, 77–8
    draft, invitation to dodge
        64–5
    entertainment division 68
    London posting 67
    United States, return to 78
Mother, Jugs and Speed 189
Nervous Set, The 100
New York, move to 14
Nixon 263
Ojai move 260–1
Once Around the Block 85–6
Orleans 285–6
peyote 165–6
pneumonia 58

Primary Colors 287–90
Queen Mother's 80th-birthday
    celebration 221–2
*Return of the World's Greatest
    Detective, The* 187
Rhinemann Exchange, The 189
rifle, gift of 18
Ringling Brothers Circus 55–7
Rogues, The 133–4
Romania 291–4
Rome 122
Romeo and Juliet 42
Royal Ascot 216–17
St John Terrel productions 54–5
*Sarah T.—Portrait of a Teenage
    Alcoholic* 187
school play 32
Sea Hunt 90
Ship of Fools 128
Sidekicks 176
silent Sundays 158–9
Skin of Our Teeth, The, walk-on
    76, 77
smoking 23
South Pacific 58–63
Spotlight Review, The 69
Stairway to the Stars 69
Stardust 178–9
Superman 192, 194–5
Sweden 38–40
Taming of the Shrew, The 45
This Girl Business 32
Three's a Crowd 161–2
Times Square apartment 91
tobacco:
    antismoking campaign 227–9
    quitting 142
Trinity prep school 14–15
Twelfth Night 41
Wales 173
Warm Peninsula, The 99–100
Watts Workshop, teaching at 151
West Point Story, The 89–90
What Are Best Friends For? 171
Woodstock Country School,
    Vermont 21–4
Hagman, Maj *See* Axelsson, Maj
Hagman, Preston (son) 156, 173–4
    Beware! The Blob 169
    birth 99

Hall, Jess, Jr. 34, 35, 206
Hall, Jess, Sr. 32–4
Hall, Larry 34, 147
Halliday, Didi 79
Halliday, Heller (half-sister) 14, 16
    Annie Get Your Gun 25
Halliday, Richard 13–16, 17,
    18–19, 60–2, 83, 91, 162
    death 173
Hamilton, Alexander 85
Hammerstein, Oscar II 9, 15
Hammond, Jake 241–2
Hammond, Nancy 241
Hansen, Joachim 119–20
Harris, Jack 168–9
Harris, Julie 99
Harris, Richard 218–19
Havoc, June 99–100
Hayes, Helen 76
Hayward, Leland 15
Hedman, David 263
Heifetz, Jascha 116
Heinmann, Klaus 23
Hiroshima and Nagasaki, bombing
    of 21
Hopper, Dennis 163–4
Hopper, Hedda 9
Houser, John 169
Howard, Trevor 193

Indianapolis 500 189–91
Ives, Burl 109

Jacobs, David 204
Johnson, Ben 170
Jones, Billy (nanny) 7–8
Jones, Margot 41–2
Jones, Parnelli 189–90

Kanaly, Steve 198
Katzman, Leonard 197, 199, 220–1,
    244, 253, 284
    Dallas, leaves 237–8
    Dallas, returns to 239
Keitel, Harvey 189
Kelly, Gene 11
Kennedy, John F., assassination of
    121–2
Kennedy, Robert, assassination of
    151

Kercheval, Ken 198–9, 284
Kern, Jerome 9, 15
Kidder, Margot 193
King, Martin Luther, assassination
    of 150–1
Kleiman, Henri 68, 70–71, 75, 117,
    215
Korean War 21, 46, 64

Lahr, Bert 101, 103–4
Larkin, John 101–2
Leigh, Vivien 63
Lewis, Richard 268
Logan, Josh 62–3, 107, 109–10,
    111
Long, John 288
Lopez, Trini 173
Lorimar 196, 200, 214–15, 217,
    218, 233
Lumet, Sidney 104–5, 139–40
Lynley, Carol 169

McClory, Kevin 188, 216–18, 219
McEachin, James 170
McGiver, John 108
McGuane, Thomas, Jr. 281
Machuzsek, Michel 264, 267
MacKenzie, Ken 48, 49
MacKenzie, Millie 48, 49
McQueen, Steve 280
Makowka, Dr. Leonard 248, 264,
    266, 272, 276, 283
Mancini, Henry 221
Mantle, Mickey 267
Marantz, Irving 85
Marchand, Nancy 45
marijuana 113–15
Marsh, Jean 188
Marshall, Peter 109
Martin, Mary (mother) viii, 3–4,
    6–16, 76–7, 196, 224–5, 230–2
    Annie Get Your Gun 24–5, 45
    Ben, divorce from 9
    Ben, marriage to 5
    car crash 230–1
    colon cancer 248
    death 249
    finishing school 5
    Great Victor Herbert, The 13
    Halliday, meets 13–14

Heller, gives birth to 14
Leave It To Me 11–12
Los Angeles, move to 8
Lute Song 15
Maj's rapprochement attempt 86–7
One Touch of Venus 14
Paramount contract 13
Peter Pan viii, 79
Queen Mother's 80th-birthday celebration 221–2
singing jobs 8, 9
Skin of Our Teeth, The 76
South Pacific 58, 63
Martin, Preston (maternal grandfather) 4, 7, 12
death 12
Marvin, Betty 128
Marvin, Lee 128–9
Mary Hagman's School of Dance 5
Matthau, Walter 105, 109
Mazursky, Paul 186
McKay, Peggy 42
Meredith, Burgess 97, 123, 125, 169, 184–5, 259–60
Batman's Penguin role 184
Merman, Ethel 196
Mills, Donna 163
Moon, Keith 179–83
death 183
Moore, Irving 208, 222
Moore, Victor 11
Morton, Dr. John 265

Nash, Ogden 14
National Kidney Foundation 295–6
National Weather Service 262
Neal, Patricia 123
Nelson, Gene 131, 137
Nettleton, Lois 97
Nichols, Mike 287, 288, 289
Nicholson, Jack 109, 113, 146
Nimoy, Leonard 170
Niven, David 133

Oates, Warren 163
Obre, Taylor 257
O'Connor, Carroll 97–8, 123, 155, 163, 257
O'Connor, Hugh 155–6

O'Connor, Nancy 108, 155
O'Connor, Tim 226
Olivier, Laurence 63
O'Rourke, Captain 60, 67
Owlsley, Stanley 146

Parker County 132
Paul, Prince 291
Peaker, E. J. 162
Pearl (friend from Canton Village) 91–2
Pelican, Joe 54
Peppard, George 127–8
Perelman, S. J. 14
Perrine, Valerie 194–5
Phillips, Roger 21–2, 24, 40
Preminger, Otto 122–5
Presley, Juanita (maternal grandmother) 4, 6–7, 12
death 14
Holmby Hills home, buys 13
Los Angeles, move to 8–9
Presley, Priscilla 240, 243
Prince, Sidney 141, 144–5
Principal, Victoria 198, 202
Dallas, leaves 242
Puttnam, David 179

Quayle, Anthony 187

Rae, Charlotte 102
Rambo, Dack 242
Redgrave, Lynn 187
Reed, Donna 233
Reeves, Christopher 192
Remick, Lee 76
Remington Raiders 68
Rich, Lee 200, 238
Rodgers, Richard 15
Roone, Nels 39
Rorke, Hayden 130, 141
Rose Lee, Gypsy 99–100
Rosenberg, Howard 210
Rubio, Paul 246
Rudnick, Dr. Paul 257–8
Ryan, Peggy 107–8

Salmon, John 88
Sandal, Jim 152–3
Sanders, George 134

Sands, Tommy 109, 110
Sangster, Bob 188
Sarandon, Susan 189
Savage, Archie 62
Saxon, John 118
Schiaffino, Rosanna 118
Schwab, Lawrence 11, 47
Scott, George C. 86, 92–6
Screen Gems 129, 131, 161, 162
segregation 117
Sellers, Peter 185
Sheldon, Sidney 129, 130–1, 134–5,
    137, 141
Shokouh, Oliver 287
Simmons, Tom 28
Simpson, Dan 273
Smith, Cecil 207
Solar Electric Light Fund 296
Stanton, Griffith 20
Stone, Peter 77, 128
Stone, Sharon 260
Stritch, Elaine 57
Sturges, John 187–8
Sutherland, Donald 187
Swackhamer, Edward Wandrink
    129–30, 140

Talbot, Nita 171, 175
Taylor, Dallas 267–8, 272, 283
Terrell, St. John 47–8, 54, 55, 59
Thornton, Artist 151
Tilton, Charlene 198
Travolta, John 288
Trip, The 146
Tryon, Tom 123–4
Tucker, Sophie 11

Uglies (motorcycle club) 287
Ulmer, Edgar 117–18
United Network for Organ Sharing
    274

Vaccaro, Brenda 186

Vadim, Roger 183
Van Patten, Dick 169
Ventura Coalition Against Radiation
    Emissions 262–3
Verdugo, Elena 170
Victor, Lucia 45
Vidal, Gore 84, 122
Vierling, Dr. John 258–9, 263
Vietnam War 150

Walker, Bob (casting director)
    133–4
Walker, Robert (actor) 109, 113
Walter, Jessica 161–2
War of the Worlds, The (radio
    drama) 12
Warden, Jack 42
Washer, Ben 173, 224, 230–1
Watts, Alan 143
Waver, Fritz 105
Wayne, David 163, 206, 236
Wayne, John 123
Weatherford, Texas 6
Webb, Richard 169
Weill, Kurt 14
Welch, Raquel 189
Williams, Cindy 169
Williams, Tennessee 42
Williams, Treat 187
Wilson, Sheree 240
Wolfington, Iggy 57, 58
Woods, Mildred 8, 9
Woolbrech, Michael 184
Wright, Jim 27
Wynn, Bob 1–2, 3, 184
Wynn, Melinda 1

Yellowstone National Park 108
Young, Gig 133
Young, John Sacret 285

Zuber, Allison 286